国家级一流本科课程配套教材

语言学教程

主　编　项成东　曲　莉
副主编　王晓军
编　者　李云靖　郭中子
　　　　晏尚元　李　彦
　　　　张　蕾　李昊平
　　　　刘晓萍　魏　梅

清华大学出版社
北京

内 容 简 介

本书系统讲解了英语语言学各个分支中最基本、最重要的概念和理论，涵盖了语言学的核心分支（微观语言学）和跨学科领域（宏观语言学）。通过学习，学生能够掌握语言学的基础知识和最新发展，并运用于各种语言的描述和分析中。作为一本入门性教材，本书兼具易读性、系统性、前沿性和实践性的特点。

本书既可以作为英语语言文学专业本科生的专业课程或通识课程教材，也可供对语言学感兴趣的相关读者阅读学习。本书还有配套的慕课课程，读者可在"学银在线"学习。读者可在www.tsinghuaelt.com 下载本书配套练习题的答案。

版权所有，侵权必究。举报：010-62782989，beiqinquan@tup.tsinghua.edu.cn。

图书在版编目（CIP）数据

语言学教程/项成东，曲莉主编．—北京：清华大学出版社，2022.4（2025.1重印）
国家级一流本科课程配套教材
ISBN 978-7-302-59125-2

Ⅰ．①语… Ⅱ．①项… ②曲… Ⅲ．①语言学—教材 Ⅳ．①H0

中国版本图书馆CIP数据核字（2021）第182172号

责任编辑：刘　艳
封面设计：子　一
责任校对：王凤芝
责任印制：刘海龙

出版发行：清华大学出版社
　　网　　址：https://www.tup.com.cn, https://www.wqxuetang.com
　　地　　址：北京清华大学学研大厦A座　　邮　编：100084
　　社 总 机：010-83470000　　邮　购：010-62786544
　　投稿与读者服务：010-62776969, c-service@tup.tsinghua.edu.cn
　　质量反馈：010-62772015, zhiliang@tup.tsinghua.edu.cn
印 装 者：三河市龙大印装有限公司
经　　销：全国新华书店
开　　本：185mm×260mm　　印　张：15.5　　字　数：292千字
版　　次：2022年6月第1版　　印　次：2025年1月第3次印刷
定　　价：65.00元

产品编号：091940-01

前 言

2019年10月24日，教育部发布了《关于一流本科课程建设的实施意见》，实施本科课程"双万计划"，即经过三年左右时间，建成万门左右国家级和万门左右省级一流本科课程。在此背景下，天津外国语大学"语言学概论"本科课程于2020年被教育部评为国家级一流本科建设课程。要打造好国家一流课程，教材建设势在必行。为了保证教材质量并充分体现一流课程教材的特性，我们组织本课程教学团队认真学习和贯彻领会教育部关于实施"双万计划"的精神，以教育部提出的"面向未来、适应需求、引领发展、理念先进、保障有力"为指导原则，精心策划和编写本教材，重点突出教材的四大特点：易读性、直观性、系统性、实践性。

易读性：每一章前面有一个中文导言，简要概括本章的主要内容，以帮助学生清晰地了解本章涉及的概念和理论。同时，每章都设定了学习目标，使学生对各章的学习任务一目了然。

直观性：本教材配有大量的图片和图表，学生根据图片和图表既能更加直观、清晰地理解语言学相关概念和理论，又能提高他们的学习兴趣。

系统性：本教材介绍语言学的核心分支（微观语言学），包括语音学、音系学、形态学、句法学、语义学和语用学，同时也讲解了语言相关的跨学科研究（宏观语言学），包括语篇分析、社会语言学、认知语言学、心理语言学和语言习得研究。

实践性：本课程教学团队成员均有十年以上的语言学教学经验，教材编写时充分重视理论与实践相结合、概念介绍与实例分析相结合，每章后面还配有相关练习，供学生进一步思考。本教材还有配套的慕课课程，读者可在"学银在线"学习使用。

本教材共12章，下面简要介绍每章的主要内容。

第1章"概要"，介绍语言学的定义、分类和容易混淆的概念，并对语言的定义、特征、功能和起源进行讲解。（项成东编写）

第2章"语音学"，介绍语音学的定义和分类，并从多个维度对语音进行讲解。另外，也对国际音标表进行了说明。（李云靖编写）

第3章"音系学"，介绍音位系统的建立、音节的组成方式及音与音的搭配规律、语音的共时变异和历时变化。（李云靖编写）

第 4 章 "形态学"，介绍词的内部结构和构词规则，讲解词素的定义和分类、主要构词法和次要构词法。（曲莉编写）

第 5 章 "句法学"，介绍语言的不同成分组成句子的规则或句子结构成分之间的关系，主要讲解树型图在展示句子结构中的作用，并介绍句子的表层结构和底层结构。（郭中子编写）

第 6 章 "语义学"，介绍意义的定义和分类，即概念意义、内涵意义、社会意义、情感意义、反射意义、搭配意义和主题意义。同时，也对词语之间的语义关系和句子之间的语义关系进行了讲解。（晏尚元编写）

第 7 章 "语用学"，介绍语境中语言使用的意义并讲解言语行为理论，即一个言语行为分成三个层面：言内行为、言外之意和言外之果。另外，结合真实语境对合作原则和礼貌原则的基本思想进行了阐释。（李彦编写）

第 8 章 "语篇分析"，介绍学者们如何从不同视角对语篇进行分析，并从以下五个领域进行讲解：信息结构、衔接与连贯、话语标记语、会话分析和书面语篇结构。（张蕾编写）

第 9 章 "社会语言学"，介绍语言的变体，包括语言、标准语、方言、语域等。此外，也介绍了社会发展和社会活动决定语码选择，语言系统在社会变量的影响下表现出语音、词汇、句子结构和语体等多方面的变异形式。（李昊平编写）

第 10 章 "认知语言学"，介绍认知语言学的基本概念和理论，包括象似性原则、范畴化、一词多义和辐射网络、隐喻和转喻、构式语法、语法化等。（项成东编写）

第 11 章 "心理语言学"，介绍语言理解、语言产生等，主要涉及词汇通达、句子理解、语篇加工、语言产生的相关心理语言学模型，并解释其中的认知加工过程。（刘晓萍编写）

第 12 章 "语言习得"，介绍母语习得、二语习得和二语/外语教学的基本概念、假设和理论，包括认知派与社会派在语言习得和二语教学方面的不同观点。（魏梅编写）

全书由主编项成东和曲莉设计、统稿、协调和分工安排，副主编王晓军对全书进行校对和内容调整。由于时间有限，错漏在所难免，恳请读者批评指正。

项成东、曲 莉
于天津马场道钟楼
2022 年 5 月 30 日

◀ Contents

Chapter 1
Introduction 1
  1.1 What Is Linguistics? 2
  1.2 Scopes of Linguistics 3
  1.3 Some Distinctions in Linguistics 5
  1.4 What Is Language? 7
  1.5 Summary 11

Chapter 2
Phonetics 13
  2.1 The Speech Chain 15
  2.2 The Organs of Speech 15
  2.3 Consonants According to Places of Articulation 18
  2.4 Consonants According to Manners of Articulation 20
  2.5 Aspiration: A Vital Feature for Chinese Consonants 23
  2.6 Vowels 24
  2.7 Suprasegmental Features 26
  2.8 Phonation Types 28
  2.9 Air Stream Mechanism 29
  2.10 The International Phonetic Alphabet (IPA) and Sound Transcription 30
  2.11 Observing Speech Production Through Instruments 32
  2.12 Acoustic Characteristics of Speech Sounds 35
  2.13 Summary 42

Chapter 3
Phonology 43
  3.1 Phonemes 45

. iii .

3.2　Syllabic Structure and Phonotactics 47
3.3　Phonological Processes 49
3.4　Constraints in Phonological Processes 52
3.5　Historical Sound Change 53
3.6　Summary 54

Chapter 4
Morphology 57

4.1　Definition of Morphology 59
4.2　Morpheme 59
4.3　Word Formation 63
4.4　Summary 72

Chapter 5
Syntax 75

5.1　Introduction 76
5.2　Constituency 77
5.3　Tree Diagrams 78
5.4　Major Constituents of Sentences: Noun Phrases and Verb Phrases 81
5.5　Active and Passive Sentences 83
5.6　Testing Constituency 84
5.7　Phrase-Structure Expansions 85
5.8　Grammatical Relations: Subject, Direct Object, and Others 88
5.9　Surface Structures and Underlying Structures 91
5.10　Syntactic Operations: Question Formation and the Auxiliary 92
5.11　Summary 94

Chapter 6
Semantics 97

6.1　Some Views on Meaning 99
6.2　Lexical Meaning 102
6.3　Sense Relations Between Words 109

6.4	Sense Relations Between Sentences	114
6.5	Summary	116

Chapter 7
Pragmatics ... 121

7.1	What Is Pragmatics?	122
7.2	Speech Act Theory	125
7.3	The Cooperative Principle	127
7.4	The Politeness Principle	130
7.5	Summary	131

Chapter 8
Discourse Analysis ... 135

8.1	What Is Discourse Analysis?	136
8.2	Information Structure	137
8.3	Cohesion and Coherence	138
8.4	Discourse Markers	144
8.5	Conversation Analysis	146
8.6	Textual Patterns	149
8.7	Summary	151

Chapter 9
Sociolinguistics ... 153

9.1	Introduction	154
9.2	Language Variety	155
9.3	Languages in Contact	158
9.4	Summary	165

Chapter 10
Cognitive Linguistics ... 169

10.1	Introduction	170
10.2	Organizing Principles of Iconicity	171

10.3 Prototype Theory and Categorization 172
10.4 Polysemy and Radial Networks 173
10.5 Metaphor and Metonymy 174
10.6 The Relation of Grammar to Cognition 176
10.7 Cognitive Grammar in Operation 177
10.8 Construction Grammar 178
10.9 Mental Spaces 179
10.10 Grammaticalization 180
10.11 Summary 181

Chapter 11
Psycholinguistics 183

11.1 Overview of Psycholinguistics 184
11.2 Language Comprehension Models 186
11.3 Language Production Models 192
11.4 Summary 194

Chapter 12
Language Acquisition 197

12.1 First Language Acquisition 199
12.2 Second Language Acquisition 204
12.3 Instruction and Second Language Learning 213
12.4 Summary 215

References 219

语言学术语表 227

Chapter 1

Introduction

The learning objectives of this chapter are:
1. to master the definition and scope of linguistics;
2. to distinguish some concepts in linguistics;
3. to understand the design features of language;
4. to identify the functions of language.

导言

语言学是系统研究人类语言的学科，或关于语言的科学研究。它探索语言的起源、定义、功能、发展和运用等，以及其他与语言相关的问题。语言学分为微观语言学和宏观语言学两大类。微观语言学只研究语言现象本身，包括语音学、音系学、形态学、句法学、语义学和语用学；宏观语言学注重研究语言与其他领域之间的关系，如心理语言学、社会语言学、认知语言学、神经语言学、应用语言学等。语言学几个容易混淆的概念包括语言和言语、语言能力和言语行为、规定性与描述性、现时语言学与历时语言学、横组合关系与纵聚合关系。语言是人类特有的、任意的、有声的符号系统。语言本身独有的特征，包括任意性、二重性、创造性、文化传承性等。语言在人类交流中有寒暄功能、指令功能、信息功能、表达功能、情感功能、疑问功能和施为功能等。语言的起源有各种假说，包括拟声说、达达说和劳动喊声说等。

Every aspect of language—sound, structure, meanings of words and more complex expressions—is narrowly restricted by the properties of the initial state; these same restrictions underlie and account for the extraordinary richness and flexibility of the systems that emerge.

—Avram Noam Chomsky[1]

1.1 What Is Linguistics?

Linguistics is generally defined as the scientific study of language. There is zero article preceding the word "language" implying that linguistics studies not only any particular language (e.g., English, Arabic, Chinese), but language in general. The word "study" does not mean "learning", but "investigation" or "examination". "Scientific" refers to the way in which language is studied. A scientific study of language is based on the systematic investigation of data, conducted with reference to some general theories of language structure. In order to discover the nature of the underlying language system, i.e., to see how language is actually used, linguists formulate some hypotheses about the language structure. However, the hypotheses thus formed have to be checked repeatedly against the observed facts. In linguistics, as in any other

---

1 Avram Noam Chomsky (1928–) is an American linguist, philosopher, cognitive scientist, logician, political commentator and activist. He has authored over 100 books and is described as the "father of modern linguistics".

disciplines, data and theory stand in a dialectal complement; that is, a theory without the support of data can hardly claim validity, and data without being explained by some theories remain a muddle mass of things. Therefore, the process of linguistic study is as follows:

- Linguistic facts observed;
- Generalization made about the linguistic facts;
- Hypotheses formulated to account for the linguistic facts;
- The hypotheses tested by further observations;
- Linguistic theories of language constructed.

1.2 Scopes of Linguistics

Linguistics can be divided into microlinguistics and macrolinguistics. The former is the core branch of linguistics which includes phonetics, phonology, morphology, syntax, semantics, and pragmatics. Microlinguistics studies the language itself.

Phonetics is the scientific study of speech sounds. It studies how speech sounds are produced, transmitted and perceived.

Phonology focuses on the study of how speech sounds function in a language. It studies the way of how speech sounds are put together and used to convey meaning in communication.

Morphology is the study of formation of words. It can be considered as the grammar of words, as syntax the grammar of sentences.

Syntax deals with the combination of words into phrases, clauses and sentences which are governed by rules.

Semantics is concerned with the study of meaning in all of its formal aspects. What one is really trying to do in semantics, is to explicate, or to make explicit, the ways in which words and sentences of various grammatical constructions are used and understood by native or fluent speakers of a language.

Pragmatics can be defined as the study of meaning in the context of use. It deals with how speakers use language which cannot be predicted from the linguistic knowledge alone.

Macrolinguistics studies the relationship between language and other fields. The major subbranches of macrolinguistics are as follows.

Sociolinguistics studies the relationship between language and society. It mainly studies how social factors influence the structure and use of language.

Psycholinguistics is the study of the relationship between language and psychology. It focuses on the mental structure and processes which are involved in the acquisition, comprehension and production of language.

Neurolinguistics is the study of the relationship between language and brain. It typically studies the disturbances of language comprehension and production caused by the damage of the certain areas of the brain.

Stylistics is the study of language style. It is concerned with the linguistic choices that are available to a writer and the reasons why particular forms and expressions are used rather than others.

Discourse analysis is the study of the relationship between discourse and its contexts. It deals with how sentences in spoken or written language form larger meaningful units such as paragraphs, conversations and interviews, and the various devices used by speakers or writers when they connect single sentences together into a coherent whole.

Cognitive linguistics is the study of the organizing, processing and cognition of language. It mainly studies categories and categorization, conceptual metaphor and metonymy, iconicity and grammaticalization, etc.

Applied linguistics is primarily concerned with the application of linguistic principles and theories to the solution of practical problems, especially methods and findings to the language problems which have been arising in other areas of experience. Narrowly speaking, it refers to the application of linguistic principles and theories to language teaching and learning.

Ecolinguistics, linking language with ecology, is a field which explores the role of language in the life-sustaining interactions of humans, other species and the physical environment. It addresses language loss and language maintenance in the age of globalization and the question of how language construes our view of nature and environment.

Computational linguistics is the study of the applications of computers in processing and analyzing language, as in automatic machine translation and text analysis. Much of this exploits the capacity of computers to accept, retain, and process vast amounts of information, thus freeing human research workers for the more vital interpretation of the results of the computer's calculations, sortings, and listings.

Legal linguistics is the application of linguistic research and methods to the law. It studies law with linguistic methods and the outcome of the studies can help legal scientists and legal practitioners do and understand their work better through an increased understanding of how language works in general and in legal domains in particular.

1.3 Some Distinctions in Linguistics

1.3.1 Langue and Parole

These two terminologies were proposed by the famous linguist F. de Saussure in the early 20th century. Langue and parole are French words. Langue refers to the abstract linguistic system shared by all the members of a speech community. Parole is the realization of langue in actual use. Specifically, langue is the set of conventions and rules which language users all have to abide by. Parole is the concrete use of the conventions and the application of the rules. Langue is abstract; it is not the language people actually use. Parole is concrete; it refers to the naturally occurring language events. Langue is relatively stable; it does not change frequently. Parole varies from person to person, from time to time, and from situation to situation. Saussure makes this distinction in order to single out one aspect of language for a series of studies. According to Saussure, parole is simply a mass of linguistic facts, too varied and confusing for systematic investigation, and what linguists should do is to abstract langue from parole, that is, to discover and study the regularities governing the actual use of language.

1.3.2 Competence and Performance

The distinction between competence and performance was proposed by an American linguist N. Chomsky in the late 1950s. Chomsky was the founder of traditional grammar (TG), which is most influential in modern linguistics. Competence is an ideal user's internalized knowledge of a language. Performance is the actual use or realization of the knowledge by individuals in linguistic communication. According to Chomsky, speakers have internalized a set of rules about their language. This rule system enables them to produce and understand an infinitely large number of sentences and recognize sentences that are ungrammatical and ambiguous. Despite the perfect knowledge of one's own language, a speaker can still make mistakes in actual use, e.g., a slip of tongue, and unnecessary pauses. These imperfect performances are usually caused by social and psychological factors, such as stress, anxiety, and embarrassment. Similar to Saussure, Chomsky thinks that what linguists should study is the ideal speaker's competence because the speaker's performance is too haphazard to be studied. The task of the linguists is to discover and specify the speaker's internalized rules.

While there is similarity between Saussure and Chomsky's notions. Saussure's distinction takes a sociological view of language. His notion of langue is a matter of social conventions. Chomsky looks at language from the psychological point of view and considers linguistic competence as the property of the mind of the speaker.

1.3.3 Prescriptive and Descriptive

Modern linguistics is descriptive, not prescriptive. It aims to describe and analyze the language people actually use. It tries to eliminate a series of grammatical rules which are forced on the language users. Most modern linguists regard linguistic study as a scientific and objective undertaking, and their major task is to describe the language that people actually use, be it "correct" or not. In other words, what actually occurred in the language use should be described and analyzed in linguistic investigation.

Traditional grammar is prescriptive in the sense that it tries to lay down a series of grammatical rules which are forced on the language users, that is, to tell people what they should say and what they should not say. For example:

It is not right to say sentences like "I runs away". (prescriptive)

People do not say sentences like "I runs away". (descriptive)

1.3.4 Synchronic and Diachronic

Language exists in time and changes through time. The description of a language at some point in time is the synchronic study. The description of a language as it changes through time is the diachronic study. A diachronic study of language is a historical study; it studies the historical development of language over a period of time. For example, a study of the features of the English used in Shakespeare's time would be a synchronic study, and a study of the changes English has undergone since then would be a diachronic study. In modern linguistics, synchronic study seems to enjoy priority over diachronic study. The reason is that unless the various states of language are successfully studied, it would be difficult to describe the changes that have taken place in its historical development. Synchronic descriptions are often regarded as the descriptions of a language as it exists at the present day and most linguistic studies are of this type.

1.3.5 Syntagmatic and Paradigmatic Relations

Saussure has put forward another pair of concepts: syntagmatic and paradigmatic relations. The former refers to the horizontal relationship between linguistic elements, which form linear sequences. The latter refers to the vertical relationship between forms, which might occupy the same particular place in a structure. Paradigmatic relationships between linguistic elements can be established by the use of the substitution test at the vertical level. Thus, the initial consonants in "beer" "deer" and "peer" form a paradigmatic relation as well as the words "today" and "tomorrow" in the sentence "She will arrive today/tomorrow." Syntagmatic relationships are defined by the ability of elements to be combined horizontally (linearly). For example, the relationship between "She will arrive" and "today".

1.4 What Is Language?

Language comes differently. If we say "Chinese is a language", it refers to language in particular. If we say "Linguistics is the systematic study of language", it refers to language in general. If we say Shakespeare's language, it refers to a typical style of using a particular language. If we say C language in computer science, it refers to an artificial language. If we say the language of bees, it refers to a system of communication.

Till now, there is no standardized definition of language. Most definitions suggested by modern linguists share some important characteristics of human language that are included in the following statement about language:

Language is a system of arbitrary vocal symbols used for human communication.

Language is a system of rules and it is constructed according to certain rules. Language is arbitrary. There is no intrinsic connection between the word and its meaning. Words are just symbols associated with objects, actions, ideas, etc., by convention. Language is vocal, for the primary medium of language is sound for all languages. Language is used for human communication in the sense that language is human-specific.

1.4.1 Design Features of Language

Design features refer to the defining properties of human language that distinguish it from any animal system of communication. The following six design features are specified by the American linguist Charles Francis Hockett.

1. Arbitrariness

Language is said to be arbitrary because there is no natural relationship between the words and the concepts that they represent. It is the matter of convention. For example, there is no intrinsic connection between the word "desk" and the object it refers to. In Chinese the word "桌子" is used for the same concept, and so on with other languages.

2. Duality

Human language has two levels of structure. The alphabet for writing and the phonemes for speech are at the lower level, which have no meaning on their own. At the higher level, the meaning emerges as a result of the combination of the units from the lower level.

3. Creativity (Productivity)

By creativity we mean language is resourceful and productive in that it makes possible the construction and interpretation of new signals by its users. That is, language has the potential to create endless sentences, including the sentences people have never heard before.

4. Displacement

Displacement means human language enables its users to refer to things that are not present in time or space at the moment of communication.

5. Cultural Transmission

Language is culturally transmitted, not genetically transmitted. It is passed down from generation to generation through teaching and learning, rather than by instinct.

6. Interchangeability

Interchangeability means any human being could be both a producer and a receiver of a message. The role of a speaker and a hearer is changeable at any moment.

1.4.2 Functions of Language

We use language for almost infinite numbers of purposes, from writing letters to gossiping with our friends, making speeches and talking to ourselves in the mirror. The primary function of language is to transmit information and convey commands, feelings and emotions. That is, language is a tool of communication. Linguists talk about the functions of language in an abstract sense, not in terms of using language to chat, to think, to buy and sell, to read and write, to greet, praise and condemn people, etc. They summarize these practical functions and attempt some broad classifications of the basic functions of language. The following are the major functions of language.

1. Phatic Function

Language is used to establish an atmosphere or maintain social contact between the speaker and the hearer. Greetings, farewells and comments on the weather serve this function. For example:

How are you?

How do you do?

It's a nice day, isn't it?

They are used to establish a common sentiment between the speaker and the hearer.

2. Directive Function

Language is used to get the hearer to do something. Most imperative sentences are of this function. For example:

Close the book and listen to me carefully.

3. Interrogative Function

Language is used to ask for information from others. All questions expecting answers serve this function. For example:

What's your idea?

What time is it now?

4. Informative Function

Language is used to tell something, to give information, or to reason things out. Declarative sentences serve this function. The following public sign serves this function.

5. Expressive Function

Language is used to reveal the speaker's attitude and feelings. Interjections serve this function. For example:

My God!

Good Heavens!

6. Evocative Function

Language is used to create certain feelings in the hearer. Jokes, advertising and propaganda serve this function.

7. Performative Function

Language is used to do things or to perform acts. The judge's imprisonment sentences, the president's declaration of war or the Queen's naming of a ship, etc., serve this function.

8. Metalingual Function

Language can be used to talk about itself. For example:

"Man" is a noun.

"Man" is composed of three phonemes.

1.4.3 The Origin of Language

There are some famous theories about the origin of language, but many of them have been discredited. The following are three well-known theories.

1. The Bow-Wow Theory

The basic idea of this theory is that primary words could have been imitations of the natural sounds which early men and women heard around them. Onomatopoeic words seem to be convincing evidence for this theory. However, we find they are very different in the degree of resemblance they express with the natural sounds. This theory lacks supportive evidence.

2. The Pooh-Pooh Theory

In the hard life of our primitive ancestors, they uttered instinctive sounds of pain, anger and joy. As for evidence, we could only cite the universal use of sounds as interjections. What makes this theory problematic is that there is only a limited number of interjections in almost all languages.

3. The "Yo-He-Ho" Theory

As primitive people worked together, they produced some rhythmic grunts which gradually developed into chants and then into language. We do have prosodic use of rhythms in language, but rhythmic grunts are far different from language in its present sense. This theory is again at most a speculation.

1.5 Summary

Linguistics is a scientific study of language. The scope of linguistics is divided into microlinguistics and macrolinguistics. The former studies language itself. The latter studies the relationship between language and other fields. When we study linguistics, we have to make a distinction between some concepts: langue and parole, competence and performance, prescriptive and descriptive, synchronic and diachronic, and syntagmatic and paradigmatic. Language is a system of arbitrary vocal symbols used for human communication. It has its own design features and functions.

Exercises

I Decide whether each of the following statements is true or false.

1. Linguistics is the scientific study of a language.
2. Psycholinguistics is the study of the relationship between language and psychology.
3. Parole is the abstract linguistic system shared by all the members of a speech community.
4. Performance is the actual use of the knowledge by individuals in linguistic communication.

5. Traditional grammar is prescriptive in the sense that it tries to lay down a series of grammatical rules which are forced on the language users.
6. Saussure has put forward another pair of concepts: syntagmatic and paradigmatic relations. The former refers to the vertical relationship between linguistic elements.
7. Language is a system of arbitrary vocal symbols used for human communication.
8. Language is productive in that it makes possible the construction and interpretation of new signals by its users.
9. Language is used to establish an atmosphere or maintain social contact between the speaker and the hearer. This is the expressive function of language.
10. Language is culturally transmitted. A language is taught and learned within a particular cultural background.

II Define the following terms.

1. parole   2. duality   3. competence   4. paradigmatic relation   5. syntax

III Answer the following questions.

1. What's the difference between prescriptive linguistics and descriptive linguistics?
2. Why do linguists say language is human specific?

Chapter 2

Phonetics

The learning objectives of this chapter are:
1. to understand how linguistic sounds are produced;
2. to know about the International Phonetic Alphabet;
3. to know how to observe linguistic sounds by tools.

语言学教程
A Coursebook for Linguistics

导言

语音学是语言学中研究与语音有关问题的一个分支。语音是语言的最初形式，也是语言的基本载体。在文字被发明出来以前，语音是语言存在的唯一形式。对语音的了解和研究是语言学学习和研究不可或缺的一个方面。本章将从多个维度对语音进行介绍。

语音在物理属性上是一种振动，由人类的发音器官通过控制气流产生。气流一般从肺部发出，经由气管、喉部、咽部、口鼻腔排出体外。气流经过喉部的时候，可以使声带振动，发出声音。这个振动继续向外传播，经过咽腔、口鼻腔的时候会因为腔体形状的不同而使音质发生改变，听起来就是不同的语音。最灵活多变的腔体是口腔，舌、唇以及下颚等部位的运动使语音变化多样，满足了人类丰富的语言表达的需要。如果在气流通过过程中有的位置比较窄，也会产生不同程度的摩擦音效果。气流通过鼻腔，还会产生鼻音效果。这都为人类语音提供了更多可能。

语音既然是一种振动，它就有自己独特的波形。本章还将简单介绍各类语音在声学语图上的表现。波形图的幅度反映的是声音响度的大小，因此，比较响亮的元音振动幅度比较大，辅音振动幅度相对较小。塞音的闭塞段有时候会完全没有声音，振动幅度接近零。不同的元音主要通过不同的共振峰来区别，反映的是口腔形状的不同。辅音由于在有无声带振动、有无摩擦气流、有无阻塞等方面的差异，在语图上表现出完全不同的特点。

本章我们还将对国际音标表进行简单介绍，认识世界语言中可能出现的各种语音及其符号。辅音方面，最主要的类别是我们最常用到的肺部气流音，包括 /k/、/s/、/f/、/r/ 等；对一些我们并不太熟悉的非肺部气流辅音，本章也会进行介绍。元音方面，我们将会基于四边形元音图进行简单讲解，/æ/、/u/、/ɔ/、/i/ 等也会提到。

When I speak, it is in order to be heard.

—*Roman Jakobson*[1]

Language is basically in form of sounds. Though we can write down what we want to say, and read written words silently, writing is only secondary, and usually regarded as a visual transcription of sounds we say and hear. Therefore, the study of speech sounds must be a vital part of linguistics. The study of speech sounds is often separated into two relatively distinct though related fields. One is called phonetics,

---

1 Roman Jakobson is a Russian-born American linguist and Slavic language scholar, a principal founder of the European movement in structural linguistics known as the Prague School. Jakobson extended the theoretical and practical concerns of the school into new areas of study.

and the other, phonology. The former mainly deals with the question what speech sounds really are, and the latter, how speech sounds are organized to function in languages. The present chapter, phonetics, will make a brief introduction to the basics of producing speech sounds and the quality of the sounds produced. Examples in this chapter are mainly from English and, sometimes, Chinese.

2.1 The Speech Chain

Figure 2.1 illustrates the process of a speech event. When a person wants to speak, he first formulates words in his brain, then sends neural signals through the motor nerves to activate muscles to move those parts of body in charge of producing speech sounds, making sound waves which go through the air to the ears of the listener. At last, sound waves change again into neural signals and are understood by the listener's brain. Sound waves may also be heard by the speaker himself serving as feedback information for him to know what he has just said and do some adjustments if necessary.

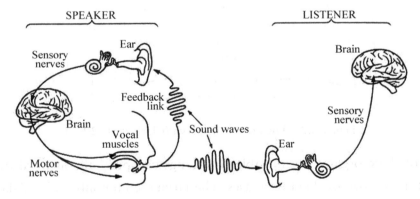

Figure 2.1   The speech chain (Peter et al., 1993)

2.2 The Organs of Speech

The term "organs of speech" refers to all those parts of human body involved in various ways in the production of speech sounds (Clark et al., 2007:15), though speaking is only the secondary function of most of them. Figure 2.2 is a simplified illustration of the body parts contributing to the speech process.

The organs of speech as shown in Figure 2.2 form a tube-like system called vocal tract. The upper end of the tube is open with the mouth and the nose, while the lower end is close to the lungs.

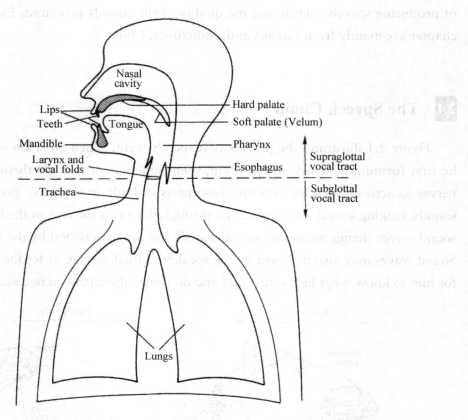

Figure 2.2 The organs of speech (Clark et al., 2007)

Some of these organs are movable. The lungs can push air outward through the vocal tract as the size of them decreases. The larynx, commonly called Adam's apple, can move up and down. In the larynx, there are two pieces of tissue called vocal folds (or vocal cords), which can move apart or close together as shown in Figure 2.3. The aperture formed by the two folds is called glottis. The air stream initiated by the lungs going through a narrow glottis makes the two folds vibrate regularly, therefore, producing periodic sound waves. This process of vocal vibrating is called voicing. The sounds with vibrating vocal folds are called voiced sounds, and those without, voiceless sounds. The soft palate can rise and contact with the back wall of the pharynx, directing the airflow to go out through the mouth, or fall, allowing the airflow to go out through both of the oral and nasal cavities, or the nasal cavity only, if certain other place in the mouth is closed (Figure 2.4). The tongue is the most flexible part of human body. It can make innumerable shapes and stretch to contact with nearly every other part of the oral cavity. The lower jaw (mandible), with the lower teeth and the lower lip on it, can move up and down, and slightly left and right. The lips can be open or closed, and spread or rounded (Figure 2.5). The other parts, such as the nasal cavity, the hard palate, and the pharynx, normally cannot change their shape and position.

Functionally, the lungs serve as the initiator of the air stream, and all the other organs are modifiers to the air stream. The vocal folds make the air vibrate, serving as the source of periodic sound waves. All those above the larynx make various modifications to the air stream and/or the sound waves. The part of the vocal tract above the larynx is called the supraglottal vocal tract, and that below, the subglottal vocal tract.

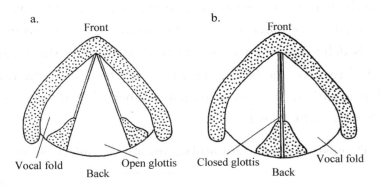

Figure 2.3   The glottis: open and closed, viewed from above (Hewlett & Beck, 2006: 30)

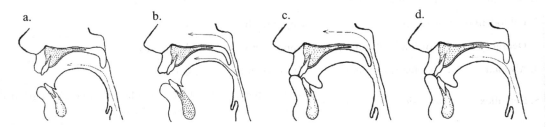

Figure 2.4   The soft palate alternating the direction of the air stream (Hewlett & Beck, 2006: 43)

Figure 2.5   Shapes of lips (Hewlett & Beck, 2006: 59)

2.3 Consonants According to Places of Articulation

Sounds of language are generally divided into two groups, consonants and vowels, judged by the presence or absence of obstacle to the air stream in the vocal tract. Consonants are sounds produced with some degree of obstacle at some place in the vocal tract, while vowels without.

Consonants can normally be described in three dimensions—voicing, place of articulation, and manner of articulation. As mentioned above, voicing refers to the state of vocal folds. Consonants produced with vocal folds vibrating are voiced, and those without, voiceless. Place and manner of articulation refer to where and how, respectively, the obstacle is formed in the vocal tract. In this section, we will make a brief introduction to the places of articulation, and the next section, the manners of articulation.

An obstacle or a stricture is formed usually by a movable part of the vocal tract moving toward the part at the opposite side of the vocal tract. The two parts involved are therefore called active articulator and passive articulator respectively. The place of articulation is defined by the two articulators involved. In theory, any contact or approximation of two parts impeding the air stream in some degree can be regarded as a place of articulation, but only a limited number of them are normally used in languages (Table 2.1 and Figure 2.6).

Table 2.1 The principal places of articulation: Articulators involved and example sounds

	Active articulator	Passive articulator	Examples (the consonants in the following words)
1. Bilabial	Upper and lower lips		my, bye, pie
2. Labiodental	Lower lip	Upper teeth	fee, vow
3. Dental	Tip or blade of tongue	Upper teeth	they, thigh
4. Alveolar	Tip or blade of tongue	Alveolar ridge	sigh, zoo
5. Retroflex	Lower side of tip of tongue	Back of the alveolar ridge	Chinese "zhi" (to know), "chi" (to eat), "shi" (poem)
6. Postalveolar	Blade of tongue	Back of the alveolar ridge	shy
7. Palatal	Dorsum of tongue	Hard palate	yeah
8. Velar	Back of tongue	Soft palate (Velum)	guy, cow
9. Uvular	Back of tongue	Uvula	French "rai" (ray)
10. Glottal	Vocal folds		how

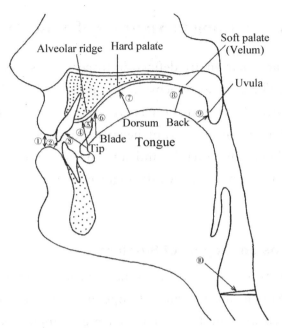

a. Articulators involved (the numbers are in corresponding with the places of articulation in Table 2.1)

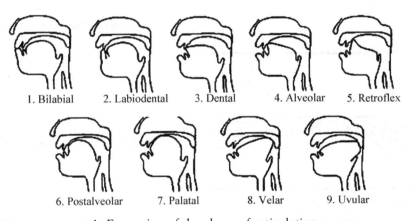

b. Formation of the places of articulation

Figure 2.6   The principal places of articulation (Hewlett & Beck, 2006: 33)

Table 2.1 lists the ten main places of articulation most frequently found in world languages. Figure 2.6a shows the movement of the active articulators in the production of the ten places of articulation, in which the tongue is further divided into four zones, namely tip, blade, dorsum and back. Figure 2.6b shows the contact patterns of these places of articulation, except that of the glottal. A glottal stop is obtained by tightly closing the glottis, blocking the air stream from passing the larynx, as shown in Figure 2.3b.

2.4 Consonants According to Manners of Articulation

The manners of articulation are defined in three dimensions, i.e. vertical, time and traverse dimensions. The vertical dimension is represented by the degree of closeness between the active articulator and the passive articulator, or in other words, degree of stricture. Time dimension is relevant because some consonants are intrinsically momentary while others maintainable, and some are temporal concatenation of basic gestures. In the traverse dimension, we distinguish central and lateral location of the oral airpath.

2.4.1 Vertical Dimension: Degree of Stricture

For each place of articulation, it is possible to form continuous degrees of stricture ranging from complete closure to complete openness, in other words, the air stream can be totally blocked or completely free. But most languages distinguish no more than four degrees of stricture as shown in Figure 2.7.

	Degree of stricture	Sound class
a. 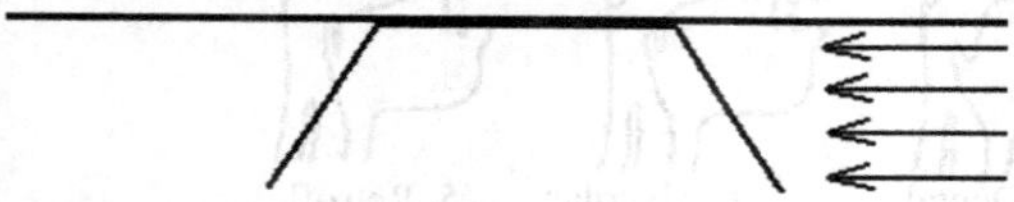	Complete closure	Stop
b. 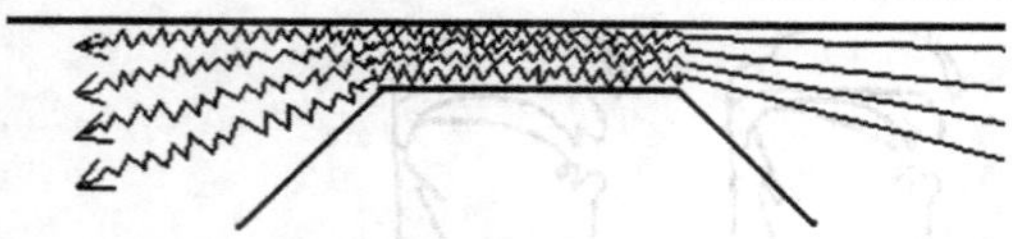	Close approximation	Fricative
c. 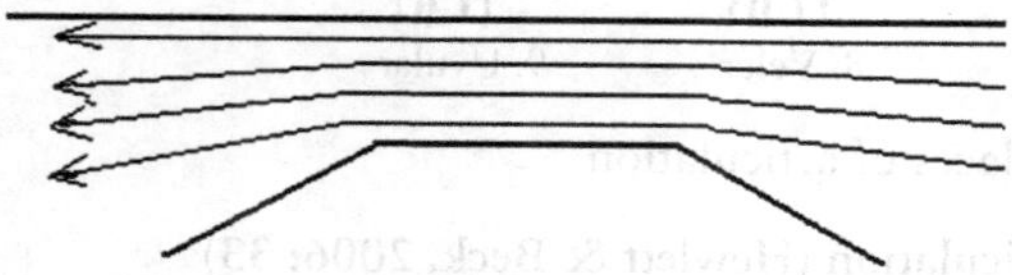	Open approximation	Approximant
d. 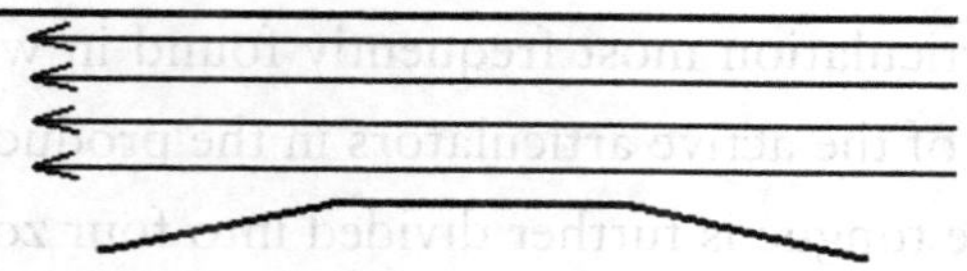	Complete openness	Vowels

Figure 2.7 Different degrees of stricture

A complete closure blocks the airflow totally. A close approximation leaves only a narrow passage for the airflow. This makes the airflow turbulent, producing a hissing sound. The degree of turbulence depends on the width of the passage way and the speed of the airflow: The narrower the passage way and the faster the airflow, the higher the degree of turbulence. Normally, the speed of the airflow of voiced sounds is much slower than that of the voiceless ones, therefore, less turbulent. An open approximation, though the articulators involved are considerably close to each other, is not narrow enough to cause turbulence. The complete openness makes no constriction to the airflow. The former three kinds correspond to three manners of articulation of consonants: stop, fricative and approximant. And the fourth one is used when vowels are being produced.

1. Stop

A complete closure can be formed in any places of articulation mentioned in the previous section, blocking the air stream from going out through the mouth. If the soft palate is raised, and at the same time a closure is formed, as shown in Figure 2.4d, the air is jailed in the oral cavity, and the air pressure rises. If a sudden release of the closure follows, the jailed air will burst out, producing an oral stop sound, which is also called a plosive, because of the sudden explosion of air stream. If the soft palate is lowered, as shown in Figure 2.4c, the airflow will go out through the nose, producing a nasal stop sound, or a nasal in short.

If the vocal folds are vibrating during the closure, the sound produced is a voiced stop, and if not, a voiceless stop. Stops, both oral and nasal, at all the places mentioned above except the glottal, can be either voiced or voiceless, though voiceless nasals are not often found in human languages. As the vocal folds cannot form a closure and let air go through to make them vibrate and/or make a nasal airflow, only a voiceless glottal plosive is possible to be produced at this place.

You can say and pay attention to the consonants in "bye", "pie" and "my", voiced bilabial stop, voiceless bilabial stop and voiced bilabial nasal stop respectively, to feel how stops are produced.

2. Fricative

When you move an active articulator toward a passive articulator in your mouth to form a passage narrow enough to cause a hissing sound, a fricative sound is produced. Fricatives can be produced at most places of articulation, either voiced or voiceless. In English, there are several fricative sounds, for example, the voiceless labiodental fricative in the word "fee", the voiced dental fricative in "thigh", the voiced and voiceless alveolar fricatives in "sigh" and "zoo", and the voiceless postalveolar fricative in "shy". In Chinese, voiceless and voiced retroflex fricatives are found in words "shi" (stone) and "zhi" (to know).

3. Approximant

Approximants are normally voiced. The passage way for the airflow in producing approximants is not narrow enough to cause a hissing sound, which is typical in the production of fricatives. Therefore, if the vocal folds do not vibrate too, there would be no sound hearable at all.

Examples of approximants in English are the initial consonants in "ray", "year" and "way". The latter two are also called semi-vowels.

2.4.2 Time Dimension

1. Affricate

An affricate is just like a combination of an oral stop and a fricative. In producing an affricate, the active articulator first forms a complete closure with the passive articulator, and then releases not to a complete openness immediately, but a close approximation first. Examples in English are the initial consonants in "cheer" and "joy".

2. Tap and Flap

When producing a tap or a flap, a complete closure is formed, but lasts for a very short time, much shorter than a stop does. Figure 2.8a shows schematically the rapid contact between the articulators.

Taps and flaps are different in how the active articulator moves to contact with the passive articulator. In producing a tap, the active articulator moves straightly toward the passive articulator, and leaves rapidly after a contact, while in producing a flap, the active articulator strikes the passive articulator just in its way of passing by.

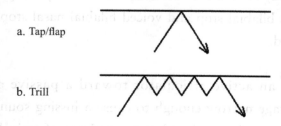

Figure 2.8 Contact patterns of taps and trills

An example of a tap sound in many varieties of American English is the consonant between two vowels in the word "latter", where the voiceless alveolar plosive turns into an alveolar tap. Many English speakers use a flapped "r" in words such as "throw" and "three", where the tip of the tongue strikes the alveolar ridge on its way from dental position to the position for the following vowels.

3. Trill

A trill is produced by the vibration of one or both articulators, resulting in a series of rapid contact and release (as shown in Figure 2.8b). Articulators able to vibrate in this way are the uvula against the back of the tongue, the tip of the tongue against the alveolar ridge and the lips. The uvular and the alveolar trills are found in European languages, such as the uvular trill in French word "rai" (ray), and the alveolar trill in Spanish word "perro". The bilabial trill, though frequently used for expressing certain feelings, presents itself only in one or two languages in the world.

2.4.3 Traverse Dimension: Central vs. Lateral

The tongue can raise either its median part or one or both of its right and left sides to direct the airflow in the oral cavity to go through either the central or the lateral part, which can be seen in Figure 2.9.

Figure 2.9 Median and lateral positions of the tongue

All sounds involving oral air stream such as fricatives and approximants can be produced either centrally or laterally. All the fricatives and approximants discussed earlier are central sounds. Examples of lateral sounds in English are the lateral approximant in "low" and its devoiced form in "slow".

2.5 Aspiration: A Vital Feature for Chinese Consonants

Though it is not a key feature for distinguishing English consonants, aspiration is vital for Chinese plosives and affricates. Chinese plosives and affricates are all voiceless, and can be divided into two groups, aspirated and unaspirated, based on aspiration.

An aspirated plosive, like the initial consonants in "pa" (afraid), "ta" (he) and "ka" (card), is produced with a period of breathing between the release of the closure and the voiced segment, while an unaspirated plosive, like the initial consonants in "ba" (eight), "da" (big) and "gai" (should), is produced with a voiced segment following the release of the closure immediately.

The period of breathing in aspirated plosives can be easily felt. Putting your hand before your mouth and say "pa" (afraid) and "ba" (eight), you can feel a more powerful flow of air out of your mouth when the former one is produced.

Aspirated affricates can be found in words "ca" (to erase) and "cha" (to insert), and the corresponding unaspirated affricates in "za" (circle) and "zha" (dregs).

Aspiration is only a secondary feature of English voiceless plosives. English voiceless plosives are aspirated except when following the voiceless alveolar fricatives, where they are unaspirated. Say "pie" and "spy", "toe" and "stow", "cool" and "school", and pay attention to the difference between the plosives in each pair.

2.6 Vowels

Articulation of vowels can be described in five dimensions: height, backness (or fronting), roundedness, length and nasalization.

The height of a vowel refers to the vertical position of the nearest point of the tongue to the roof of the mouth; it can be high, mid or low. If a vowel is high, the passage way for the airflow between the tongue and the roof of the mouth is narrow, and if it is low, the passage way is wide; therefore, high vowels are also called close vowels, and low vowels, open vowels. You can try to say "heed", "head" and "had", and pay attention to the height of the tongue changing from high to mid and at last to low, when producing the vowels in the words.

The backness refers to the longitudinal position of the point in the oral cavity, whether it is front, central or back. English examples of front, central and back vowels are the vowels in "beat", "but" and "boot".

The roundedness refers to the shape of the lips. Figure 2.5 shows the three basic shapes the lips can form: spread, neutral and rounded. To be spread or neutral mostly does not distinguish different sounds in world languages, While to be rounded or not is relevant to the distinction of different vowels. Vowels produced with rounded lips are called rounded vowels, and those with spread or neutral lips, unrounded vowels. Chinese words "yi" (aunt) and "yu" (fish) are different only in roundedness. English back vowels are often rounded, such as the vowels in "boot" and "bought".

The length of a vowel refers to the temporal duration of the vowel. Many languages distinguish between long vowels and short vowels. The vowel in "heat" is much longer than that in "hit", distinguishing them apart, though their qualities are also not exactly the same.

Nasalization of a vowel is achieved by lowering the soft palate to allow the air stream to go out from both oral and nasal cavities as shown in Figure 2.4b. Vowels produced in this way are called nasalized vowels. In contrast, vowels produced with the airflow going out through the oral cavity only are called oral vowels. There is a big set of nasalized vowels in French, such as vowels in "un" (one) and "sang" (blood).

A vowel quadrilateral is often used to describe vowel quality, as shown in Figure 2.10. Eight primary cardinal vowels and eight secondary cardinal vowels were proposed by British phonetician Daniel Jones (1881–1967), serving as landmarks in the quadrilateral space. The four corners of the quadrilateral correspond to the four extremes the tongue can reach in producing vowel sounds. The two points, mid-high and mid-low, are equally distanced from the highest and lowest ends. The cardinal vowels are supposed to be independent of particular languages, though vowels similar in position are always found. In the eight primary cardinal vowels, /i/, /e/, /ɛ/, /a/ and /ɑ/ are unrounded, while /u/, /o/ and /ɔ/ are rounded. The eight secondary cardinal vowels are related with the primary ones by reversing the lip's posture.

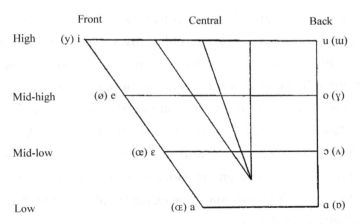

Figure 2.10 The primary cardinal vowels and secondary cardinal vowels (in the parentheses)

So far, the vowels we have discussed are all pure vowels, which are also called monophthongs. In languages there are vowels changing their qualities constantly in their process of articulation, such as the vowels in "bye", "how", "go", and so on.

This type of vowel is called diphthong. In producing a diphthong, the tongue moves from the position of a vowel to that of another, resulting in an ever changing quality. A diphthong is usually produced by a combination of the two vowels representing the starting and the end position of its movement. For example, the vowel in "bye" is written as /ai/, suggesting that it is produced by a movement of the tongue from the position of /a/ to the position of /i/. Triphthongs, vowels involving a movement of the tongue from one position to another, and then to a third one, are also always found in languages, such as the vowels in Chinese words "niao" (/niəʊ/, bird) and "sui" (/suei/, age).

2.7 Suprasegmental Features

Consonants and vowels are called segments, each of which occupies a period of time in the flow of speech, and is generally separable from others. In speech, there are several other properties, which may go across more than one segment. In this section, we will discuss about three suprasegmental features: syllabicity, tone and stress.

2.7.1 Syllabicity

Though speech is a sequence of sounds, the shortest stretch of speech a person actually makes in a fairly natural way is always a syllable. A syllable is a group of consecutive sounds pronounced like one pulse, always containing a prominent part, usually a vowel, which is necessary, and some optional consonants. An English word can be made of one syllable or more. Examples of monosyllabic words are "I", "bee", "ask" and "strange". "I" consists of only one dipthong /ai/; "bee", a consonant /b/ and a vowel /iː/; "ask", a vowel /æ/ and two consonants /s/ and /k/; and "strange", a dipthong /ei/, three consonants /s/, /t/ and /r/ before it, and two consonants /n/ and /dʒ/ after. Examples of words containing more than one syllable are "papa" (/ˈpɑːpə/), "basket" (/ˈbæs.kit/) and "international" (/in.tə.ˈnæ.ʃə.nəl/), in which the dots serve as the dividing line between syllables.

2.7.2 Tone

Tone refers to the pitch pattern of speech. Tone in some languages distinguishes one word from another. The tones in this case are called lexical tones, and the languages, tone languages. Chinese is a typical tone language, employing four lexical tones: high-level, rising, dipping and falling, as exemplified in "ma" (mother), "ma" (hemp), "ma" (horse) and "ma" (to scold) respectively.

In all languages, including the tone languages, the general pitch pattern of a sentence or a phrase is related with the overall meaning of the sentence or the phrase, larger than the meaning of a word. The tone in this case is called intonation. In Chinese for example, "zhe shi ni de" (this is yours) is a declarative sentence making a statement about the ownership of something being talked about, if it is pronounced with a falling intonation, but an interrogative sentence inquiring for whether the thing is a possession of the listener, if it is pronounced with a rising intonation. In English, though usually the syntactic structure of declarative sentences and that of interrogative sentences are different, the former always has a falling intonation, and the latter always has a rising one, just like those sentences in Chinese.

We should notice that pitch in languages is a relational feature. The absolute pitch height of a Chinese word, for example "ma" (mother), may vary among different speakers, and even different times of the same speaker, but this does not influence people's recognition of it as a high-level tone, because it is always high in the four-tone system of a certain speaker at a certain time. The pitch pattern, whether it is level, rising or falling, is something of a comparison between the pitch heights of the internal parts of a pitch contour, having nothing to do with the absolute pitch height. The same is the intonation of a sentence.

2.7.3 Stress

Stress is a relational feature indicating that one syllable is produced with more energy, and therefore more prominent over another, usually the neighboring one. Whether one syllable is stressed or more prominent over another is usually shown in a combination of factors: length, loudness and pitch. A stressed syllable may be longer and louder than its neighbors, and have some kind of change in its pitch pattern.

Every multisyllabic word in English must have at least one stressed syllable. English word stress system is very complex. Though some rules can be formulated, exceptions are often found. Some English words, such as ",concen'tration", have two stresses: a primary stress, indicated by "'" and a secondary stress, indicated by ",". Stress in English sometimes distinguishes word classes. For example, "in'sult" is a verb, but "'insult" is a noun. Vowel quality is also often correlated with stress in English:

the vowel of a stressed syllable is often a strong vowel, diphthong or a weak vowel followed by at least two consonants.

The paragraph above is all about stress as a property of words, called word stress or lexical stress. But a sentence has its own stress pattern, called sentence stress or rhythmic stress. The ultimate stress pattern of a sentence is actually a combination of the sentence stress and the word stress. For example, the last syllable of the word "afternoon" is more stressed when in isolation, but the first syllable is more stressed when in the phrase "afternoon tea". Content words in a sentence are often stressed, while functional words, unstressed. Unstressed words in a sentence often lose their word stresses. For example, in the sentence "John is a teacher", "John" and "teacher" are normally stressed, retaining their stresses, and "is" and "a" are normally unstressed, losing their stresses. If the speaker intends to emphasize a certain word, the word may get extra energy, therefore it is more stressed. Take the sentence again as an example, if the speaker wants to emphasize John's status as a teacher, the word "teacher" will usually become the most stressed word in the sentence.

2.8 Phonation Types

The vibration of the vocal folds not only produces sound waves for the articulators to modify into different qualities, the nature of the vibration itself may also be significant. The process of making sound waves by the vocal folds is called phonation, and it actually has several types. A type of phonation, called normal or modal voice, is used most frequently in every language, and is the easiest and most comfortable to produce. Other widely used phonation types are breathy voice, creaky voice and whispery voice.

Breathy voice is produced with the glottis closed incompletely, causing audible breath noise while the vocal folds are vibrating. Some syllables in Shanghai Chinese are produced with a breathy voice, such as "t^{h}a" (to wash). The first part of the vowel in it is produced with a breathy voice.

Creaky voice is produced with the vocal folds vibrating very slowly, slowly enough for people to recognize the sporadic individual vibrations. A syllable with the concave third tone in Beijing dialect, when spoken by a male adult slowly, often turns into a creaky voice at its lowest pitch point.

When whispering, the glottis is sufficiently narrow, but not narrow enough to cause vibrations, generating an aperiodic noisy sound. Whispery voice is often used when speakers want to speak very quietly or secretly.

2.9 Air Stream Mechanism

What we have talked about so far are all sounds made by an outward air stream initiated by the compression of the lungs. Actually, the air stream in language can be produced in other ways. The three mechanisms that will be talked about in this section are egressive and ingressive glottalic air stream and ingressive velaric air stream. The sounds produced with these three types of air stream mechanisms are ejectives, implosives, and clicks.

Egressive and ingressive refer to the directions of the air stream, i.e., whether it is pushed outward or sucked inward. The sounds produced with the air stream initiated by lungs are called pulmonic sounds. Pulmonic sounds found so far are all egressive, but you can easily make sounds by sucking air into your lungs, though it is not very comfortable to do that.

2.9.1 Egressive and Ingressive Glottalic Air Stream

If the velum rises to block the passage to the nasal cavity, the glottis is tightly closed, and a closure is made in the oral cavity, the part of vocal tract above the glottis will become an enclosed space, as shown in Figure 2.11a. Keeping the velum, the glottis and the oral closure in their status, and at the same time raising or lowering

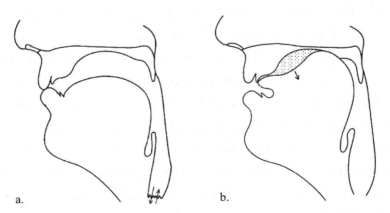

Figure 2.11 Glottalic and velaric air stream mechanisms (Ladefoged, 2006: 14)

the larynx will cause the air pressure in the enclosed space to increase or decrease. A release of the closure in the former case will cause an audible burst of air outward, producing an ejective. A release of the closure in the latter case will cause an audible burst of air inward, producing an implosive.

2.9.2 Ingressive Velaric Air Stream

Clicks are made by raising the back and the left and right sides of the tongue to contact with the velum at the back side and the palate and the teeth at the left and right sides, and at the same time making a closure by the tip or blade of the tongue with the part of the roof of the oral cavity before the velum, forming an enclosed space with a small volume of air trapped in it, then lowering the tongue body, causing the air pressure in the enclosed space to decrease, and then releasing the closure made by the tip or the blade, causing a sudden rushing in of the air stream, making an audible sound, a click. Please see Figure 2.11b.

2.10 The International Phonetic Alphabet (IPA) and Sound Transcription

The International Phonetic Alphabet (IPA) is a set of symbols and diacritics proposed by the International Phonetic Association aiming to provide for every sound used distinctively in every human language a separate representation. It has been revised many times to include new findings in the development of phonetics since its first appearance more than one hundred years ago.

Figure 2.12 is the 2018 version of the IPA. The upper most part of it is the consonant table, the columns of which are different places of articulation, and the rows of which are different manners of articulation. The symbols inside stand for sounds produced at particular place in particular manner. The white boxes without symbols mean the sounds supposed to be placed in the boxes are possible in speech production, but have not found yet. The shaded boxes suggest that the sounds supposed to be placed in the boxes are impossible in speech production.

Below the consonant table is a table containing symbols of sounds produced with non-pulmonic air stream mechanisms and the vowel quadralateral. Other symbols below are various diacritics and suprasegmental symbols. Students interested in Chinese tones may pay a little more attention to the tone symbols at the bottom right corner.

Chapter 2 Phonetics

CONSONANTS (PULMONIC)

	Bilabial	Labiodental	Dental	Alveolar	Postalveolar	Retroflex	Palatal	Velar	Uvular	Pharyngeal	Glottal
Plosive	p b			t d		ʈ ɖ	c ɟ	k g	q ɢ		ʔ
Nasal	m	ɱ		n		ɳ	ɲ	ŋ	N		
Trill	B			r					R		
Tap or flap		ⱱ		ɾ		ɽ					
Fricative	ɸ β	f v	θ ð	s z	ʃ ʒ	ʂ ʐ	ç ʝ	x ɣ	χ ʁ	ħ ʕ	h ɦ
Lateral fricative				ɬ ɮ							
Approximant		ʋ		ɹ		ɻ	j	ɰ			
Lateral approximant				l		ɭ	ʎ	L			

Where symbols appear in pairs, the one to the right represents a voiced consonant. Shaded areas denote articulations judged impossible.

CONSONANTS (NON-PULMONIC)

Clicks		Voiced implosives		Ejectives	
ʘ	Bilabial	ɓ	Bilabial	ʼ	Examples:
ǀ	Dental	ɗ	Dental/alveolar	pʼ	Bilabial
ǃ	(Post)alveolar	ʄ	Palatal	tʼ	Dental/alveolar
ǂ	Palatoalveolar	ɠ	Velar	kʼ	Velar
ǁ	Alveolar lateral	ʛ	Uvular	sʼ	Alveolar fricative

OTHER SYMBOLS

- ʍ Voiceless labial-velar fricative
- w Voiced labial-velar approximant
- ɥ Voiced labial-palatal approximant
- ʜ Voiceless epiglottal fricative
- ʢ Voiced epiglottal fricative
- ʡ Epiglottal plosive
- ɕ ʑ Alveolo-palatal fricatives
- ɺ Voiced alveolar lateral flap
- ɧ Simultaneous ʃ and x

Affricates and double articulations can be represented by two symbols joined by a tie bar if necessary. k͡p t͡s

VOWELS

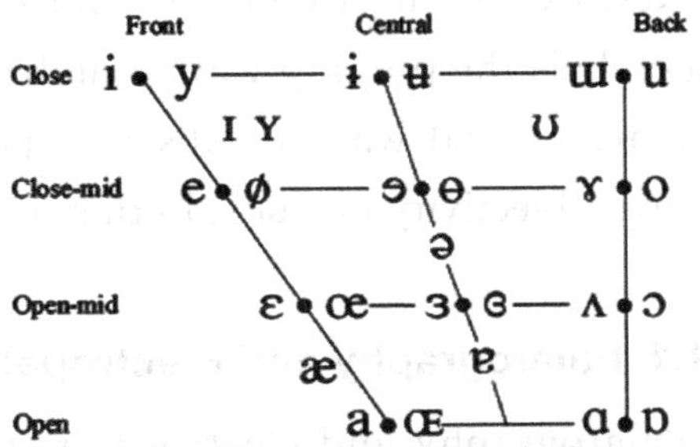

Front   Central   Back
Close   i•y — ɨ•ʉ — ɯ•u
        ɪ ʏ   ʊ
Close-mid e•ø — ɘ•ɵ — ɤ•o
                ə
Open-mid   ɛ•œ — ɜ•ɞ — ʌ•ɔ
           æ   ɐ
Open   a•ɶ — — — ɑ•ɒ

Where symbols appear in pairs, the one to the right represents a rounded vowel.

SUPRASEGMENTALS

- ˈ Primary stress
- ˌ Secondary stress ˌfoʊnəˈtɪʃən
- ː Long eː
- ˑ Half-long eˑ
- ̆ Extra-short ĕ
- | Minor (foot) group
- ‖ Major (intonation) group
- . Syllable break ɹi.ækt
- ‿ Linking (absence of a break)

DIACRITICS Diacritics may be placed above a symbol with a descender, e.g. ŋ̊

	Voiceless	n̥ d̥		Breathy voiced	b̤ a̤		Dental	t̪ d̪
	Voiced	s̬ t̬		Creaky voiced	b̰ a̰		Apical	t̺ d̺
ʰ	Aspirated	tʰ dʰ		Linguolabial	t̼ d̼		Laminal	t̻ d̻
	More rounded	ɔ̹	w	Labialized	tʷ dʷ		Nasalized	ẽ
	Less rounded	ɔ̜	j	Palatalized	tʲ dʲ	ⁿ	Nasal release	dⁿ
	Advanced	u̟	ˠ	Velarized	tˠ dˠ	ˡ	Lateral release	dˡ
	Retracted	e̱	ˁ	Pharyngealized	tˁ dˁ	̚	No audible release	d̚
	Centralized	ë	~	Velarized or pharyngealized	ɫ			
	Mid-centralized	ẋ		Raised	e̝	(ɹ̝ = voiced alveolar fricative)		
	Syllabic	n̩		Lowered	e̞	(β̞ = voiced bilabial approximant)		
	Non-syllabic	e̯		Advanced Tongue Root	e̘			
	Rhoticity	ɚ ɑ˞		Retracted Tongue Root	e̙			

TONES AND WORD ACCENTS
LEVEL

- e̋ or ˥ Extra high
- é ˦ High
- ē ˧ Mid
- è ˨ Low
- ȅ ˩ Extra low
- ↓ Downstep
- ↑ Upstep

CONTOUR

- ě or ˩˥ Rising
- ê ˥˩ Falling
- ᷄ ˦˥ High rising
- ᷅ ˩˨ Low rising
- ᷈ ˧˦˧ Rising-falling
- ↗ Global rise
- ↘ Global fall

Figure 2.12 The International Phonetic Alphabet

By using the IPA system, all the aspects of a sound can be described. But a simplified way of representation with more familiar symbols and less diacritics is also allowed. The full representation is called narrow transcription, and the simplified, broad transcription. Phonetic symbols are usually put into square brackets "[ ]" or a pair of slashes "/ /".

2.11 Observing Speech Production Through Instruments

Researchers mostly take the introspection of the movement of their own organs of speech as the primary way of understanding speech production. In addition to this, there are several ways to observe speech production through instruments, helping improve objectivity in study. In this section, we will discuss some of them.

2.11.1 Palatography and Electropalatography (EPG)

Palatography and electropalatography both help us to know how the tongue and the palate contact with each other in speech production. In palatography, some kind of black powder is pasted onto the surface of the tongue of the speaker first. If the tongue makes a contact with the palate, the powder on the contacted part of the tongue will transfer to the contacted part of the palate; therefore, by observing which part of the palate becomes black and which part of the tongue becomes less black after pronouncing a sound, researchers can know how the tongue and the palate contact with each other in producing the sound. Figure 2.13 is a configuration of the photograph of the palate after saying the Chinese word "zha" (dregs).

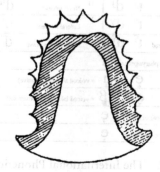

Figure 2.13   A palatogram of Chinese "zha" by
a female speaker (Wu et al., 1988)

Chapter 2　Phonetics

Electropalatagraphy is a digitalized form of palatography. In electropalatography, the speaker wears a pseudo palate about 2 millimeters thick, made of plastic with 62 electrodes on it, covering the alveolar ridge and the hard palate (Figure 2.14). When speaking, if there is contact between the tongue and the pseudo palate, the electrodes in the contacted area will be excited, and the contact pattern will be displayed on the computer screen at the same time. The most important advantage of the electropalatography over the palatography is that it can display the contact pattern between the tongue and the palate in real time, and record the process, but in palatography, what a researcher gets is an ultimate accumulated result of the whole process. Figure 2.15 shows the process of formation and release of the contact

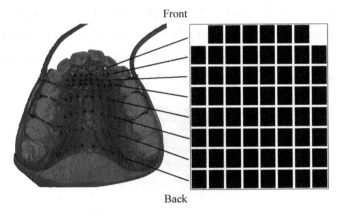

Figure 2.14　A pseudo palate on a dental model and the palatogram displayed on the computer screen if all the electrodes are contacted

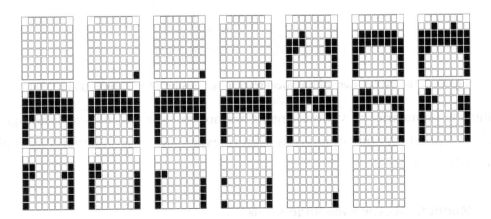

Figure 2.15　The contact patterns showing the formation and release of the closure in saying a nonsense word "azha". The sampling rate is 100 Hz. (Palatograms without contacts are not included.)

between the tongue and the palate in saying a Chinese nonsense word "azha" by a native Beijing female speaker.

The contact pattern between the tongue and the palate shown by palatography and electropalatography is very useful to researchers in the study of sounds involving certain degree of constriction in the alveolar and palatal areas, especially concerning their places of articulation. However, the drawback is also very obvious: They cannot be used in studying sounds without much constriction in the alveolar and palatal areas.

2.11.2 X-ray Photography and Cinematography

Through X-ray researchers can observe directly the movement of various organs in speech production. Figure 2.16 is an X-ray photograph of an adult male speaker saying a Russian mid central vowel. X-ray cinematography is the video recording of viewing speech production through X-ray.

Figure 2.16　X-ray view of the vocal tract in the position for a vowel (Fant, 1960)

But the boundaries of various organs are not so clear cut in X-ray photographs; therefore, a good interpretation needs a lot of experience. The radiation risk is also a big trouble to the speaker.

2.11.3 Magnetic Resonance Imaging (MRI)

Comparing with X-ray, MRI is a much safer technique to the speaker, and the picture is even clearer and easier to interpret (see Figure 2.17). The working procedure

Chapter 2 Phonetics

is very complex and should not be contained in this introductory book. MRI is too slow to get moving pictures of the vocal tract.

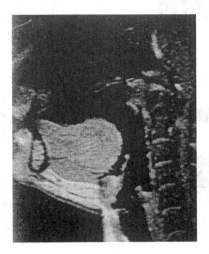

Figure 2.17 An MRI picture in producing an alveolar fricative [s] (Narayanan et al., 1995)

2.12 Acoustic Characteristics of Speech Sounds

Speech sounds are sound waves themselves. The scientific study of sound and how sound is heard is acoustics. The acoustical study of speech sounds is termed as acoustic phonetics. This section shows what various kinds of speech sounds appear in acoustics.

Waveform and spectrogram are two basic techniques to display speech sounds on a computer screen and to do analysis. Figure 2.18 shows the waveform and spectrogram of the English word "see". This and all the other samples of English in this section are spoken by a native American English male speaker, and the analyses of them are all made by the software Praat 4.6.

The upper half of the large picture in Figure 2.18 is a waveform, and the lower half, a spectrogram.

Sounds are transmitted in air by successive changes in air pressure. A waveform is a representation of the air pressure, converted into decibels, along the time line. The horizontal axe is time in seconds. The vertical axe is amplitude in decibels. Amplitude is the base for the loudness of sound, though human ears do some modifications in detecting sound energy.

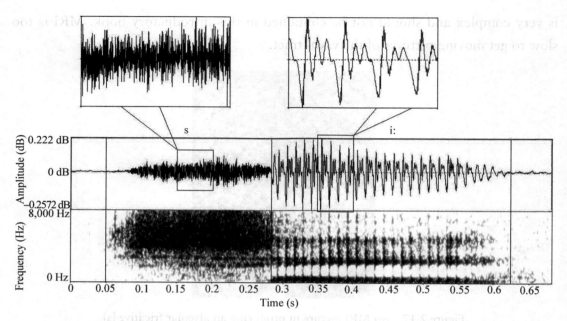

Figure 2.18 The waveform and spectrogram of the word "see" spoken by a native American English male speaker

Sound is usually composed of many waves of different frequencies. A spectrogram shows the energy of the component waves of different frequencies along the time line. A spectrogram is three dimensional. The horizontal axe is still time in seconds; the vertical axe is frequency in hertz, and the thickness of color corresponds to the energy of the component waves.

In Figure 2.18 we can find that the sounds /s/ and /iː/ look very different in waveform and spectrogram. /iː/ shows regular ups and downs in waveform and pulses of energy in spectrogram, while the waveform and distribution of energy in /s/ are generally random.

Periodicity is a common characteristic of all voiced sounds, because they are produced with regular vibration of the vocal folds, or in other words, the successive opening and closing of the glottis. The randomness or noisy characteristic of the sound /s/ is a common characteristic of all sounds produced with turbulence of air in the vocal tract. Vibration of the vocal folds generates periodic sound, and turbulence of air generates a periodic or noisy sound. /iː/ is a vowel without any friction in the vocal tract, and /s/ is a voiceless alveolar fricative, therefore /iː/ is purely periodic, and /s/ is purely noisy.

A combination of periodic sound and noisy sound is possible, by vibrating the vocal folds and generating turbulence at certain place above the larynx at the same time. This is how a voiced fricative is produced. Please have a look at Figure 2.19 to see how the voiced alveolar fricative /z/ looks like in waveform and spectrogram. The waveform of /z/ has overall ups and downs corresponding to the regular vibration of the vocal folds, and minor zigzags originated from the air turbulence caused by the friction at the alveolar position. The spectrogram also shows two kinds of distribution of energy at the same time: The energy at the lower frequencies is periodic, forming a so-called voiced bar in the lower part, while that at the higher frequencies is generally randomized along the time line. The sameness of /z/ and /i:/ on voicing in production, and therefore in periodicity in acoustics makes them not so clear cut as /s/ and /i:/ are, and the transition between them is gradual. The vertical line drawn between /z/ and /i:/ in Figure 2.19 intends only to show the position of the transitional area.

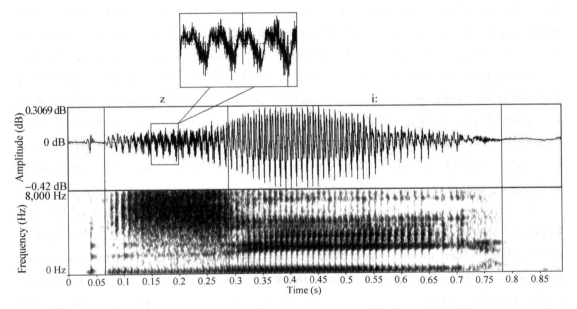

Figure 2.19 The waveform and spectrogram of the letter "z" /zi:/

A plosive is made by a blocking of air in the vocal tract followed by a sudden release causing an often hearable burst. The closed period, called gap in acoustic phonetics, of a voiceless plosive is totally silent, while in that of a voiced one, the vibration of the vocal folds can often be heard. In Figure 2.20 we can see that in the gap of /b/ there are several circles of waves in the waveform, and a voiced bar in the spectrogram, but in the gap of /p/, both of these are not found. The burst of the air stream following the closure makes a sudden increasing of energy in a wide range of frequencies, resulting in a spike in the spectrogram.

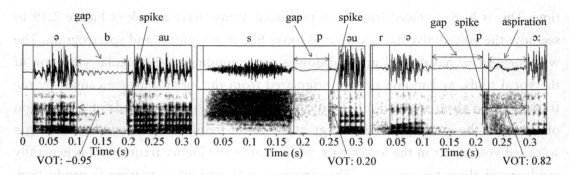

Figure 2.20 Parts of the waveforms and spectrograms of the words "about", "spoke" and "report"

One term that must be mentioned here is the Voice Onset Time (VOT), the value of which is very important in distinguishing voiced plosives from voiceless plosives, and aspirated plosives from unaspirated plosives. The VOT is measured from the start of the explosion of a plosive to the point where vocal fold vibration begins. The value is negative in a voiced plosive, but positive in a voiceless plosive, because the start of voicing precedes the explosion in producing the former but follows in producing the latter. The VOT of an aspirated voiceless plosive is much longer than that of an unaspirated one, because of the aspiration part of the former one. In Figure 2.20, /b/ in "about" is a voiced plosive, so the VOT is –0.95 seconds. The VOT of the aspirated /p/ in "report" is 0.82 seconds, which is much longer than the VOT of the unaspirated /p/ in "spoke", which is only 0.20 seconds in length.

An affricate is a combination of an explosion followed by a period of friction. Let's take the two /dʒ/ sounds in "George" as examples (see Figure 2.21). Notice that the English voiced plosives and affricates at the word's initial position sometimes appear to be voiceless, that is to say, there is no voiced bar and wave before the explosion. Consequently, the starting point of the closure of the first /dʒ/ is not known,

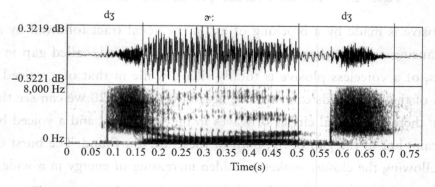

Figure 2.21 The waveform and spectrogram of the word "George"

because it is totally silent, without any acoustic signals. This is just the case of the first /dʒ/ in Figure 2.21.

Fricatives of various kinds show different patterns of energy distribution in frequencies, as shown in Figure 2.22. /f/ in the word "feeling" spreads its energy almost equally from about 1,000 Hz to 8,000 Hz. /s/ in "see" concentrates more energy at about 4,000–5,000 Hz, and distributes most of the rest from 5,000 Hz to 8,000 Hz and above. Two areas of energy concentration are found in /ʃ/ of "she" at about 2,000–3,000 Hz and 5,000–6,000 Hz respectively. The palatalized /hʲ/ in "he" has its energy distributed from about 3,000 Hz to 7,000 Hz with relatively more at the lower frequencies. The differences between plosives of different places of articulation are mostly in the transitional period from the plosive to the vowel following it in the spectrogram, which will not be dealt with in this book.

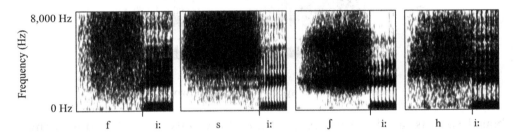

Figure 2.22 Spectrographic patterns of /f/, /s/, /ʃ/ and /hj/ in "feeling", "see" "she" and "he" (time not in proportion)

Vowels and voiced approximants distinguish each other by different patterns of formants. Please look at the generally horizontal black bars in the vowel parts in Figure 2.23. These black bars are called formants, numbered from the bottom upward. The lowest formant is called F1, and the formants above are F2, F3, F4, and so on. Recognition tests show that only F1 and F2 are sufficient for people to distinguish different vowels, though the formants above help in some degree. If the quality of a vowel does not change throughout, the formants, at least F1 and F2, are totally horizontal. Therefore, we can find that /ə/, /uː/ and /æ/ in Figure 2.23 are not purely monophthongs. In general, the value of F1 is related with the backness of a vowel and that of F2 with the height. You can find this correlation in Figure 2.23.

The formant pattern of a semivowel is similar to that of the corresponding vowel, except that it is more dynamic, changing all the time, because it is basically not maintainable. Please have a look at the ever changing contours of the formants of /w/

from and to the two /iː/ sounds preceding and following it respectively in Figure 2.24 and make a comparison with the /uː/ in Figure 2.23.

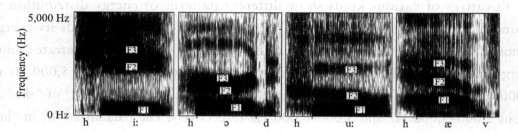

Figure 2.23　Formant patterns of /iː/, /ə/, /uː/ and /æ/ in "he", "heard", "who" and "have" (time not in proportion)

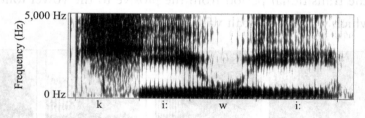

Figure 2.24　The spectrogram of the word "kiwi"

Nasal sounds, as those in Figure 2.25, show only several strong formants at the lower frequencies. Nasals at various places of articulation are quite similar in spectrogram, and distinguish between each other mainly in their transition from or to the adjacent vowels.

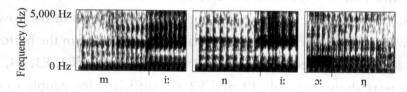

Figure 2.25　Nasals /m/, /n/ and /ŋ/ in "me", "need" and "wrong"

The lateral approximant /l/ in English before a vowel looks similar to a nasal sound in the spectrogram. (see Figure 2.26)

Human's perception of pitch is mainly based on fundamental frequency (F0), with some minor modifications by human ears. F0 is measured in Hertz, corresponding to the number of vocal fold vibrations in a second. For example, if the pitch of a sound is 100 Hz, that means in producing the sound, the vocal folds of the speaker vibrate 100 times in a second. Researchers often make a contour to show the changing of

F0 through time and to extract data. Figure 2.27 presents the F0 contours of an English declarative sentence and an interrogative sentence. You can find that only voiced segments have F0 contours. That is because only when voiced segments are produced, there are vocal fold vibrations. In the declarative sentence (see Figure 2.27a), the pitch starts highest in the beginning, and goes down gradually to the end. In the interrogative sentence (see Figure 2.27b), the pitch goes upward from the beginning to the word "go", then turns down a little, but becomes a little higher again in the last word. The different pitch patterns of the two sentences are typical of the declarative and interrogative sentences in English.

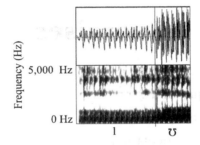

Figure 2.26 The spectrogram of /l/ in the word "look"

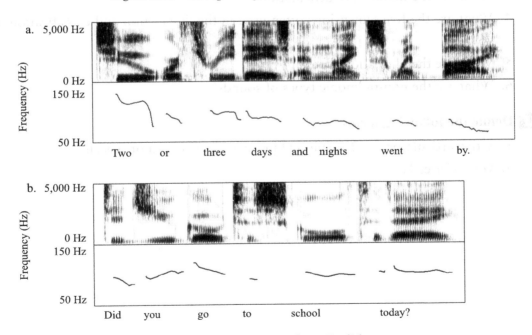

Figure 2.27 The F0 contours of two English sentences

2.13 Summary

Language is a system of human voice at the first place. In this chapter, we have discussed the organs of speech, the places and manners of consonant articulation, the phonation types, the dimensions of vowels, the International Phonetic Alphabet, the ways to see the production of sounds, and the acoustic phonetics in its simplest form. By learning the knowledge of phonetics, students will get a preliminary understanding of sounds in language and be prepared for further study.

Exercises

I Answer the following questions.

1. What are the organs of speech?
2. What are the places of articulation?
3. What are the manners of articulation?
4. What are the five dimensions often used in the description and classification of vowels?
5. What are the phonation types?
6. What are the non-pulmonic types of sounds?

II Define the following terms.

1. active articulator   2. aspirated plosive   3. organ of speech
4. Voice Onset Time

Chapter 3

Phonology

The learning objectives of this chapter are:
1. to master the basic concepts in phonology;
2. to do basic analyses of phonological phenomena;
3. to know preliminarily about the sound pattern of language at present and in the past.

语言学教程
A Coursebook for Linguistics

导言

上一章已经学习了语音学，这一章我们继续学习"音"。音系学与语音学相比，主要研究的是音与音之间的组织方式及语音的共时变异和历时变化。在本章中，我们首先学习语音在语言系统中的确定，即音位系统的建立。音位指在一个语言系统中能够区别意义的一个音。我们平时说的音，一般在语言学中对应的是一个音位。有的情况下，两个读音不完全相同的音也可能属于同一个音位，比如英文的 sport 和 port 中的 /p/，在两个单词中读音不完全一样，但是并不算作两个不同的音位。

本章还介绍了音节的组成方式及音与音的搭配规律等。音节一般至少含有一个元音，也可以同时在元音的前后加上辅音。比如英文第一人称单数 I 只是一个双元音 /ai/ 即可单独成词。元音 /ai/ 之前加上一个辅音 /t/ 就构成一个辅音加元音的音节 /tai/，在英文中成为 tie 这个单词。继续在 /tai/ 后面加上辅音，比如 /d/，可以构成一个辅音加元音再加辅音的更复杂的音节 /taid/，在英文中成为 tide 这个单词。在极少数情况下，一个音节中可以不含有元音，而由一个辅音代替。比如 lesson 的第二个音节可以读作 /sn/，也是可以接受的。英语的语音搭配组成音节，音节单独或者与其他音节再组成单词。这种组合方式并不是完全自由的，有许多限制。比如在英语中，/h/ 一般是不出现在音节末尾的，也不会出现在单词末尾。

在语言中经常会遇到同一个音在不同情况下并不完全一样的情况，这一般被称为语音的共时变异。上面说到的 sport 和 port 中的 /p/ 音位在两个单词中的不同表现就是这方面的典型代表。在处理这样的情况时，有的语言学家喜欢用公式一样的规则来描述，也有的语言学家喜欢用表格排序的方法来演示。

最后，本章还会对历史上的语音变化进行简单介绍。

Writing is nothing but the representation of speech.

—*Jean-Jacques Rousseau*[1]

In the previous chapter, we have learned the speech sounds in human languages. In the present chapter, we will learn how speech sounds are organized and how they function in languages. This area of study is called phonology.

---

[1] Jean-Jacques Rousseau is a Swiss-born philosopher, writer and political theorist whose treatises and novels inspired the leaders of the French Revolution and the Romantic generation.

Chapter 3 Phonology

3.1 Phonemes

We human beings can produce a great number of speech sounds, but not every sound can function as a "significant" sound in a language. /ə/ and /ð/ are two English sounds, but not found in Chinese phonological system. If you replace the /s/ in saying /sai/ (赛) with /ə/ when speaking Chinese, people most likely would still recognize it as /sai/, but with a little weird accent. In this case, it seems that the sound /ə/ is not as "significant" as /s/ in Chinese.

Not only a sound from another language may appear like this, sounds of the same language may also be more or less "significant" against one another. In English, the /p/ in "sport" is an unaspirated bilabial stop, different from the /p/ in "port", which is aspirated and should be better transcribed as /pʰ/, but the former is regarded as a variant of the latter in the English phonological system.

The fact is that sounds in a language are always reduced into a limited number of "significant" sounds, which are important in recognizing a word or distinguishing different words. These significant sounds of a language are called phonemes. /s/ in Chinese is a phoneme, while /ə/ is not. And due to the fact that they are acoustically similar, /ə/, heard by Chinese natives in a Chinese sentence, would most likely be recognized as /s/. Correspondingly, the members of the same phoneme, /p/ and /pʰ/, are usually called allophones.

How do we pin down phonemes in a language? Suppose that you are invited to construct the phonological system of an untested language, how do you find the phonemes in this language? Linguists usually compare one word to another which is different only in one sound, like comparing /kæt/ to /hæt/, or /kil/ to /kił/ in English, and ask the native speakers to tell whether the two are different words. English native speakers mostly can tell /kæt/ from /hæt/, but deny /kił/ as a separate word different from /kil/. So, /k/ and /h/ should be two separated phonemes, while /l/ and /ł/ though a little different are members of the same phoneme. These pairs of words used to distinguish phonemes are usually called minimal pairs. Other minimal pairs in English can be /pein/ vs. /vein/ or /ˈmeni/ vs. /ˈmʌni/. Examples from Chinese can be /tan˥/ (单) vs. /tʰan˥/ (摊) or /suŋ˥/ (松) vs. /səŋ˥/ (僧).

But things are not always as clear as shown by the examples mentioned above. If we compare phonological systems across languages, we can sometimes find that the same sound may be identified as allophones of different phonemes in different languages. Here is an example. In the Japanese word /sakɯɾa/ (桜さくらsakura), the consonant of the third syllable is an alveolar flap /ɾ/. In the American English, the consonant of the second syllable in the word /leɾɝ/ (letter) is the same one sound /ɾ/. But in Japanese it is identified as an allophone of the phoneme /r/, while in American English, as an allophone of the phoneme /t/.

This can happen even in the analysis of the same language. Let's take the romantizaton of the Chinese syllable /tʰiɛn/ (天) as an example. In pinyin, the standard romantization system of Chinese at present, it is written as "tian", in which the open vowel is phonologically identified as an allophone of the phoneme /a/, along with other variants like the open vowels in /ta/ (da搭), /kʰai/ (k'ai开), /san/ (san三) and /fɑŋ/ (fang方). But in Wade-Giles romanization system, it is written as "t'ien" as in "T'ients'in" (天津), in which the same open vowel is identified as an allophone of the phoneme /e/, along with the open vowels in /tsɤ/ (tse噴), /tiɛ/ (tieh跌), /pei/ (pei背), /pʰən/ (p'en噴) and /məŋ/ (meng蒙). Which way is better, in your opinion? Actually, this is not the only one difference between pinyin and Wade-Giles romanization system. If you are interested, you can make a thorough study of both of them, and find out why pinyin is more preferable than Wade-Giles and other competing romantization systems in the past.

Allophones of the same phoneme are usually in complementary distribution in the phonological system; they don't appear in the same phonological context. For example, in English, the clear /l/ can be found only at the initial position in a syllable or before vowels, while the dark /ɫ/ can be found only at the end of a syllable or after vowels. In Chinese, the three variants of /i/ phoneme, /i/ as in /tɕi/ (鸡), /ɣ/ as in /tsɤ/ (姿) and /ʅ/ as in /tʂʅ/ (知), never confuse with each other, because they always follow different consonants.

In some cases, a sound, identified as a separate phoneme by some linguists, may instead be identified as only a feature of the adjacent sound, like the /i/ in Chinese syllable /ɕia/ (虾) based on pinyin system. Some linguists have argued that the syllable should be transcribed as /ɕʲa/ or even /ɕa/, and the /i/ in pinyin system is only a feature of the initial consonant.

Chapter 3 Phonology

3.2 Syllabic Structure and Phonotactics

To say the sounds in a word, we usually don't say them one by one. We often say them in groups, especially when we speak very slowly. These groups are called syllables in linguistics. Think of the word "international", we are most likely to divide it into five syllables like /in.tə.næ.ʃən.əl/. The dots represent the boundaries between syllables. Words consisting of more than one syllable are called multisyllabic words. Words consisting of only one syllable are called monosyllabic words, like /kit/ (kit).

Syllables in a language often fall into a limited number of patterns. Combinations of sounds not fit into the patterns are often thought as not grammatical. If we use C and V to stand for consonants and vowels, English syllables mostly are in one of the following formats, as shown in Table 3.1.

Table 3.1 English syllabic patterns

English syllabic patterns	Example words	
V	/ai/	eye
CV	/biː/	bee
CCV	/plei/	play
CCCV	/strɔː/	straw
VC	/iːtʃ/	each
VCC	/ækt/	act
CVC	/ruːm/	room
CVCC	/film/	film
CCVC	/frɔg/	frog
CCVCC	/slænt/	slant
CCCVC	/spraut/	sprout
CCCVCC	/skript/	script
CVCCC	/nekst/	next

A vowel is nearly always necessary in a syllable. It is called the nucleus. The consonants before the vowel are called onsets, and the ones following the vowel, codas.

The number of consonants in the onset or coda position ranges from one to three, even though CC and CCC clusters are highly restricted. CCC coda is found only in words /nekst/ (next) and /tekst/ (text). CCC onsets can only be one of the following combinations. They must have an /s/ at the beginning, a /t/, /p/ or /k/ in the middle, and a /j/, /w/, /l/ or /r/ at the end. At the coda position, only one kind of combination of three consonants is usually found, if words with reflexional affixes are excluded from consideration. It is /-kst/, as in /nekst/ (next). The number of CC onsets and codas is much larger, though they are still very restricted. At the onset position, while combinations like /sk-/, /sm-/, /fl-/, /br-/ and /dr-/ are frequently found, others such as /mb-/, /sŋ-/, /hr-/ and /wt-/ are not found in English. At the coda position, CC clusters like /-nt/, /-ks/, /-ld/ and /-sp/ are allowed, others like /-ht/, /-pg/, /-sg/, /-bm/ and /-tw/ are not grammatical in English. Table 3.2 lists some examples of the CCC onsets and coda in English.

Table 3.2   English CCC onsets and coda

CCC onsets	Example words	
/str-/	/striːt/	street
/spr-/	/sprɪŋ/	spring
/skr-/	/skriːn/	screen
/spl-/	/splæʃ/	splash
/skl-/	/ˈsklɪərə/	sclera
/skw-/	/skwɛɚ/	square
/stj-/	/ˈstjupid/	stupid
/spj-/	/spjuː/	spew
/skj-/	/ˈskjubə/	scuba
CCC coda	Example word	
/-kst/	/nekst/	next

This area of study, analyzing the rules of combining sounds to make words, is called phonotactics. In Chinese, there are also specific rules governing the construction of syllables. Let's also have a glance of some examples of phonotactics of Chinese, though we will not go very deep into it. /ɕi/ (xi西), /ɕin/ (xin新) and /ɕiŋ/ (xing星) are good Chinese syllables, while /si/, /sin/ and /siŋ/ sound weird. While /tɕia/ (jia家), /lia/ (lia俩) and /tia/ (dia嗲) are members of the Chinese syllable inventory, /fia/, /nia/ and /kʰia/ are not possible syllables.

Chapter 3 Phonology

3.3 Phonological Processes

3.3.1 Velarization

A sound doesn't always stay the same in all contexts. When talking about allophones, we get to know that allophones of the same phoneme or sound usually can be found in different contexts. If we take one of the allophones as the basic form and other ones as derived forms, phonological rules may be constructed between them. Let's take the phoneme /l/ in English as an example.

The two allophones of the phoneme, the clear /l/ and the dark /ɫ/, are in complementary distribution. The former appears mostly before vowels, while the latter after vowels. If we define the clear /l/ as the basic form of this phoneme, the dark /ɫ/ can be derived through the following rule.

$$l \rightarrow ɫ / V\_\sigma$$

In this rule, the symbol before the arrow stands for the basic or original form, and the one after the arrow stands for the derived form. The symbols following the slash indicate the environment or context where the variation happens. Here the blank is an indication of the position of the sound in issue, the V before it stands for a vowel, and the σ after it stands for a syllabic boundary. This rule describes the phonological process that the sound /l/ is always realized as /ɫ/ when it is the last sound of a syllable and the penultimate sound is a vowel.

The dark /ɫ/ is produced with the tongue closer to the velum than the clear /l/ is. Therefore, the phonological process of producing dark /ɫ/ is called velarization of the clear /l/.

3.3.2 Assimilation

Of course, velarization is not the only one phonological process taking place in languages. Assimilation, changing of a sound to be more similar in some way to its neighboring sound, is one of the most commonly found phonological processes across languages.

In English, the plural form marker "-s" is usually pronounced as a voiceless /s/ after voiceless sounds, as in "caps" /kæps/, or as a voiced /z/ after a voiced sound, as in "bags" /bægz/. The voice of the sound is always in accordance with the sound before it, presenting a classic instance of phonological assimilation. If the voiceless form /s/ is regarded as the basic form, the phonological process of assimilation in voice can be formalized as a rule in the following. In it, the feature [+ voiced] stands for voiced sounds before the plural marker "-s", and the # after it stands for the word boundary.

$$s \rightarrow z / [+ \text{voiced}]\_\#$$

Phonological assimilation can also be found in Chinese. The phoneme /a/ can precede both alveolar and velar nasals, as in "ban" (班) and "bang" (帮), though pronounced a little differently. In the former one, it is produced as a front vowel /a/, as it is usually written as, while in the latter syllable, it is produced as a back vowel /ɑ/ in accordance with backness of the velar nasal /ŋ/ following it.

$$a \rightarrow ɑ / \_ŋ$$

3.3.3 Elision

In the flow of words, some sounds may be omitted due to various reasons. This kind of phonological process is called elision. In English, when saying phrases like "last day" and "next week", the /t/ at the end of the first words is often missing, and the actual productions of them are /læs dei/ and /neks wi:k/. The reason causing the elision of the sound /t/ may be that long consonant clusters in the middle of a phrase are difficult in production, and people tend to omit some of them to save their efforts. This phonological process of elision can be represented by the rule in the following, in which the slashed circle Ø stands for the deletion of the sound before the arrow.

$$t \rightarrow Ø / s\_C$$

In Chinese, an example of elision is the missing of /u/ after /f/ in the word "doufu" /toufu/ (豆腐), where the syllable /fu/ is unstressed which makes the effort consuming process of producing a round vowel /u/ after a spread /f/ difficult to completely fulfill. A rule as the following may well describe the process.

$$[- \text{stressed}]\ u \rightarrow Ø / f\_\#$$

3.3.4 Epenthesis

Adding a sound can also be found in languages, even though deleting a sound is more commonly found. Let's take the English plural form again as an example. When the last sound of a word is /s/ or /z/, there is always an additional vowel /i/ inserted into between the word and the plural marker "-s", like in "buses" /bʌsis/. This type of phonological process of adding a sound is called epenthesis in linguistics. The voiced and voiceless alveolar fricatives /s/ and /z/ can be referred as sibilant sounds. If we employ [+ sibilant] to represent them, the rule can be written as the following:

$$\emptyset \rightarrow i\ /\ [+\ \text{sibilant}]\_s$$

3.3.5 Neutralization

Neutralization refers to the phenomenon that two or more sounds may appear as the same sound in some contexts, and as a result lose their differences. For example, in American English, various vowels in stressed syllables usually reduce into a schwa /ə/ when they are unstressed, as shown in Table 3.3.

Table 3.3 Neutralization in English

Vowels in stressed syllables		Neutralized forms	
compete	/iː/	competition	/ə/
photograph	/æ/	photography	/ə/
solid	/ɔ/	solidity	/ə/
phone	/əu/	phonetic	/ə/

3.3.6 Tone Sandhi

Tones in tonal languages may vary in different contexts too. Chinese, as a well-known tonal language in the world, is no exception. Tone sandhi is the linguistic term standing for the phenomena of tones, especially lexical tones, varying according to the phonological contexts they are in.

In Chinese, there are four distinctive tones, namely Tone 1, 2, 3 and 4. The pitch contours of them are high-level, rising, dipping and falling respectively. While most of them stay the same throughout all environments, the third tone may surface as a rising tone, identical to the second tone, when followed by another third tone syllable inside the same phonological phrase. There are some examples in Table 3.4.

Table 3.4 The third tone sandhi in Chinese

Words	Pinyin	Original tones	Actual tones
理想	li xiang	T3.T3	T2.T3
恐鸟	kong niao	T3.T3	T2.T3
警醒	jing xing	T3.T3	T2.T3

The rule representing this phenomenon can be written as:

$$T3 \rightarrow T2\ /\ \_T3$$

3.4 Constraints in Phonological Processes

In the description of phonological processes, the using of rules makes things simple and easy to understand. However, according to Alan Prince and Paul Smolensky (1993/2004), the forces underlying the process are not often properly revealed and represented in rules. Let's take an example from English. Nasalization is one type of assimilation we have mentioned above, where the feature in issue is nasality. In English, the vowel of the word "on" /ɔn/ is always nasalized to /ɔ̃/, an assimilation to the nasal /n/ following it. The rule describing this process can be written as the following:

$$ɔ \rightarrow ɔ̃ / \_n$$

The rule is extremely clear, and it does very good in helping people to understand the process. However, it tells nothing about why that has to happen in the first place. The reason for the vowel /ɔ/ to become /ɔ̃/ is in fact that there is a force in language production preferring an overall consistency in nasality across the whole rhyme of a syllable. Therefore, whenever there is a nasal at the end of a syllable, the vowel before it is preferably nasalized. So an /ɔn/ should always be /ɔ̃n/ instead.

But how can we formalize this force underlying a phonological process theoretically? Alan Prince and Paul Smolensky proposed that this kind of force can be called and formalized as constraints, and the various possible output forms of a word are candidates competing with each other and judged by those constraints involved. This theory is called Optimality Theory.

A classical tableau dealing with these candidates and constraints is like the following in Table 3.5. In it, the two possible pronunciations of the word "on" are listed as two candidates. They are judged by two phonological constraints, Nasal-Consistency and No-Change, one by one, in which the former one should go earlier in the process of evaluation. Nasal-Consistency is a formalization of the force preferring the overall consistency of nasality in a rhyme, while No-Change represents the force preferring stability or faithfulness to the original sound. The first round of competition between the two candidates is judged according to the higher ranked constraint Nasal-Consistency, and the candidate /ɔn/ loses the game, and an asterisk (*) is assigned to it as a marker of failing the game, while the candidate /ɔ̃n/ wins the game, and a tick (√) is assigned to it as a marker of winning the game. The second round of competition between them judged by the constraint No-Change is no longer necessary, because the best candidate has already been selected, though it favors the loser instead of the winner. This phonological process is summarized in Table 3.5.

Table 3.5 The analysis of nasalization in Optimality Theory

/ɔn/ → /ɔ̃n/

	Constraints	
Candidates	Nasal-Consistency	No-Change
/ɔn/	*	
/ɔ̃n/	√	*

This approach shows us another way of describing a phonological process, not only presenting us the process itself, but also helping us in the understanding of underlying forces motivating the process.

3.5 Historical Sound Change

Language is always changing. What we speak now is not necessarily the same as what our ancestors spoke. The classical Chinese or wenyan is the written form of the language spoken by ancient Chinese people, and a lot of differences in vocabulary and grammar can be found between it and the present Chinese language. The pronunciation should not be the same either, though people, except linguists, commonly don't know it, because Chinese characters were coined mostly according to their senses. English scripts as a phonetic writing system, on the other hand, preserve more information about the sounds of English in the past. Linguists generally agree that there have been a lot of sound changes in English in the past. The Great Vowel Shift is one of the best known events taking place in the history of English.

The Great Vowel Shift refers to the strikingly different pronunciations of the long stressed vowels in Middle English before the 15th century and in Modern English, as shown in Table 3.6.

Table 3.6 The Great Vowel Shift and example words

Middle English	Modern English	Example words
/iː/	→ /ai/	kite

(Continued)

Middle English	Modern English	Example words
/eː/	→ /iː/	sheep
/ɛː/	→ /iː/	leap
/aː/	→ /ei/	late
/uː/	→ /au/	house
/oː/	→ /uː/	boot
/ɔː/	→ /əu/	boat

Most words went through the change quite regularly, but some words do retain their old pronunciations. Some words containing "ea", for example, do not take on the new pronunciation /iː/, like "bear" and "pear". Some words containing "oa" remain unchanged as in "broad". The sound of the final unstressed "e", as in "kite" and "late", was pronounced as a schwa /ə/ in the earlier stage of Middle English, but was muted altogether in later times. The word "kite" at that time should be pronounced as /ˈkiːtə/.

Consonants mostly remain the same at present, as they were pronounced in Middle English, but still there were a small number of consonantal changes taking place around the same time as the vowels were moving crazily. The letter "r" at that time was an alveolar trill, like its Spanish counterpart. The "k" in the combination "kn" was still pronounced as /k/, so that the word "knife" was /kniːfə/ at that time. The nowadays muted "gh" was pronounced as a velar fricative /x/, similar to the consonant in the Chinese word /xɤ/ (he喝). Therefore, the word "light" at that time was pronounced as /lixt/.

3.6 Summary

In this chapter, we have learned about some basic concepts in phonology, like phoneme, assimilation, etc., and two ways to describe and/or analyze phonological phenomena by using rules or OT tableaus. And we have also discussed preliminarily about the sound patterns of language at present and in the past. Students can get an overall understanding of phonology and a preliminary ability to do research in this area after studying this chapter.

Chapter 3 Phonology

Exercises

I **Define the following terms.**
  1. phoneme   2. assimilation   3. epenthesis   4. neutralization
  5. tone sandhi   6. the Great Vowel Shift

II **Recognize whether the following pairs of words are minimal pairs or not.**
  1. cat/kit   2. wave/waffle   3. hour/our   4. light/night
  5. church/churl   6. god/dog

III **Count the number of syllables in the following words.**
  1. sight   2. broadcasting   3. penicillin   4. vehicle
  5. incomprehensibility   6. preside

IV **Answer the following question.**
  What does the following phonological rule stand for?
  $$i: \rightarrow ai / \_\_\#$$

Chapter 4

Morphology

The learning objectives of this chapter are:
1. to master the definition and classification of morphemes;
2. to familiarize students with the major and minor processes of word formation;
3. to analyze the word formation in English newspaper headlines.

语言学教程
A Coursebook for Linguistics

导言

　　形态学是语言学的分支，它研究词的内部结构和构词规则。例如，英语名词 worker 由两部分构成：work 和 er，依此可以总结出一条规则：在动词后添加 er 可以生成名词。更多的例子如 writer、reader、murderer、commuter 等。词是由词素构成的。根据单独出现的能力，词素分为自由词素和粘着词素。自由词素是可以独自成词的词素，如 book、poor、bottle 等。与此相反，books 中的 s 和 worker 中的 er 都不能单独出现，它们必须与至少另外一个词素一起出现，因此被称为粘着词素。词根是词的基础形式，它是词中去掉词缀后的剩余部分，如在 denationalization 一词中，去掉 de、al、iz(e)、ation 之后，剩下的成分就是词根 nation，它表达的是词的基本含义。词缀是只能依附于别的词素之上使用的构词成分，它分为屈折词缀和派生词缀。屈折词缀体现的是语法关系，如数、人称、限定、体以及格等。派生词缀一般分为前缀、中缀和后缀，分别取决于它们在词中的位置。构词法有多种，根据使用的频率，构词法分为主要构词法和次要构词法。主要构词法有复合法、派生法和转类法。次要构词法有拼缀法、截短法、首字母缩略法、专有名词转化法和逆生法等。复合法是将两个或两个以上的独立词合并生成一个词的方式，如 blackboard、roller coaster、round-the-clock 等。派生法就是派生构词，指在词根上加词缀构成新词，如 beauty + ify = beautify。转类法，又称"零派生"，是指通过词类转化构成新词的方法。也就是说，一种词类加上零形式转化为另一种词类，词的原形不变，但转类后的词性体系和语法功能都改变了，如 bottle 可由名词不加任何形式变化直接转化为动词 to bottle。拼缀法是把两个词同时进行裁剪，或截头或去尾，或只裁剪两个词中的一个，保留另外一个，然后把两部分拼合在一起，构成一个新词，如 *smoke + fog = smog*。将单词缩写，词义和词性保持不变的英语构词法称为截短法，主要有截头、去尾、截头去尾等形式，如 dormitory 去掉 itory 就变成了截短词 dorm。首字母缩略法指用单词首尾字母组成一个新词的英语构词法。这种形式的英语构词法生成的新词，读音主要有两种形式，即各字母分别读音，如 NBC；作为一个单词读音，如 AIDS。专有名词转化法是指专有名词（人名、地名、书名、商标名）转化为普通名词，如 china（瓷器）是由 China 转化的。逆生法被看作是派生法的逆向构词法，就是把原词词尾去掉，生成新词。这里的词尾并不是派生词中定义的后缀，所以又被称为"假后缀"，如 edit 的原式是 editor。

　　Grammar thus operates between the upper limit of the sentence and the lower limit of the morpheme or minimal grammatical unit. Between these limit structures given such titles as clause, phrase, and word may be abstracted and formally delimited.

—*R. H. Robinson*[1]

1　R. H. Robinson is a renowned British linguist. His most influential works are *General Linguistics* and *A Short History of Linguistics*.

Chapter 4　Morphology

4.1　Definition of Morphology

Morphology is about the structure of words. The word "morphology" originates from German *morphologie* (1817) and it contains two roots: "morpho-" (meaning "shape") + "-logy" (meaning "study of"). Morphology is the branch of linguistics that studies the internal structure of words and the rules that govern the formation of words. Words have an internal structure imposed by the word-formation rules which produce them, such as the word "face" and the words stemmed from "face" (see Figure 4.1).

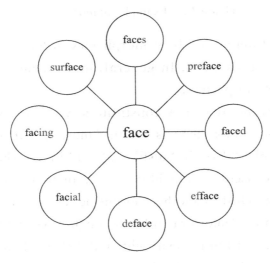

Figure 4.1　Words stemmed from "face"

4.2　Morpheme

Morpheme is the smallest meaningful linguistic unit, not divisible or analyzable into smaller forms. For instance, the word "cats" consists of "cat" and "-s"; the word "workers" is made up of "work", "-er" and "-s". These smaller components are known as morphemes, but they themselves cannot be further analyzed. Therefore, a morpheme is the smallest meaningful unit of language, a unit that cannot be divided into further smaller units without destroying or drastically altering the meaning, whether it is lexical or grammatical. The following examples would help us to have a deep sense of morpheme: "nation", "national", "nationalize", "denationalize" and "denationalization" (see Figure 4.2).

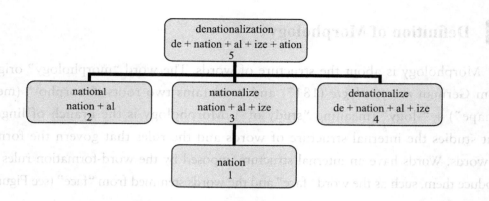

Figure 4.2 Examples of morphemes

There are many different kinds of morphemes in language and linguists have classified them in various ways. In general, morphemes are divided into free morphemes and bound morphemes.

Free morpheme is one that may constitute a word by itself, such as "book", "rich" and "take". Bound morpheme is one that must appear with at least one other morpheme, for example, "dis-" in "dislike", "-ed" in "worked". In other words, morphemes are free to occur as individual words, or they may be bound, in which case they are always attached to another morpheme. The distinction between free and bound morphemes can be demonstrated by the English word "dogs": "Dog" is a free morpheme since it is a word in its own right, and "-s" is a bound morpheme, as it is not a word in its own right. If we divide the word "polygamy" into morphemes, we will find that each morpheme is bound: None of the morpheme units can stand alone. If we do the same with the word "landlady", we find that each morpheme can stand alone; they are all free. More examples of free and bound morphemes are given in Table 4.1.

Table 4.1 Examples of free and bound morphemes

Words	Free morphemes	Bound morphemes
trying	try	ing
remove	move	re
worked	work	ed
enrich	rich	en
drinkable	drink	able
poorest	poor	est

(Continued)

Words	Free morphemes	Bound morphemes
hers	her	s
slowness	slow	ness
boxes	box	es

Free morphemes are also called free roots. What is a root? A root is the basic unchangeable part of a word, and it conveys the main lexical meaning of the word. Root morphemes may be bound or free. For instance, "work" is a free root; in "monologue", "logue" is a bound root which means "to talk". It conveys the basic meaning of the word "monologue", but it cannot stand in its own right. More examples of bound roots are shown in Table 4.2.

Table 4.2 Examples of bound roots

Words	Bound roots	Meaning
inject	ject	to throw
conceive	ceive	to take
detain	tain	to hold
dialogue	logue	to talk
polygamy	gamy	marriage
defence	fence	to hit
location	loc	to position
dentist	dent	tooth
audience	audi	to hear
annual	ann	year
inspect	spect	to see
scripture	script	to write
revise	vise	to see
process	cess	to go
contradictory	dict	to say

4.2.1 Morph and Allomorph

A morpheme may have different phonetic (sound) and orthographic (written) realizations. For instance, the plural marker "-s" is realized phonetically and orthographically in the words "book*s*"(/s/), "train*s*" (/z/), and "box*es*" (/iz/) respectively. To distinguish the phonetic realizations from the functional morphemes, linguists often call "-s" a morph. Thus, morphs are the phonetic and orthographic forms which realize morphemes. Each of these realizations, namely /s/, /z/, /iz/, /iː/, and /n/, is an allomorph of the morph "-s", such as in the words "texts", "bags", "families", "feet", "oxen", etc. Therefore, an allomorph is a member of a set of morphs which represent the same morpheme. A typical example is the prefix "in-". When "in-" precedes "b", "p" and "m", its allomorph is "im-", such as "imbalance", "impossible" and "immature". When "in-" occurs before "r" and "l", its allomorphs are "ir" (irregular) and "il" (illegal).

4.2.2 Derivational Affixes and Inflectional Affixes

Bound morphemes are subdivided into bound roots and affixes. A bound root conveys the basic meaning of a word, but it cannot stand alone by itself in a word. An affix does not convey the basic meaning and cannot stand alone by itself in a word. Affixes may be divided formally into three major positional classes according to the position they occur in relation to the root morpheme. For instance, in "unkind", "un" is a prefix; in "kindness", "ness" is a suffix; in "feet", "ee" is an infix.

Affixes are categorized into derivational affixes and inflectional affixes. Derivational affixes are so called because when they are added to another morpheme, they "derive" a new word. For example, "un + kind" forms a new word "unkind". Generally, derivational affixes change the meaning and the lexical category of the words which they attach to. Another category of affixes are inflectional affixes. They are not used to produce new words, but rather to indicate the syntactic relation between words and show aspects of the grammatical function of a word. Inflectional affixes serve to express such meanings as plurality, tense and the comparative or superlative degree, etc. English has only eight inflectional morphemes, as illustrated in Table 4.3.

Table 4.3 Types of inflectional morphemes

Word classes	Forms	Meanings	Examples
noun	-s/es	plural	cats/boxes
	-'s	genitive case	student's
verb	-s	third person singular	works
	-ed	past tense	worked
	-ed/en	past participle	worked/written
	-ing	progressive tense	working
adjective/adverb	-er	comparative degree	richer
	-est	superlative degree	richest

4.3 Word Formation

There are various ways of forming words. The various processes of forming words can be classified into major and minor processes on the basis of the frequency of usage. There are three major processes, namely compounding (composition), affixation (derivation) and conversion (functional shift/zero-derivation). The minor processes mainly include blending, clipping, acronymy, words from proper names, back-formation, onomatopoeia and coinage.

4.3.1 Compounding (Composition)

For English, compounding or composition is the most powerful word building process. What is compounding? Please look at the words "downtown", "workout" and "tug of war". These words consist of two or more separate words and are called compounds. To sum up, compounding or composition is a word-forming process by joining two or more separate words to produce a new unit, a compound word. Compounds are written in different ways. Some are written in a solid way, such as "airtight" and "airmail". Some are written in a hyphenated way, for instance, "air-conditioning". Some are written in an open way, like "air force" and "air raid". It's difficult to decide which form should be used as a criterion. Generally speaking, a personal preference is taken into consideration. Sometimes the same compound may appear in three different forms, for example, "flowerpot", "flower-pot" and "flower pot". In American English, compounds are usually written in solid and open forms. In British English, however, compounds are usually written hyphenated. Phonetically, many compounds have a so-called compound accent, that is, a single stress on the first element, such as "'blue bottle" (肉蝇), "'blue fish" (海豚), "'green hand" (生手), "'red meat" (牛羊肉) and "'dark horse" (黑马). Compound accent is different from normal free combination accent, which has a secondary stress on the first element, as in "blue 'bottle", "blue 'fish", "green 'hand", "red 'meat" and "dark 'horse". Hence, there is usually no difficulty in distinguishing a compound from a free combination by the phonological criterion. Another feature of a compound is that semantically it expresses a single idea. The meaning of a compound can be subdivided into transparent meaning and opaque meaning. Transparent meaning indicates that the meaning of a compound is derived from the combined lexical meaning of its components which one can easily recognize. For example, "backdoor" is a door at the back of a house or other buildings; "sunset" is the time of the sun's setting; "workday" is a day for work. However, we cannot always tell what the compound means by the words it contains. The meaning of a compound is not always the sum of the meanings of its parts. In this sense, the meaning is opaque. Examples are "love handles", "Adam's apple" and "sit-in". Therefore, semantically, a compound can be said to have a meaning which may be related to but cannot always be inferred from the meaning of its component parts. Syntactically, a compound functions as one grammatical unit in a sentence, regardless of the word classes of the combined individual elements. For example, "round-the-clock" in sentence (1) functions as an adjective to modify the noun "watch" and "mass produce" in sentence (2) plays as a verb. In sentence (3), the word class of "downtown" is a noun.

(1) They kept a *round-the-clock* watch on the house. (adjective)

(2) The factory is now able to *mass produce* instruments of high quality. (verb)

(3) The city is providing free transportation to the stadium from *downtown*. (noun)

The features of compounds stated above are criteria for distinguishing compounds and free phrases. For instance, the compound "greenhorn" has stress on "green", while the free phrase "green horn" is stressed on "horn". Moreover, the free phrase "green horn" is necessarily green, while the compound "greenhorn" refers to someone who lacks experience of something and it has nothing to do with the color green. That is to say, "green" does not mean green in "greenhorn". We cannot defer the meaning of the whole just from the meanings of the parts of the compound. More examples of compounds and free phrases are listed in Table 4.4.

Table 4.4 Examples of compounds vs. free phrases

Compounds	Free phrases
greenroom (玻璃暖房)	green house
greenback (美钞)	green back
greenline (轰炸线，敌我分界线)	green line
greenfly (蚜虫)	green fly
greentail (步鱼)	green tail
greengrocer (蔬菜水果商)	green grocer
dog days (暑天)	dog days
blackguard (恶棍)	black guard
grand piano (三角钢琴)	grand piano
blackboard (黑板〔教学用具，不一定是黑色的〕)	black board
darkroom (暗室〔专供冲洗胶卷用的房间〕)	dark room
homeplate (棒球的本垒打)	home plate

4.3.2 Affixation (Derivation)

Affixation or derivation is a word-formation process by which new words are created by adding a prefix, or a suffix, or both, to an already existing word. For example, the word "dislike" is formed by prefix "dis-" and free morpheme "like". This process of word building is called prefixation. Vice versa, if we add a suffix to an existing word, such as "death" plus suffix "-ist", we create a new word "deathist" which means a person who is prejudiced against the belief that science and technology will someday overcome human death. This process is called suffixation. In general, prefixes are non-class changing, for instance, "natural" to "unnatural", the word class does not change. Prefixes change the meanings of the words. Few prefixes are class-changing, such as "force" to "enforce". Unlike prefixes, suffixes mainly change the word class, such as nouns to verbs, verbs to adjectives, adjectives to adverbs, and so forth, as in "success" to "successful".

4.3.3 Conversion (Functional Shift/Zero-derivation)

What is conversion? First, let's look at the two sentences.

(4) Please use *Google* to do a research. (noun)

(5) Please *Google* it. (verb)

In sentence (4), "Google" is a noun. It refers to an American multinational technology company specializing in Internet-related services and products. In sentence (5), "Google" is a verb, meaning to search for something on the Internet using the Google search engine. In these sentences, the word "Google" has shifted from a noun to a verb, whereas its spelling and pronunciation remain the same. This type of word-forming process is called conversion or functional shift. Therefore, conversion is a word formation in which a word of certain class is shifted into a word of another word class without the adding of an affix. In this sense, conversion is also called zero derivation. More examples of conversion are as below.

(6) Please *email* me tomorrow. (verb)

　　Please send me an *email* tomorrow. (noun)

(7) The doctor *eyed* (verb) my swollen *eye* (noun).

(8) My grandmother *microwaved* the lunch. (verb)

　　My grandmother heated the lunch in the *microwave*. (noun)

(9) The man *named* (verb) his baby a beautiful *name* (noun).

(10) The man just needs a good *cry*. (noun)

　　　The baby *cried* all night. (verb)

In general, during the process of conversion, the spelling and pronunciation of words do not change, but there are a few exceptions which are illustrated in Table 4.5.

Table 4.5　Some exceptions of changes of word forms in conversion

a. Voiceless to voiced consonant	
Noun	**Verb**
house /-s/	house /-z/
use /-s/	use /-z/
mouth /-θ/	mouth /-ð/
shelf /-f/	shelve /-v/
sheath /-θ/	sheathe /-ð/
advice /s/	advise /z/
belief /f/	believe /v/

Chapter 4 Morphology

(Continued)

Noun	Verb
grief /f/	grieve /v/
abuse /s/	abuse /z/

b. Initial to end stress

Noun	Verb
'conduct	con'duct
'extract	ex'tract
'permit	per'mit

Apart from the three major types of word formation, there are also minor types of word formation, such as blending, clipping, acronymy, words from proper names, back-formation, onomatopoeia and coinage.

4.3.4 Blending

Blending is a process of word formation in which a new word is formed by combining parts of two or more words or a word plus a part of another word. The result of such a process is called a blend. For example, the word "smog" is formed by combining parts of "smoke" and "fog" and "newscast" is formed by combining the word "news" and part of the word "broadcast". More examples of blending are shown in the following.

- situation + comedy = sitcom
- lunar + astronaut = lunarnaut
- medical + care = medicare
- motor + town = motown

Blends can be divided into four types: head + head, head + tail, word + tail and head + word. Some examples are illustrated in Table 4.6.

Table 4.6 Types of blends

head + head		
First word	Second word	Blend
*commu*nications	*sat*ellite	comsat
*mot*or	*ped*al	moped
*tele*printer	*ex*change	telex

(Continued)

head + head		
*fo*rmula	*trans*lation	fortran
*sit*uation	*com*edy	sitcom
head + tail		
First word	**Second word**	**Blend**
*br*eakfast	*lunch*	brunch
*m*elt	*weld*	meld
*fan*tastic	*fabulous*	fantabulous
*mo*tor	*tel*	motel
*cre*mate	*mains*	cremains
word + tail		
First word	**Second word**	**Blend**
lunar	astro*naut*	lunarnaut
work	wel*fare*	workfare
tour	auto*mobile*	tourmobile
slim	gym*nastics*	slimnastics
talk	mar*athon*	talkathon
death	ann*iversary*	deathiversary
head + word		
First word	**Second word**	**Blend**
*psy*chological	*war*	psywar
*medi*cal	*care*	medicare
*gu*ess	*estimate*	guestimate
*Euro*pe	*Asia*	Euroasia
*auto*mobile	*camp*	autocamp

4.3.5 Clipping

The process of clipping involves the deletion of one or more syllables from a word, which is also available in its full form. An example is "phone" from "telephone". Clipping is mainly categorized into four types.

1. Apocope

Apocope is the omission or deletion of the last part of the word. This is the most common type of clipping. Examples are: exam (← examination), kilo (← kilogram), dorm (← dormitory), homo (← homosexual), memo (← memorandum), comfy (← comfortable), etc.

2. Aphaeresis

Aphaeresis is the omission or deletion of the first part of the word. Examples are: bus (← omnibus), phone (← telephone), copter (← helicopter), quake (← earthquake), plane (← airplane), wig (← periwig), burger (← hamburger), van (← caravan), scope (← telescope), etc.

3. Front and Back Clipping

Front and back clipping is the deletion which occurs at the front and back of the word. Such type of clipping is not common in English. Examples are: flu (← influenza), tec (← detective), fridge (← refrigerator), and script (← prescription).

4. Phrase Clipping

Phrase clipping is the shortening of a phrase. Examples are: perm (← permanent wave), zoo (← zoological garden), pub (← public house), pop (← popular music), daily (← daily paper), weekly (← weekly paper), etc.

4.3.6 Acronymy

Acronymy is the process of word formation in which a word is formed from the initial letters of the name of an organization or a scientific term. For example, "WTO" is formed from "World Trade Organization" and "SAM" is formed from "Surface to Air Missile". Acronymy is subdivided into initialism and acronym. Acronyms differ from initialisms in that they are pronounced as words rather than as sequences of letters.

There are more illustrations of initialisms and acronyms in the following part.

1. Initialism

IOC: International Olympics Committee
ISBN: International Standard Book Number
UN: United Nations
AP: Associated Press
VIP: very important person
ATM: Automatic Teller Machine
HSK: Hanyu Shuiping Kaoshi
c/o: care of
B.A.: Bachelor of Arts
ID: identification card

CIA: Central Intelligence Agency
H-bomb: hydrogen bomb
2. Acronym
AIDS: Acquired Immune Deficiency Syndrome
TOEFL: Test of English as a Foreign Language
IELTS: International English Language Testing System
UNESCO: United Nations Educational, Scientific and Cultural Organization
radar: radio detection and ranging

4.3.7 Words from Proper Names

Another minor type of word formation is the coinage of common words from proper names. A proper noun is a noun belonging to the class of words used as names for specific or unique individuals, events, or places, and may include real or fictional characters and settings. The transition from proper names to common words is gradual. They come from all sources, such as names of people, names of places, names of books and trade marks, etc. The names of many scientists have been used in the particular fields of study in which they were distinguished, like "diesel" from Rudolf Diesel and "mackintosh" from Charles Mackintosh. In a similar way, quite a few of our familiar words are derived from the names of places. Examples are "china", "champagne" and "afghan". Some common words are derived from the names of books, such as "godfather", "catch 22" and "utopia". Although a trademark is owned by a particular company and used for a specific class of products, some trademarks become so familiar that they are used by many people for similar products. That is, some trademarks become common words. Examples are "Mickey Mouse", "Mr. Clean" and "rayon".

4.3.8 Back-formation

Back-formation is a term used to refer to a type of word formation in which a shorter word is coined by the deletion of a supposed affix from a longer form already present in the language.

The following are major types of back-formation.

1) Verbs created from nouns ending in "-er", "-or", "-ar":
   editor—to edit

Chapter 4 Morphology

    escalator—to escalate
    house sitter—to house sit
    stoker—to stoke
2) Verbs created from abstract nouns:
    diagnosis—to diagnose
    television—to televise
    enthusiasm—to enthuse
    automation—to automate
    concordance—to concord
3) Verbs created from adjectives:
    lazy—to laze
    cosy—to cose
    gloomy—to gloom
4) Verbs created from compound nouns:
    match-maker—to match-make
    merry-making—to merry-make
    dress-maker—to dress-make

4.3.9 Onomatopoeia

Onomatopoeia is the process of word formation in which a word is created by the imitation of sounds. A word formed in this way is called an onomatopoeic word (imitative word or echoic word), whose pronunciation suggests the meaning of the word. The words "bang" and "crash" are clearly imitative of the sounds that they denote. More examples are the "meow" of a cat, the "coo" of a pigeon, the "hiss" of a snake, etc.

4.3.10 Coinage

Coinage is the process of word formation in which new words are coined by analogy. Some examples are listed below.

    eye candy → arm candy (an extremely beautiful person who accompanies a member of the opposite sex to a party or event, but is not romantically involved with that person)

    cat fishing → kitten fishing (embellishing or exaggerating one's online dating profile) cat fishing → hat fishing (tricking a potential dating partner by wearing a hat to hide one's baldness or receding)

nearsighted → nerd sighted (the inability to see beyond a technology's interesting technical aspects, particularly to miss its ethical implications; to see the world from the perspective of a nerd)

face blindness → tree blindness (the disregard of the trees in one's environment)

man spreading → beach spreading (taking up more than one's fair share of space on a crowded beach)

4.4 Summary

Morphology is about the structure of words. Words consist of morphemes. A morpheme is, by definition, a meaningful linguistic unit that contains no smaller meaningful units. Morphemes vary in kind and function. We can classify morphemes into several categories: free versus bound and derivational versus inflectional.

There are many ways in which the lexicon of a language can be enlarged. The major processes of word formation are compounding, affixation and conversion. The minor processes mainly include blending, clipping, acronymy, words from proper names, back-formation, onomatopoeia and coinage.

Exercises

I Decide whether each of the following statements is true or false.

1. Morphology studies the internal structure of words and the rules by which words are formed.
2. A morpheme is the smallest linguistic unit of language.
3. A free morpheme is one that can be uttered alone with meaning, such as the word "richer".
4. Conversion is a word-formation process whereby a word of a certain word class is shifted into a word of another word class without the addition of an affix.

5. Derivational affixes are added to an existing form to create a word.
6. Phonetically, the stress of a compound always falls on the second element, while the first element receives a secondary stress.
7. Acronymy is a type of shortening, using the first letters of words to form a proper name or a phrase. An acronym is pronounced letter by letter.
8. Clipping often alters spelling. For example, "comfortable" is changed into "comfy"; "handkerchief" becomes "hanky".
9. On the morphemic level, words can be classified into simple, complex and compound words, according to the number and type of morphemes they are composed of.
10. Compounding, affixation and blending are the three major types of word formation in contemporary English.

II Divide the following words into morphemes and identify each morpheme as free or bound, derivational or inflectional.

1. blackboard   2. deform   3. working   4. receive   5. comfortable

III Change the construction of the following sentences by converting the nouns into verbs according to the example.

Example: David removed the snow with a *shovel.*
            David *shoveled* the snow.

1. She looked after the orphan like a *mother*.
2. Tom repeated what the boss had said by rote like a *parrot*.
3. The police followed the suspected spy closely like a *shadow*.
4. Will you please send the parcel by *mail*?
5. This is the *divide* between the two rivers.

IV Express the following expressions in one compound word.

1. someone who writes songs
2. someone who cleans windows
3. the rise of the sun
4. the lights for the control of the traffic
5. the control of one's own emotions and actions
6. to tan by the sun
7. walk in sleep

8. dream during the day
9. as cheap as dirt
10. as white as snow

V Answer the following questions.

1. List as many pairs of "-ee" and "-er" examples as you can. What do "-ee" and "-er" mean in all your examples?
2. Two or more negative prefixes can be applied to the same word. What difference in meaning is signaled by the prefixes?
   a. uninterested/disinterested
   b. unarmed/disarm
   c. counter-culture/uncultured
   d. disconnected/unconnected
   e. imbalance/unbalanced

VI Explain the formation and meaning of each of the following blends.

1. sitcom   2. smog   3. motel   4. brunch
5. lunarnaut

VII Give clippings for the following words and phrases.

1. refrigerator   2. comfortable   3. helicopter   4. debutante
5. limousine   6. memorandum   7. permanent wave   8. public house
9. zoological garden   10. handkerchief

Chapter 5

Syntax

The learning objectives of this chapter are:
1. to master the definition of syntax and constituency;
2. to familiarize students with the syntactic operations;
3. to conduct an analysis of sentence structure in literary works.

> **导言**
>
> 句法学是语言学的核心分支之一。句法是研究语言的不同成分组成句子的规则或句子结构成分之间的关系。句子的内部结构是对结构组成成分的描述，可用主语、谓语、宾语、限定词、名词等术语。在句子结构分析中，成分用来指任何语言单位，而该单位又是更大的语言单位的一部分，若干成分共同组成一个结构。树形图不仅能显示出句子的线性结构，而且能清楚地表明其阶层结构，这种阶层关系用"支配"这一术语来定义。句子结构分为表层结构和底层结构。句法操作可将一种句法结构转换为另一种句法结构。

Chomsky's ultimate goal is to devise a theory of Universal Grammar/UG which generalizes from the grammars of particular I-languages to the grammars of all possible natural (i.e., human) I-languages.

—*Andrew Radford*[1]

5.1 Introduction

In this chapter we explore how words are organized in phrases and sentences. We also explore the relationships between certain kinds of sentence pairs such as actives and passives. We investigate how a finite grammar can generate an infinite number of sentences and how the "creative" aspects of producing and understanding novel sentences are normal parts of everyone's competence.

All languages have ways of referring to entities—people, places, things, ideas, events, and so on. The expressions used to refer to entities are noun phrases. The proper nouns "Pam" and "Pennsylvania", the common nouns "cows" and "calories", and the personal pronouns "he", "she" and "them" are noun phrases. So are more complex expressions such as "Pam's mother", "that bag of tricks", "the star of the show", "a judge from Jersey" and "that feisty federal judge in Massachusetts who was nominated by Nixon in 1972". All are referring expressions; all are noun phrases.

Languages also have ways of saying something about entities. They have ways of making affirmative and negative statements about entities. They enable speakers to ask questions, issue directives, and so on. Let's illustrate with affirmative statements. In

---

1 Andrew Radford is a British linguistic professor in the University of Essex. His main works are *Analyzing English Sentences* and *Colloquial English: Structure and Variation*, etc.

the following sentences, reference is made to an entity and then a predication is made about it.

Referring Expression	Predication
Judge Jensen	married a butcher.
A poltergeist	appeared last night.
Julian	bought an iPad.

In the first example, reference is made to "Judge Jensen," and then something is predicated of her: She "married a butcher".

Syntax is the part of grammar that governs the organization of words in phrases and sentences—the sentences speakers utter to make statements, ask questions, give directives, and so on. The study of syntax addresses the structure of sentences and their structural and functional relationships to one another. What are called referring expressions in functional terms are called noun phrases in syntactic terms. From a functional perspective, expressions such as "married a butcher" and "bought an iPad" are predicates or predications; from a syntactic point of view, they're verb phrases. Languages may differ from one another in many ways, but every language has noun phrases that act as referring expressions and verb phrases that act as predicates.

A simple sentence—often called a clause—contains a verb and, at a minimum, any other expressions required by the verb as part of its structural characteristics. We noted that some verbs require a noun phrase complement, as in "Britney bought a new raincoat". Others do not allow a noun phrase complement, as in "Danny tripped" or "He fell into the pool". From a syntactic point of view, the verb is the pivotal element in a clause, and the verb's subcategorization determines the kinds of complements it may have. Verbs may consist of a single word, like "bought", "tripped" and "fell", or of several words such as those underlined in "She <u>had hidden</u> the gifts under a tree" and "The physician <u>should have alerted</u> the authorities".

5.2 Constituency

When analyzing sentences, it's essential to recognize that they consist not simply of words strung together like beads on a string, one after another, but of organized groups of words called constituents. We saw in earlier chapters that words and even syllables have linear and hierarchical organizations, so it shouldn't be surprising to learn that words in a sentence are organized not just in an obvious linear order but also hierarchically.

Consider the sentence "The elusive poltergeist frightened Alison's boyfriend during the night". Plainly, it's made up of words in a particular order, and each word has sounds associated with it, so we could say that the sentence is made up of sounds (such as /d, u, r, ɪ, ŋ/) or of words (such as "poltergeist" and "night"). Though accurate to some degree, those analyses would miss a crucial point. Describing this sentence in terms of sounds or words would be akin to describing a shopping mall in terms of steel girders and copper wires—not wrong but beside the point. In any analysis the aim is to identify the structural units that are relevant to some purpose or level of organization. To characterize a shopping mall, we'd want to say that it comprises retail shops, restaurants, parking areas, movie theaters, and so on. We could go further and describe the composition of these units and their relationship to one another. In analyzing a sentence, the relevant structural units are its constituents. Thus, in this sentence, we'd want to say that "the elusive poltergeist" and "Alison's boyfriend" are unified while "boyfriend during" and "during the" are not unified; "boyfriend during" and "during the" are not constituents of the sentence. For the moment we rely on native speaker intuitions in making those judgments. In the course of this chapter, we'll be more explicit about identifying constituents.

5.3 Tree Diagrams

A useful way to represent constituents and their relationships to one another is using a tree diagram. Figure 5.1 represents the fact that the sentence "Harry liked Peeves" consists of two parts: the referring expression "Harry" and the predicate "liked Peeves". In the tree diagram, S stands for sentence, N for noun or pronoun, and V for verb. Notice that there are two branching nodes in the tree. The topmost branching node is labeled S, and the lower node to the right (not labeled for the moment) has two branches, one leading to V and the other to N.

This same tree diagram can represent other sentences, such as "Harry saw it" in Figure 5.2.

Chapter 5 Syntax

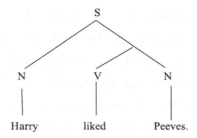

Figure 5.1   Tree diagram of "Harry liked Peeves"

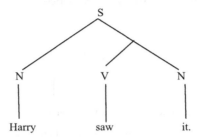

Figure 5.2   Tree diagram of "Harry saw it"

5.3.1 Linear Ordering of Constituents

The words of every sentence occur in a particular—and obvious—order. To put it simply, sentences are expressed as an ordered sequence of words: "Harry liked Peeves", "Hillary hated the harp", "Xavier comes from Xanadu" and "A plump plumber from Portland poked a poltergeist in the park".

5.3.2 Hierarchical Ordering of Constituents

As is apparent in the tree diagrams of Figures 5.1 and 5.2, there is more to the organization of a sentence than the linear order of its words. Figure 5.1 illustrates that "Harry liked Peeves" contains two constituents—one is "Harry" and the other is "liked Peeves".

To explore the notion of internal structure a bit further, consider the expression "gullible boys and girls". It has two possible interpretations: "gullible boys and gullible girls" and "girls and gullible boys". This ambiguity reflects the fact that "gullible boys and girls" has two possible constituent structures, depending on whether "gullible" modifies "boys and girls" or only "boys". Notice in the tree diagram of Figure 5.3 that from the highest node there are two branches, representing two constituents. By contrast, Figure 5.4 shows three branches—and thus three constituents—stemming from the highest node. Two observations are worth making. In Figure 5.3, the string "boys and girls" branches from a single node and thus forms a constituent, but the words "gullible" and "boys" do not branch from a single node and thus do not form a constituent. In Figure 5.4, however, the words "gullible" and "boys" do branch from a single node and thus form a constituent, whereas the string "boys and girls" does not branch from a single node and does not form a constituent. Figures 5.3 and 5.4 represent the two possible constituent structures for "gullible boys and girls" and capture the fact that the linear string has two possible internal organizations—and therefore two interpretations.

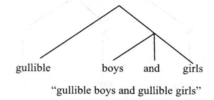

"gullible boys and gullible girls"

Figure 5.3 Tree diagram of "gullible boys and gullible girls"

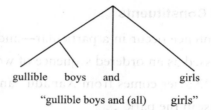

"gullible boys and (all) girls"

Figure 5.4 Tree diagram of "gullible boys and (all) girls"

5.3.3 Structural Ambiguity

Just as structural ambiguity can occur in phrases like "gullible boys and girls", it can occur in sentences. Examine sentence (1) below.

(1) He sold the car to a cousin in Boston.

Although the individual words are not ambiguous, the sentence has more than one possible interpretation, and its ambiguity arises because the linear string of words has two possible constituent structures. We can use brackets to represent the possible constituent structures of sentence (1), as in (2) and (3) below.

(2) He sold the car [to [a cousin in Boston]].

(3) He sold the car [to a cousin] [in Boston].

Sentence (2) can be paraphrased as in (4) below, but not as in (5) or (6). By

Chapter 5 Syntax

contrast, sentence (3) can be paraphrased as in (5) or (6), but not as in (4):

(4) It was to a cousin in Boston that he sold the car.

(5) It was in Boston that he sold the car to a cousin.

(6) In Boston he sold the car to a cousin.

These examples illustrate that the words in a sentence have an internal organization that is not apparent from direct inspection. The linear order—which word is first, second, and so on—is obvious from inspection, but only a speaker of English can recognize constituent structure in an English sentence and the fact that a given string of English words may have more than one possible internal organization.

5.4 Major Constituents of Sentences: Noun Phrases and Verb Phrases

Besides their obvious linear order, then, the words in a sentence are organized into constituents that, while not apparent, are nevertheless understood by speakers. Consider the sentence in Figure 5.5, with its two constituents, and more elaborate sentences such as those in Figure 5.6.

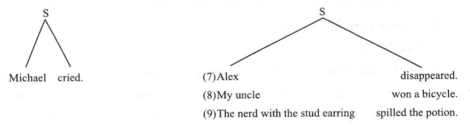

Figure 5.5 Simple form of noun phrases and verb phrases

Figure 5.6 Elaborate sentences of noun phrase and verb phrase

Sentences like those we've examined consist of two principal constituents: a noun phrase and a verb phrase, or NP and VP. (These structures correspond roughly to the functional features of referring expression and predicate discussed earlier.) In turn, each noun phrase contains a noun (Alex, uncle, nerd) and each verb phrase contains a verb (disappeared, won, spilled). As a matter of definition a noun phrase crucially contains a noun as its head, and a verb phrase crucially contains a verb as its head. The head of a phrase is its pivotal, central element. Noun phrases and verb phrases can be identified by the slots they fill in the architecture of a sentence and often by their functions. Thus in Figure 5.6, "Alex" in (7), "My uncle" in (8), and

"The nerd with the stud earring" in (9) function as referring expressions about which a predication is made. Similarly, "_____ disappeared", "_____ won a bicycle", and "_____ spilled the potion" make predication about a noun phrase.

Noun phrases can also be identified by substitution procedures such as those implied in the list of alternatives to the two-part structure shown in Figure 5.6.

For "Alex" we could substitute "My uncle" or "The nerd with the stud earring". All three are NPs and can occur in these slots: _____ disappeared; _____ won a bicycle; _____ spilled the potion.

In sentence (11) below, the verb phrase is "liked the song". Unlike the VP of (10), which consists of the single word "vanished", the VP of (11) contains the verb "liked" and the NP "the song". Thus, a VP may contain a noun phrase. Further, as (12) shows, a verb phrase may also contain a prepositional phrase (on a bet).

(10) [Tina] [vanished].

(11) [Genaro] [liked the song].

(12) [The neighbor with the iPad] [won a bike on a bet].

The noun phrases in the sentences above include "Tina", "Genaro", "the neighbor", "the iPad", "the song", "a bike" and "a bet".

A word string you can insert in the slots below would be an NP:

She enjoyed talking about _____.

Invariably, _____ upset her.

Inserted into either slot, the following expressions would produce well-formed English sentences and are therefore NPs; in each case, the head noun is italicized.

wild *wolverines*   that *loyalty* to his latest love
the *weather*   his *resolve* to reside in Riverdale
her yellow *yarn*   Wally's foolish *wager*

Notice, too, that a noun phrase can be a pronoun:

She enjoyed talking about *it/him/them/us*.

Invariably, *it/they/we* upset her.

Noun phrases and pronouns have the same distribution in sentences; where a noun phrase can occur, a pronoun can occur instead. Thus, pronouns are a kind of noun phrase (and a pronoun may be the head of a noun phrase). Later, we'll see how to exploit this fact in determining noun-phrase constituency.

Verb phrases can be identified by using similar substitution procedures. Consider the sentence "Lou cried", in which "cried" constitutes the verb phrase. Among many others, the following strings can substitute for "cried" in that sentence. They thus fit the frame and are verb phrases (the head in each verb phrase is italicized):

Lou { *fell*.
lost the race.
won a prize for her success in the tournament. }

To this point, we have seen two major constituents of a sentence: noun phrase and verb phrase.

5.5 Active and Passive Sentences

Regardless of how many words an NP contains, it may operate as a constituent in a sentence. Even elaborate NPs such as "the neighbor with the iPad" or "what she hoped to receive for her twenty-first birthday" are syntactic units, just like simple NPs such as "she", "Genaro" and "wolverines". To see more clearly what is meant by a syntactic unit—a constituent—consider the sentences below. In each pair, the first sentence is characterized as "active", the second as "passive":

(13) a. The coach blamed the referee. (active)
　　　b. The referee was blamed by the coach. (passive)
(14) a. Zimmershied discovered that dinosaur skeleton. (active)
　　　b. That dinosaur skeleton was discovered by Zimmershied. (passive)
(15) a. A jaunty judge from Jersey fined a plump plumber from Portland. (active)
　　　b. A plump plumber from Portland was fined by a jaunty judge from Jersey. (passive)

Speakers of English implicitly know how active and passive sentences are related to one another (even if we don't know the terms "active" and "passive"), but it is not possible to make that knowledge explicit without relying on the notion of constituency. For example, without knowledge of constituents, we might characterize the operation that relates sentences (13) a and (13) b above as follows: To transform an active sentence to its passive counterpart, interchange the first two words (the coach) with the last two (the referee). For present purposes, we ignore the additional steps needed, including introducing the verb "was" and the preposition "by", but in a complete statement of the operation, those steps would have to be specified as well. The operation of exchanging the first two and last two words produces the well-formed string (13) b when applied to (13) a. But if the same operation were applied to (14) a, it would produce not (14) b but the ill-formed string—"Dinosaur skeleton was that by Zimmershied discovered", and if applied to (15) a, it would likewise produce an ill-formed string. Clearly, what speakers know about the relationship between active and passive counterparts involves something other than counting words. Implicitly, speakers know that active and passive sentences are related by a structure-dependent operation that interchanges noun phrase constituents, irrespective of the number of words contained in them.

Refer again to the constituents that get interchanged in the active and passive sentence pairs of (13), (14), and (15) above, and note that the word strings in each set below in (16) and (17) must share a structural property because the strings function similarly in those sentence pairs:

(16) the coach; Zimmershied; a jaunty judge from Jersey

(17) the referee; that dinosaur skeleton; a plump plumber from Portland

The NPs in (16) and (17) move as units in the operation that relates active and passive sentences: They are constituents.

5.6 Testing Constituency

For emphasis, we say it again: A sentence is not merely an ordered string of individual words but a structured string of words grouped into constituents that function as syntactic units. The tree diagrams earlier in this chapter relied on informal notions in determining constituency. Now we describe two kinds of tests that can be used for that purpose.

5.6.1 Movement

In examining active and passive sentences, we rely on movement to identify noun phrase constituents. We regard any group of words that can be moved in transforming a sentence between active and passive as a constituent. We also rely on movement in paraphrasing the earlier sentences that present structural ambiguity. In exploring the ambiguity of "He sold the car to a cousin in Boston", we note that one reading can be paraphrased as "In Boston he sold the car to a cousin". Moving "in Boston" to the front of the sentence demonstrates that it functions as a syntactic unit—a constituent.

Chapter 5 Syntax

Generally speaking, we say that a string of words that can be moved in a syntactic operation functions as a unit and is a constituent.

5.6.2 Substitution

Substitution of pro-forms offers another method of identifying constituents. When a pro-form (for example, a pronoun or a "pro-verb") can substitute for a string of words in a sentence, that string is a constituent. In each of the sentences below, the substitution of a pro-form (underlined and boldfaced) for a preceding underlined string provides evidence that the preceding string is a constituent.

(18) Josh gained a lead, and Beth gained **one**, too. (Thus, "a lead" is a constituent.)

(19) Josh gained a huge lead, and Beth gained **one**, too. (Thus, "a huge lead" is a constituent.)

(20) Josh gained a huge lead, and Beth **did**, too. (Thus, "gained a huge lead" is a constituent.)

5.7 Phrase-Structure Expansions

5.7.1 Expanding Noun Phrase

Relying on the analysis of categories (parts of speech), we can now characterize and exemplify certain NP types:

Noun (N): Karen, oracles, justice, swimming

Determiner (Det) + Noun: that amulet, a potion, some gnomes, her coach

Determiner + Noun + Prepositional Phrase (PP): the book on the table, that rise in prices, the marketplace of ideas, her plumber in Portland

Determiner + Adjective (A) + Noun: an ancient oracle, these hellish precincts, my first Harley, a jaunty judge

These various NP patterns can be represented by phrase-structure expansion rules such as the following:

1. NP → N (NP consists of N)
2. NP → Det N (NP consists of Det + N)
3. NP → Det N PP (NP consists of Det + N + PP)
4. NP → Det A N (NP consists of Det + A + N)

These four expansions can be merged into a single rule. N is the only constituent required in every NP expansion because every NP must contain a noun as its head. Other elements are placed in parentheses to represent their optionality. The merged rule looks like this:

5. NP → (Det) (A) N (PP)

Besides the four expansions (1–4) that we aimed to capture, rule 5 represents other expansions. Because Det, A, and PP are optional, we can expand NP not only as in 1, 2, 3, and 4 above, but also as in 6 and 7:

6. NP → A N
7. NP → Det A N PP

Rule 5 thus represents expansions we did not set out to capture. If English has well-formed NP structures consisting of A N (as in 6) and of Det A N PP (as in 7) and of any other expansions 5 would represent, then 5 is valid. Otherwise, it would need to be revised to exclude any impermissible structures.

As a matter of fact, some English NPs comprise an adjective and a noun—A N (such as "tall trees", "ordinary superheroes", "natural grace" and "youthful instructors")—while others consist of Det A N PP (such as "his sorry life on the sidelines", "the huge whale on the beach" and "those whimsical clouds in the sky"). An advantage of formalisms like rule 5 is that they often entail unanticipated claims that can be checked against other data and thus provide a test of their own validity.

5.7.2 Expanding Prepositional Phrase

PP stands for prepositional phrase, such as "in the car", "from Xanadu", "to a cousin", "with the iPad" and "by a jaunty judge". PPs consist of a P (preposition) as head and typically a NP (noun phrase), so the phrase-structure expansion for PP is:

PP → P NP

If NP is treated as optional, as in "It fell off (the table)", it would appear in parenthesis:

PP → P (NP)

5.7.3 Expanding Sentence and Verb Phrase

Sentences and clauses that have two basic constituents can be captured in this phrase-structure expansion:

$$S \rightarrow NP\ VP$$

Chapter 5 Syntax

Every expansion rule can generate a tree diagram, and S → NP VP would generate this tree:

Having already explored expansions of NP, now we turn to the internal structure of VP.

(21) Lou won.

(22) Lou won a bicycle.

(23) Lou won the bike in May.

Sentences (21), (22) and (23) above indicate three VP expansions:

VP → V

VP → V NP

VP → V NP PP

V is the only constituent that occurs in all of these rules. It is the essential category in the VP constituent—its head. As is clear from sentence (21) above, NP and PP are optional constituents of VP. Using parentheses for optional elements, the three expansions above can be combined into a single phrase-structure rule:

VP → V (NP) (PP)

Just as we discovered unanticipated structural patterns when we merged four expansions of NP into a single rule, so the combined rule for VP generates an unanticipated V PP structure, which is not represented among sentences (21), (22) and (23), the basis for our VP expansion rule. We can check the validity of V PP as an expansion and see that it represents the internal structure of sentences like "(Finian) played in the yard", "(Dana) raced through the exam" and "(Pat) flew to Ballina", the last of which is illustrated below:

Pat flew <u>to Ballina</u>.
      V   PP

5.7.4 Phrase-Structure Expansions and Tree Diagrams

We have formulated four phrase-structure expansion rules:

S → NP VP

NP → (Det) (A) N (PP)

$$VP \rightarrow V \ (NP) \ (PP)$$
$$PP \rightarrow P \ (NP)$$

These represent the fact that S comprises NP and VP; NP contains N; VP contains V; and PP contains P. According to these phrase-structure expansion rules, all other possible constituents are optional.

The following tree diagram is one representation of our expansion rules:

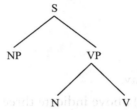

It is the simplest structure generated by our rules and would represent sentences like "Lou disappeared" and "That stinks". Now consider the more complex structure given in Figure 5.7, where "The runner from Butte won a prize at the fair" is an illustrative sentence for the structure. It is clear that our four expansion rules can represent structurally simple or structurally elaborate sentences.

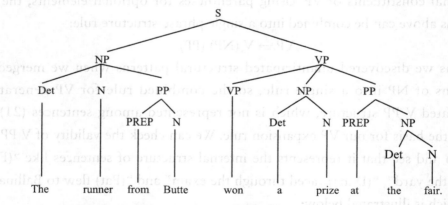

Figure 5.7 Complex structure of phrase-structure expansion

5.8 Grammatical Relations: Subject, Direct Object, and Others

Some traditional English grammar treatments offer notional definitions of subject (doer of the action) and object (receiver of the action). Others rely on structure and define a subject as the sentence constituent that a present-tense verb agrees with (for example, in "she sings" versus "they sing"). For various reasons, these and similar definitions leave a lot to be desired.

Using constituent structure, however, does enable analysts to define subject and direct object more precisely.

5.8.1 Immediate Dominance

In Figure 5.8, the circled NP is directly under the S node, the boxed NP directly under the VP node, and the VP node directly under the S node. When a node is directly under another node—that is, when there are no intervening nodes—we say it is immediately dominated by that other node. Thus, in Figure 5.8, V is immediately dominated by VP; the circled NP immediately dominated by S; the boxed NP immediately dominated by VP; and both VP and the circled NP immediately dominated by S.

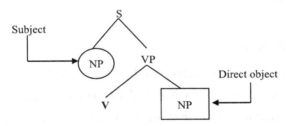

Figure 5.8 Example of immediate dominance

5.8.2 Subject and Direct Object

In English, subject is defined as the NP that is immediately dominated by S. In Figure 5.8, the circled NP is immediately dominated by S and is thus the subject. Direct object is defined as an NP that is immediately dominated by VP. In Figure 5.8 it is the boxed NP. Because NP is an optional element in the expansion of VP, not every sentence will have a direct object.

5.8.3 Transitive and Intransitive

We know that a sentence lacking a direct object contains what is called an intransitive verb. Examples are "cry", "laugh" and "disappear", all of which may occur without a direct object, as in "Hillary cried", "Geoff laughed" and "The jewels disappeared". By contrast, verbs like "make", "buy" and "find" take a direct object and are called transitive verbs, as in "made a potion", "buy a Harley" and "found a penny". While some verbs may be either transitive or intransitive, as exemplified in the first three sentence pairs below, others are only transitive, as in (27) or only intransitive, as in (28). (We use an asterisk to mark an ungrammatical structure, one that doesn't occur in the language.)

Intransitive	**Transitive**
(24) Josh won.	Josh won a prize.
(25) Taylor sings.	Taylor sings lullabies.
(26) Suze studied at Oxford.	Suze studied economics at Oxford.
(27) *Nicole frightened.	Nicole frightened the kittens.
(28) Miguel reappeared.	*Miguel reappeared the dishes.

Given the pivotal role of the verb in determining the structure of a clause, a verb's subcategorization as transitive or intransitive determines whether its clause may contain an object or not.

5.8.4 Grammatical Relations

Grammatical relation is the term used to capture the syntactic, or structural, relationship in a clause between an NP and the verb. In other words, grammatical relations indicate the syntactic role that an NP plays in its clause, and that role cannot be equated with anything else, including meaning. Besides the grammatical relations of subject and direct object, an NP in a clause can be an indirect object, an oblique, or a possessor. Oblique is the term for NPs that are not subject, object, or indirect object; in English an oblique is realized as the object of a preposition (For example, "The vampire pointed to his teeth."). Possessor is the term for entities showing possession (For example, "Josh's new Mini".).

5.8.5 Passive Sentences and Structure Dependence

Having defined subject and direct object in structural terms, we now return to the syntactic relationship examined earlier. Relying on the grammatical relations of subject and direct object, we can reformulate our description of the relationship between active and passive sentences as follows.

To form a passive sentence from an active one, interchange the subject NP with the direct object NP. (As before, provision must be made for the preposition "by" and a form of the verb "be".) Figure 5.9 provides an example.

Chapter 5 Syntax

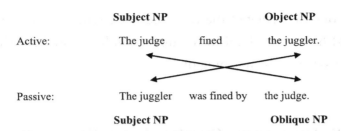

Figure 5.9 Example of relationship between active and passive sentences

You can see that the direct object of the active sentence appears as the subject of the passive sentence, and the subject of the active sentence appears as an oblique (in a prepositional by-phrase) in the passive sentence.

5.9 Surface Structures and Underlying Structures

As we have seen in several ways, we understand considerably more about the architecture of sentences than is apparent in the linear order of their words. In fact, not only do we have implicit knowledge of constituent structure within the linear string of words in a sentence—what we call its surface structure—but we often perceive or understand constituents that are unexpressed in the linear string. For example, we readily understand the meaning of "didn't" in "Lisa won a prize, but Larry didn't", as in option 5 below. But to understand that sentence requires implicit knowledge of syntactic operations.

Lisa won a prize, but Larry
1. didn't.
2. didn't care.
3. didn't tell Sarah.
4. didn't congratulate her.
5. didn't win a prize.

While the list of possible sentences following this pattern is endless, English speakers know that the only legitimate interpretation of 1 is 5 and that sentences 2 to 4 are not possible interpretations of 1.

Well, one way to account for implicit knowledge about sentence structure is to posit underlying structures for syntax. For instance, we could represent the meaning of sentence 1 by positing an underlying structure, something like "Lisa won a prize, but Larry didn't win a prize". If we assumed such an underlying structure and certain syntactic operations that deleted the repeated occurrence of the constituent "win a prize", we would have a mechanism for understanding how English speakers know that only 5 above satisfies the meaning of 1.

5.10 Syntactic Operations: Question Formation and the Auxiliary

Among examples of syntactic operations in English, we have examined movement (as in passivization) and deletion (as in "Lisa won a prize, but Larry didn't".). Now we analyze other examples.

English has two principal kinds of questions. Yes/no questions are those that can be answered with a reply of yes or no, as in "Was it a candid discussion?" Information questions, on the other hand, include a wh-word like "who", "what" or "when" and require more than a simple yes or no reply.

Examine the statements below and their corresponding yes/no questions.

(29) Suze <u>will</u> earn a fair wage.

Will Suze earn a fair wage?

(30) Last year's winner of the Tour de France <u>was</u> leading the pack on Tuesday.

<u>Was</u> last year's winner of the Tour de France leading the pack on Tuesday?

If you compare the matched declarative and interrogative sentences, you'll see that the question requires moving the auxiliary verb of the statement to a position before the subject NP. Verbs such as "will" in (29) and "was" in (30) are called auxiliary verbs, or auxiliaries, and can be moved in front of a subject NP to form a question; auxiliary verbs are distinguished from main verbs such as "earn" in (29) and "lead" in (30) above and "study" in (31) and "hurt" in (32) below.

Notice that yes/no questions contain an auxiliary even when the corresponding declarative sentence does not, as (31) and (32) show:

(31) Alvin studied journalism in college.

<u>Did</u> Alvin study journalism in college?

(32) Inflation always hurts the poor.

<u>Does</u> inflation always hurt the poor?

In addition, an auxiliary usually must appear in the surface structure of negative sentences, as in the examples below.

(33) Alvin studied journalism in college.

Alvin <u>didn't</u> study journalism in college.

Chapter 5 Syntax

Because an auxiliary often must appear in the surface structure of sentences (and also for other reasons not discussed here), a constituent representing the auxiliary is postulated in the underlying structure of every sentence. That means that, instead of the earlier expansion of S simply as NP VP, it must include AUX, as below:

$$S \rightarrow NP\ AUX\ VP$$

The operation that changes the constituent structure of the declarative sentences in (29), (30), (31) and (32) above to the constituent structure of their respective yes/no questions moves AUX to a site preceding the subject NP, as represented in Figure 5.10 below.

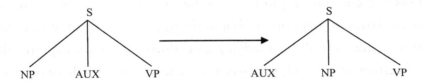

Figure 5.10 Basic form of subject-auxiliary inversion

We thus represent the underlying structure of both "Suze will earn a fair wage" and "Will Suze earn a fair wage?" as in the first tree in Figure 5.11. The second tree represents the constituent structure that results from application of the subject-auxiliary inversion operation.

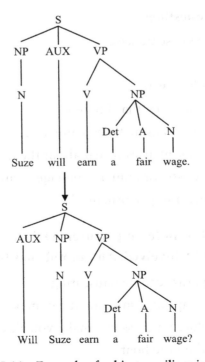

Figure 5.11 Example of subject-auxiliary inversion

· 93 ·

5.11 Summary

The operations governing the formation of sentences constitute the syntax of a language. The study of sentence structure is also called syntax. All languages have referring expressions and predication expressions. In syntactic terms, a referring expression is an NP (noun phrase) and a predication expression a VP (verb phrase). A sentence (and a clause) consists of a verb with the appropriate set of NPs. Speakers of every language can generate an unlimited number of sentences from a finite number of operations for combining phrases. Phrase-structure expansion rules generate underlying constituent structures. Syntactic operations change one constituent structure into another. Positing underlying constituent structures captures the striking regularity of certain relationships between sentences that are otherwise not apparent on the surface.

Exercises

I **Answer the following questions.**

Consider the following sentences.

a. I hate war.

b. You know that I hate war.

c. He knows that you know that I hate war.

1. Write another sentence that includes sentence c.
2. What does this set of sentences reveal about the nature of language?
3. How is this characteristic of human language related to the difference between linguistic competence and performance?

II **Paraphrase each of the following sentences in two ways to show that you understand the ambiguity involved. An example has been given.**

Example: Smoking grass can be nauseating.

a. Putting grass in a pipe and smoking it can make you sick.

b. Fumes from smoldering grass can make you sick.

1. Dick finally decided on the boat.

2. The professor's appointment was shocking.
3. The design has big squares and circles.
4. That sheepdog is too hairy to eat.
5. Could this be the invisible man's hair tonic?
6. The governor is a dirty street fighter.
7. I cannot recommend him too highly.
8. Terry loves his wife and so do I.
9. They said she would go yesterday.
10. No smoking section available.

III Explain why the following sentences are ungrammatical.
1. *The man located.
2. *Jesus wept the apostles.
3. *Robert is hopeful of his children.
4. *Robert is fond that his children love animals.
5. *The children laughed the man.

IV Draw tree diagrams to illustrate the meanings of the following sentence.
   The dog bit the man in the room.

Chapter 6

Semantics

The learning objectives of this chapter are:
1. to master the definition of sense and reference;
2. to know how to analyze the sense relations between words;
3. to understand how to analyze the sense relationship between sentences.

语言学教程
A Coursebook for Linguistics

导言

语义学，也作"语意学"，其研究对象是自然语言的意义，可以是词、短语、句子、篇章等不同级别的语言单位的意义。意义与指称是分析哲学的一个根本问题，也是哲学领域中其他问题和讨论的概念基础。意义和指称是词汇意义的两个侧面。意义是一系列抽象语义特征的集合，是抽象的，与语境无关；指称是词汇在特定的语境中所指的具体事物。意义是词的词典意思，指称是词和它所代表的客观事物或现象的关系，它表现于一定的上下文之中。根据英国语言学家利奇的说法，一个单词可以有七种意义：概念意义、内涵意义、社会意义、情感意义、反射意义、搭配意义和主题意义。概念意义也就是这个单词最基础、最通俗的意义。内涵意义是一个词除了其表面的概念意义以外的隐含意义。社会意义反映了使用这个词的社会情境（包括说话的人、使用的情境、使用的主题）。情感意义表达说话人的情感与态度，通过概念意义、内涵意义和社会意义三者的调和表达出来。反射意义是指一个词有多个概念意义，其中的一个意义构成了我们对另一个意义的反应。搭配意义即词在具体的语境中所产生的意义，是词与词的搭配习惯或词在固定的组合中具有的意思。主题意义是说话人或作者通过信息的组织方式，如词序、焦点和强调等所传达的意义。对词汇的意义和结构的研究，如义素分析、语义场、词义之间的结构关系等属于结构主义语义学，也称为词汇语义学。词义并不是孤立存在的，而是相互联系的；词之间的关系也是多样的，如同义关系、反义关系、同音异义关系、多义关系、下义关系等。词和词之间有各种意义关系，句子也一样，也可以有各种意义关系。句子语义学是在句子层面对意义进行研究，并把句子当成一个整体来看待。句义关系包括蕴含、预设（前提）、同义、矛盾等。

Lexical semantics represents the meaning of each word in the language and to show how the meanings of words in a language are interrelated; formal semantics attempts to ground semantic analysis in the external world; cognitive semantics attempts to ground its analysis in primitive level concepts derived from bodily experience.

—John Ibrahim Saeed[1]

Semantics is a technical term used to refer to the study of the communication of meaning through language. In linguistics, semantics is the study of the meaning of

---

1 John Ibrahim Saeed is a professor in Trinity College Dublin and he is interested in the relationship between grammatical knowledge and pragmatic processes. He has engaged in language description and documentation, and written grammatical descriptions of Somali, its dialects and Irish Sign Language.

linguistic units, words and sentences in particular. Its goal is to reveal how language is matched with its proper meanings by the speakers of that language.

In linguistics, compared with other branches we have discussed, semantics is very young and new. The term "semantics" is a recent addition to the English language. It has only a history of over 100 years. In 1893 the French linguist Bréal coined "sémantique" while in 1897 he first used it as the science of meaning.

6.1 Some Views on Meaning

Meaning covers a variety of aspects of language, and unfortunately there is no general agreement about what meaning is and how it should be defined.

6.1.1 Naming Things

One of the oldest views is that the form is a word in a language and the meaning is the object in the world that it stands for, refers to or denotes. Words are the names or labels for things in our mind or in our experience. That is, the semantic relationship holding between words and things is the relationship of naming. For example, the word "book" names the object book in the real world. It stands for the properties that all books have. So nouns name objects or events, and adjectives name the properties of those objects or events. Verbs name actions, and adverbs name their properties. But even with nouns, the theory of naming will encounter some difficulties. What about nouns like "ghost", "dragon" which relate to imaginative objects and creatures that do not exist?

6.1.2 Conceptualism

Inspired by the medieval grammarians, Ogden and Richards (1923) presented the classic semantic triangle, as manifested in Figure 6.1, in which the relationship between the word and the thing it refers to is not direct. It's mediated by concept.

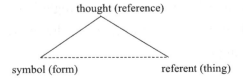

Figure 6.1　Semantic triangle (Ogden & Richards, 1923: 37)

In this figure, the symbol or form refers to linguistic elements (words, phrases); the referent refers to the things in the real world or in man's experience, and thought or reference refers to the concept about the referent. Concept is the generalization of a class of individual objects. A linguistic form symbolizes a concept and therefore, there is no direct (necessary and intrinsic) relation between the symbol (form) and the referent (thing). The word is associated with the referent by virtue of reference (concept). The symbol and concept are linked by a psychologically associative bond. For example:

(1) The dog over there looks unfriendly.

The word "dog" is directly associated with a certain concept in our mind, i.e., what a "dog" is like, but it is not directly linked to the referent (the particular dog) in this particular case. Thus, the symbol of a word signifies the thing by virtue of the concept associated with the form of the word in the mind of the speaker of a language, and the concept looked at from this point of view is the meaning of the word.

This theory avoids many of the problems of naming as it recognizes the close relation between meaning and concept and the role of concept in forming meaning. However, it has some limitations.

First, since it only looks at the meaning of words, it can't explain how the meanings of morphemes in a polymorphemic word are related to each other and how they are organized into the meaning of the word.

Second, it fails to interpret the polysemic phenomenon, that is, why a word may have several different meanings and how these meanings are related.

Third, it fails to interpret the question of why words with different meanings may have the same referent. For example, "morning star" and "evening star" are two expressions used to refer to sightings of Venus.

And according to the semantic triangle, each word in a language has its referent. However, for some words, there are no referents to them. What are the referents of "and", "so", "perhaps" and "therefore"?

Moreover, the referents of some words may vary according to the context in which they occur. To summarize, the semantic triangle basically suffers from looking at the meaning of words in isolation and ignoring the interrelation of words and the semantic structure of a language.

6.1.3 Behaviorism

Behaviorists attempt to define the meaning of a language form as "the situation in which the speaker utters it and the response it calls forth in the hearer" (Bloomfield, 1933). Bloomfield, an American behaviorist, illustrated his views with a famous account of Jack and Jill as showed in Figure 6.2.

(2) Jill is hungry. She sees an apple and gets Jack to fetch it for her by saying something to him.

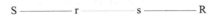

Figure 6.2　Bloomfield's stimulus–reaction model (Bloomfield, 1933: 25)

Here S means practical events (physical) which precede the act of speech, i.e., Jill's hunger. It is termed as a stimulus. And r refers to a linguistic response of Jill to this stimulus. Jill expresses this response by speaking to Jack. The sound waves reaching Jack result in creating a linguistic stimulus for Jack, which is indicated by a small letter s. R refers to the eventual physical response Jack makes in getting the apple for Jill. Thus, Bloomfield argued that meaning consists in the relation between speech (which is shown by r---s) and the practical events S and R that precede and follow it.

6.1.4 Contextualism

Contextualism is based on the presumption that one can drive meaning from and reduce it to observable contexts. Two kinds of context are recognized: a linguistic context and a situational context. Every utterance occurs in a particular spatio-temporal situation. Each utterance is limited by various factors of the situational context. These factors include:
- the setting (formal, informal…);
- the speaker and hearer (relationship, position…);
- the actions they are engaged in at the time;
- the presence or absence of other participants;
- the presence of various external objects and events.

The linguistic context is concerned with the probability of one word's co-occurrence or collocation with another, which forms part of the meaning and is an important factor in communication.

Firth's model of context of situation (1957) covers both linguistic and situational contexts. He held that "we shall know a word by the company it keeps".

6.2 Lexical Meaning

6.2.1 Sense and Reference

Sense and reference are the two terms we often encounter in the study of word meaning. They are two related but different aspects of meaning.

Sense is defined in terms of relationships which hold between the linguistic elements themselves; it is concerned with intralinguistic relations. It is the collection of all the features of the linguistic form. It is abstract and de-contextualized. It is the aspect of meaning dictionary compilers are interested in. For example, the sense of the word "bachelor" is a man who has never been married. Pairs of words can be formed into certain patterns to indicate particular kinds of sense relations. Cow/bull, sow/boar, ewe/ram, mare/stallion, etc. form a pattern indicating a meaning related to sex. Duck/duckling, pig/piglet, dog/puppy, lion/cub, etc. form another pattern indicating a relationship between adult and young. Narrow/wide, male/female, buy/sell, etc. show a different pattern related to opposition. We can find many sense relations in a language, which shows that sense relations are in fact a part of the semantic structure of a language.

Reference or extension deals with the relationship between the linguistic elements and the non-linguistic world of experience. For example, the word "dog" is given the definition "a common domestic animal kept by human beings for work, hunting, etc. or as a pet". This doesn't refer to any particular dog that exists in the real world, but applies to any animal that meets the features described in the definition, so this is the sense of the word "dog". But if we say "The dog is barking", we must be talking about a certain dog existent in the situation; the word "dog" refers to a dog known to both the speaker and the hearer. This is the reference of the word "dog" in this particular situation.

We can say every word has a sense, but not every word has a reference. For example, grammatical words like "but", "if" and "and" do not refer to anything. Words like "God", "ghost" and "dragon" refer to imaginary things, which have no reference. Linguistic forms having the same sense may have different references in different situations.

(3) I was bitten by a dog.

(4) Mind you. There is a dog over there.

Here the two "dog"s bear the same sense, but have different references in the two utterances. Sometimes linguistic forms with the same reference might differ in sense, for example, "morning star" and "evening star" can refer to the same star "Venus".

Sense and reference are very similar to connotation and denotation in philosophy. Denotation is the part of meaning of a word or phrase that relates it to the phenomena in the real world or in a fictional or possible world. Connotation refers to the additional meanings that a word or phrase has beyond its central meaning. These meanings show people's attitudes or emotions. For example, "The man is a rat." What are the denotation and connotation of "rat" respectively? The denotation of the word "rat" is an animal that looks like a large mouse with a long tail. It connotates such meanings as "disloyal, despicable".

6.2.2 Seven Types of Meaning

According to the British linguist Geoffrey Leech (1981), meaning can be classified into seven types: conceptual meaning, connotative meaning, social meaning, affective meaning, reflected meaning, collocative meaning and thematic meaning. Among them, connotative meaning, social meaning, affective meaning, reflected meaning, and collocative meaning are called associative meaning (see Table 6.1).

Table 6.1 Seven types of meaning (Leech, 1981: 9–20)

	1. Conceptual meaning	Logical, cognitive, or denotative content
Associative meaning	2. Connotative meaning	What is communicated by virtue of what language refers to
	3. Social meaning	What is communicated of the social circumstances of language use
	4. Affective meaning	What is communicated of the feelings and attitudes of the speaker/writer
	5. Reflected meaning	What is communicated through association with another sense of the same expression
	6. Collocative meaning	What is communicated through association with words which tends to occur in the environment of another word
	7. Thematic meaning	What is communicated by the way in which the message is organized in terms of order and emphasis

1. Conceptual Meaning

Conceptual meaning, also called denotative or cognitive meaning, is the essential part of what language is, and is widely regarded as the central factor in verbal communication. The conceptual meanings of language can be studied in terms of contrastive features, so that the meaning of the word "woman" could be specified as [+HUMAN, −MALE, +ADULT], as distinct from, say, "man", which could be defined as [+HUMAN, +MALE, +ADULT]. Conceptual meaning is an inextricable and essential part of what language is, such that one can scarcely define language without referring to it.

2. Connotative Meaning

Connotative meaning is the communicative value an expression has by virtue of what it refers to, over and above its purely conceptual content. If the word "woman" is defined conceptually by three features [+HUMAN, −MALE, +ADULT], then these three properties provide a criterion of the correct use of that word. But there are a multitude of additional, non-criterial properties that we have learned to expect a referent of woman to possess. They include not only some physical characteristics (biped, having a womb), but also psychological and social properties (gregarious, capable of speech, experienced in cookery). In the past, woman has been burdened with such attributes (frail, cowardly, emotional, irrational) as the dominant male has pleased to impose on her, as well as with more becoming qualities such as gentle, hardworking. Obviously, connotations are apt to vary from age to age and from society to society. It is equally obvious that connotations will vary, to some extent, from individual to individual within the same speech community: To an English-speaking misogynist, woman will have uncomplimentary associations not present in the minds of speakers of a more feminist persuasion.

It is peripheral and relatively unstable; it may vary according to culture, historical background, and the experience of the individual. Connotative meaning is indeterminate and open-ended in a sense in which conceptual meaning is not. Connotative meaning is open-ended in the way as our knowledge and beliefs about the universe are open-ended: Any characteristic of the referent, identified subjectively or objectively, may contribute to the connotative meaning of the expression which denotes it.

3. Social Meaning

Social meaning is the meaning which an expression conveys about the contexts or social circumstances of its use. In part, we decode the social meaning of a text through our recognition of different dimensions and levels of style within the same language. We recognize some words or pronunciations as being dialectal, i.e., as telling us something of the geographical or social origin of the speaker; other features of language tell us something of the social relationship between the speaker and hearer: We have a scale of status usage, for example, descending from formal and literary English at one end to colloquial, familiar, and eventually slang English at the other.

Social meaning chiefly includes stylistic meaning of an utterance. Stylistic meaning refers to the word features of formality. For example, "steed, horse, nag, and gee-gee" have the same conceptual meaning, but they belong to different contexts of use. "Steed" is poetic in style, "horse" is general and common, "nag" is slangy and colloquial, while "gee-gee" belongs to the nursery and is used by and to children. Let's see more examples.

$$\begin{cases} \text{domicile (very formal, official)} \\ \text{residence (formal)} \\ \text{abode (poetic)} \\ \text{home (general)} \end{cases}$$

$$\begin{cases} \text{cast (literary, biblical)} \\ \text{throw (general)} \\ \text{chuck (casual, slang)} \end{cases}$$

$$\begin{cases} \text{diminutive (very formal)} \\ \text{tiny (colloquial)} \\ \text{wee (colloquial, dialectal)} \end{cases}$$

The examples above are groups of near synonyms which differ in stylistic meanings. Absolute synonyms do not exist.

4. Affective Meaning

Affective meaning indicates the speaker's feelings and attitudes towards the person or thing in question. For example, "slender" is commendatory while "skinny" is derogatory; "politician" is derogatory while "statesman" is favorable.

Affective meaning is largely a parasitic category in the sense that to express our emotions we rely upon the mediation of other categories of meaning—conceptual, connotative, or stylistic. Emotional expression through style comes about, for instance, when we adopt an impolite tone to express displeasure or when we adopt a casual tone to express friendliness. On the other hand, there are elements of language (chiefly interjections like "Aha!" and "Yippee!") whose chief function is to express emotion. When we use these, we communicate feelings and attitudes without the mediation of any other kind of semantic function.

5. Reflected Meaning

Reflected meaning is the meaning which arises in cases of multiple conceptual meanings, when one sense of a word forms part of our response to another sense.

The case where reflected meaning intrudes through the sheer strength of emotive suggestion is most strikingly illustrated by words which have a taboo meaning. Since their popularization in senses connected with the physiology of sex, it has become increasingly difficult to use terms like "intercourse", "ejaculation" and "erection" in innocent senses without conjuring up their sexual associations. This process of taboo contamination has accounted in the past for dying-out of non-taboo sense of a word. Bloomfield explained the replacement of "cock" in its farmyard sense by "rooster" due to the influence of the taboo use of the former word, and the word "intercourse" is now following a similar path. The word "gay", which means "happy" decades of years ago, has a reflected meaning "homosexual" now.

6. Collocative Meaning

Collocative meaning consists of the associations a word acquires on account of the meanings of words which tend to occur in its environment. "Pretty" and "handsome" share common ground in the meaning "good-looking", but may be distinguished by the range of nouns with which they are likely to co-occur or collocate.

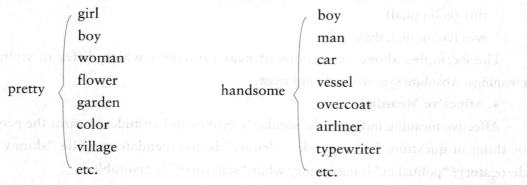

The range may well overlap: "Handsome woman" and "pretty woman" are both acceptable although they suggest different kinds of attractiveness because of the collocative associations of the two adjectives. Further examples are synonymous verbs such as "wander" and "stroll" or "tremble" and "quiver":

(5) Cows may *wander*, but may not *stroll*.

(6) One *trembles* with fear, but *quivers* with excitement.

7. Thematic Meaning

Thematic meaning is what is communicated by the way in which a message is organized in terms of order and emphasis. It is often felt, for example, that an active sentence has a different meaning from its passive equivalent, although on conceptual content they seem to be the same:

Chapter 6 Semantics

(7) Mrs. Bessie Smith donated the first prize.
(8) The first prize was donated by Mrs. Bessie Smith.

Certainly, these have different communicative values in that they suggest different contexts: The active sentence seems to answer an implicit question "What did Mrs. Bessie Smith donate?", while the passive sentence seems to answer an implicit question "Who was the first prize donated by?" That is, sentence (7) suggests that we know who Mrs. Bessie Smith is.

Thematic meaning is mainly a matter of choice between alternative grammatical constructions, as in:

(9) A man is waiting in the hall.
(10) There's a man waiting in the hall.
(11) They stopped at the end of the corridor.
(12) At the end of the corridor, they stopped.
(13) I like Danish cheese best.
(14) Danish cheese I like best.
(15) It's Danish cheese that I like best.

The kind of contrast by ordering and emphasis can also be contrived by lexical means:

(16) My brother owns the largest betting-shop in London.
(17) The largest betting-shop in London belongs to my brother.
(18) He is familiar to me.
(19) I'm familiar with him.

In other cases, it is stress and intonation rather than grammatical constructions that highlight information on one part of a sentence. If the word "electric" is given contrastive stress in (20):

(20) Bill uses an *electric* razor.
(21) The kind of razor that Bill uses is an *electric* one.

Then the effect is to focus attention on that word as containing new information, against a background of what is already assumed to be known. This kind of emphasis could have been equally achieved in English by the different syntactic construction of (21). All the examples above in this part obviously have, in a sense, the same meaning, but not all the same. We need to acknowledge that the communicative value may be somewhat different; they will not each be equally appropriate within the same context.

6.2.3 Componential Analysis

Componential analysis refers to an approach adopted by structural semanticists in describing the meaning of words or phrases. This approach is based on the belief that the total meaning of a word can be analyzed in terms of a number of distinct elements or meaning components (called semantic features).

The study of meaning in any language shows that lexical items overlap in meaning and share common properties, e.g., "lions" and "tigers" both contain an element of "wild animalness". "Calf puppy" and "baby" can be considered as both sharing an element of "non-adultness" while "cow", "woman" and "tigress" all contain an element of "female", but because of other properties each word contains, none of them will be said as being synonymous to any one of the others.

One attempt to account for this phenomenon is to assume that lexical items, like phonemes are made up of a number of component parts. Componential analysis is often seen as a process aiming at breaking down the meaning of a word into its minimal distinctive features or properties, which are also called components by some linguists. One way of describing the components of a word is to use feature symbols, which are usually written in capitalized letters, with "+" or "−" before them. The plus sign indicates the presence of a certain property, and the minus sign indicates the absence of it. For example:

man: [+HUMAN, +ADULT, +MALE]
woman: [+HUMAN, +ADULT, −MALE]
boy: [+HUMAN, −ADULT, +MALE]
girl: [+HUMAN, −ADULT, −MALE]

Words like "father", "mother", "daughter", "son", which involve a relation between two entities, may be shown as follows:

father = PARENT (X,Y) & MALE (X)
mother = PARENT (X,Y) & −MALE (X)

In the first example, the parent function takes two arguments X and Y, and the male function takes one parameter X. It can be understood as X is a parent of Y and X is male.

Verbs can also be analyzed in this way. For example:

take = CAUSE (X, (HAVE (X,Y)))
give = CAUSE (X, (−HAVE (X,Y)))

The meaning of "take" can be explained as X causes X to have Y, and "give" can be understood as X causes X not to have Y.

By specifying the semantic features of certain words, we may better account for sense relations. Those having the same semantic components are synonyms; those having a contrasting component are antonyms; those having all semantic components of another are hyponyms. But it would be senseless to analyze the meaning of every word by breaking it into its meaning components.

6.3 Sense Relations Between Words

Words are in different sense relations with each other. There are generally six sense relations recognized, namely, synonymy, antonymy, hyponymy, polysemy, homonymy and meronymy.

6.3.1 Synonymy

Synonymy is the technical term for the sameness relation. Words that are close in meaning are called synonyms. Some examples might be pairs below:

couch/sofa   boy/lad   lawyer/attorney   toilet/lavatory   large/big

English is said to be rich in synonyms, but total synonyms are rare. For example, they may have belonged to different dialects and then become synonyms for speakers familiar with both dialects, like American English "fall" and British English "autumn". Or they may differ in registers or styles of language. Thus, some synonyms are preferred in certain situations as they are believed to be colloquial, formal, literary, etc. For example, "wife" or "spouse" are more formal than "old lady" and "missus". In the following example, "Little Tom buys/purchases a toy bear", "buy" is more appropriate than "purchase" as "buy" is general while "purchase" is formal. The synonyms may portray positive or negative attitudes of the speaker. For example, "naive" or "gullible" seem more critical than "ingenuous". One or other of the synonyms may be collocationally restricted. Examples are "rotten" food, "addled" eggs, "rancid" bacon or butter, and "sour" milk. Speaker attitude is a further distinguishing factor. Some words like "statesman" show a respectful attitude, while words like "politician" reveal a derogatory attitude.

6.3.2 Antonymy

Antonymy is the name for oppositeness relation. Words that are opposite in meaning are antonyms. There are several types of lexical opposites in the English language: gradable antonymy, complementary antonymy and converse antonymy.

Gradable antonymy is the commonest type of antonymy. The members of a pair differ in terms of degree. The denial of one is not necessarily the assertion of the other. As Figure 6.3 shows, there can be some intermediate terms between the two antonyms X and Y. Take "good" and "bad" as an example. Something which is not "good" is not necessarily "bad". It may simply be "so so" or "average".

Figure 6.3 Gradable antonyms

Take "hot/cold" for another example. One can find intermediate terms such as "hot/warm/cool/cold". And it is possible to be neither "hot" nor "cold". Antonyms of this type can be modified by "very". Something may be "very good" or "very bad". They may have comparative and superlative degrees. Something may be "better" or "worse" than another. Second, antonyms of this kind are graded against different norms. There is no absolute criterion by which we may say something is "big" or "small". The criterion varies with the object described. "A big car" is in fact much smaller than "a small plane". What's more, one member of a pair, usually the term for the higher degree, serves as the cover term. We ask somebody "How old are you?" And the person asked may not be old in any sense.

Complementary antonymy is of binary taxonomies and regarded as a special case of incompatibility holding over a two-term set. The denial of one member of the pair implies the assertion of the other, and the assertion of one also means the denial of the other.

Figure 6.4 Complementary antonyms

As Figure 6.4 manifests, there is no intermediate term between the two antonyms X and Y. For example, "He is alive" means "He is not dead". "He is not alive" also means "He is dead". A man cannot be neither alive nor dead. So, the adjectives in this type cannot be modified by "very". One can't say somebody is "very alive" or "very dead". And they do not have comparative or superlative degrees. We don't say "John is more dead than Peter". Second, the norm of this type is absolute. It does not vary with the thing a word is applied to. For example, the criterion for separating "male" and "female" is the same with that for "human beings" and "animals". Third, there is no cover term for the two members of a pair. If we don't know the sex of a baby, you ask "Is it a boy or a girl?" not "How male is it?" as "male" cannot cover the meaning of "female".

Pairs of words like "buy" and "sell", "parent" and "child" belong to converse antonymy in that the members of a pair do not constitute a positive–negative opposition. This type of antonymy can also be called relational opposites. They show the reversal of a relationship between two entities. "X buys something from Y" means the same as "Y sells something to X". "X is the parent of Y" means the same as "Y is the child of X". Terms such as "above" and "below" may be transitive, that is, if X is above Y and Y above Z, then X is above Z. Some expressions are symmetric. Expressions of a symmetric relationship are exemplified as follows:

(22) John is married to Mary. = Mary is married to John.
(23) Peter is Jane's cousin. = Jane is Peter's cousin.
(24) Robert met Linda. = Linda met Robert.

Relational opposites can also be reflexive if they relate an argument to themselves as in "One equals one".

6.3.3 Hyponymy

The term "hyponymy" is a relation of inclusion, or a matter of class membership. A hyponym includes the meaning of a more general word. The more general or upper term is called superordinate or hypernym. Much of the vocabulary is linked by such systems of inclusion, and the resulting semantic networks form the hierarchical taxonomies mentioned above. As we can see in Figure 6.5, under "season", there are several hyponyms such as "spring", "summer", "autumn" and "winter". These members of the same superordinate are co-hyponyms.

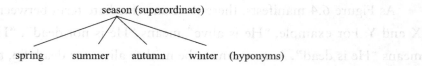

Figure 6.5   Example of hyponymy (1)

For another example, "flower" is the superordinate, while "tulip", "violet" and "rose" are co-hyponyms.

All hyponymy is transitive in the sense that there is a hierarchical relation between different terms. If a relation holds between the superordinate X and the hyponym Y, and Y in turn is the superordinate of Z, then X is also the superordinate of Z.

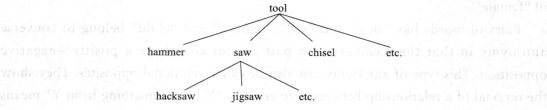

Figure 6.6   Example of hyponymy (2)

As we can see in Figure 6.6, "jigsaw" is a hyponym of "saw", which in turn is a hyponym of "tool", so "jigsaw" can be said to be a hyponym of "tool" as hyponymy is a vertical relationship in a taxonomy.

6.3.4 Polysemy

When a word has two or more meanings that are related conceptually or historically, it is said to be polysemous or polysemic. For example, the word "hand" is polysemic.

"Hand" means part of the human arm beyond the wrist. But in the following sentences, the meanings of "hand" are different.

(25) Give me a *hand*, please. (help)

(26) He is a new *hand*. (performer)

(27) We need some extra *hands*. (workman)

(28) He writes a good *hand*. (handwriting)

(29) All *hands* are on deck. (sailor)

(30) The clock has one *hand* only. (pointer)

The word "hand" can mean part of the human arm beyond the wrist, help, performer, workman, handwriting, sailor, pointer and even more. The meanings are conceptually associated with each other, so the word "hand" is polysemic.

6.3.5 Homonymy

Homonymy refers to the relation between two words that are spelled the same way but differ in meaning or the relation between two words that are pronounced the same way but differ in meaning. There are many pairs or groups of words, which, though different in meaning, are pronounced alike, or spelled alike, or both.

Perfect homonyms refer to the words identical in sound and spelling but different in meaning. For example, "bat" means a "flying creature" as well as "the tool used in sports". The two meanings are not conceptually or metaphorically associated with each other, so they are treated as homonyms, that is, two single words having the same linguistic form. Words like "pupil", "bank", "lie", "race" are also treated as examples of homonymy.

One type of homonymy is homophones. They are words which sound alike but are written differently and often have different meanings such as "rain" and "reign".

When two words are identical in spelling but differ in pronunciation and meaning, they are homographs. Homography can be illustrated from such pairs as "wind" [wind] and "wind" [waind].

It is easy to distinguish homophones and homographs with polysemants, for homophones have different spellings and homographs have different sounds. But perfect homonyms and polysemants are fully identical in spelling and pronunciation.

One important criterion is to see their etymology. Homonyms are from different sources. A polysemant is from the same source, which has acquired different meanings in the course of development.

The second principle is semantic relatedness. The various meanings of a polysemant are correlated and connected to some central meaning to a greater or less degree. Meanings of different homonyms have nothing to do with one another.

The third principle is to check the entry in the dictionary. A polysemic word is under one same entry in the dictionary, while homonyms are under different entries.

6.3.6 Meronymy

Many objects in the world are conceived as a whole consisting of different parts. The semantic relationship of this kind is called part and whole relationship or meronymy. Thus, "cover" and "page" are meronyms of "book". We can identify this relationship by using sentence frame like "X is part of Y", or "Y has X", as in "A page is part of a book", or "A book has pages". A small section of the system of body-part terms in English is shown in Figure 6.7:

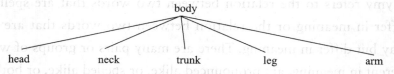

Figure 6.7   Example of meronymy (1)

Here the referent "head" is part of the referent of the term "body".

Meronymy reflects hierarchical classifications in the lexicon somewhat like taxonomies. A typical system might be:

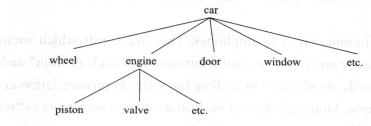

Figure 6.8   Example of meronymy (2)

Figure 6.8 shows that "piston" is part of the object "engine", while "engine" is part of the object "car", therefore, "piston" can also be said to be part of the referent "car".

Meronymic hierarchies are less clear-cut and regular than taxonomies. Meronyms vary for example in how necessary the part is to the whole. Some are necessary for normal examples, like "nose" as a meronym of "face"; others are usual but not obligatory, like "collar" as a meronym of "shirt"; still others are optional like "cellar" for "house".

6.4 Sense Relations Between Sentences

Sense relationships also exist between sentences. Semantic relations between sentences include entailment, presupposition, synonymy, inconsistency, and so on.

6.4.1 A Entails B

Entailment is concerned with the meaning of the sentence itself. It does not depend on the context in which a sentence is used. In terms of truth value, when A is true, B is necessarily true; when B is false, A is false. In formula: A→B; −B→−A. For example:

(31) a. He has been to France.

b. He has been to Europe.

(32) a. John picked a tulip.

b. John picked a flower.

(33) a. The anarchist assassinated the emperor.

b. The emperor died.

There are fixed truth relations between the pairs of sentences above. We could say if somebody tells us (31) a and we believe it, then we know (31) b without being told any more. Or we could say that it is impossible for somebody to assert (31) a but deny (31) b. So entailment is not an inference in the normal sense: We do not have to reason to get from (31) a to (31) b; we just know it instantaneously because of our knowledge of English. A truth-based definition of entailment might allow us to state the relationship more clearly and would be something like: Sentence A entails sentence B when the truth of the first guarantees the truth of the second, and the falsity of the second guarantees the falsity of the first.

Indeed, hyponymy between lexical items is a regular source for entailment between sentences. For example, the noun "dog" is a hyponym of "animal", so it follows that sentence (34) a below entails sentence (34) b.

(34) a. I bought a dog today.

b. I bought an animal today.

6.4.2 A Presupposes B

Presupposition is the situation when the speaker always assumes that the hearer already knows something of what he is going to say. So "John's son is an engineer" presupposes "John has a son". In terms of truth value, when A is true, B is necessarily true; when A is false, B is still true. See one more example:

(35) a. The queen of England is old.

b. England has a queen.

So presupposition is something that the speaker assumes to be the case prior to making an utterance. It's the speakers, not the sentences, that have presuppositions.

6.4.3 A Is Inconsistent with B

When the truth of one sentence contradicts with the truth of the other, then we say sentence A is inconsistent with sentence B. In terms of truth value, when A is true, B is false; when A is false, B is true. For example:

(36) a. John is married.
   b. John is a bachelor.

6.4.4 A Is Synonymous with B

Two sentences may have the same meaning, that is, sentence A is synonymous with sentence B. In terms of truth value, when A is true, B is true; when A is false, B is also false. For example:

(37) a. The boy killed the dog.
   b. The dog was killed by the boy.

6.4.5 A Is a Contradiction

There are statements whose parts contradict each other. When a sentence is a contradiction, it is invariably false. For example:

(38) My unmarried sister is married to a bachelor.

6.4.6 A Is Semantically Anomalous

When a sentence is semantically anomalous, it is absurd in the sense that it presupposes a contradiction. For example:

(39) The table has bad intentions.

The sentence above presupposes "A table can have intentions", which is absurd because the abstract notion "intention" can't be harbored by the inanimate subject "table".

6.5 Summary

Semantics is generally considered to be the study of meaning in language. Historically, there are different views concerning the study of meaning—the nominalist's view, the referential theory, the behaviorist theory and contextualism, but none provides a satisfactory solution to all semantic problems.

Sense and reference are two different, though related, aspects of meaning. Sense is concerned only with intralinguistic relations, while reference is about interlinguistic relations. As to the meaning of meaning, Leech presents seven types of meaning: conceptual meaning, connotative meaning, social meaning, affective meaning, reflected meaning, collocative meaning and thematic meaning.

Sense relations form an important part of the study of language. Generally, six sense relations between words can be recognized, namely, synonymy, antonymy, hyponymy, polysemy, homonymy and meronymy. Semantic relationships between sentences may be entailment, presupposition, synonymy, contradiction, and so on.

Exercises

I Decide whether each of the following statements is true or false.

1. Dialectal synonyms can often be found in different regional dialects such as British English and American English but cannot be found within the variety itself, for example, within British English or American English.
2. Sense is concerned with the relationship between the linguistic element and the non-linguistic world of experience, while the reference deals with the inherent meaning of the linguistic form.
3. Linguistic forms having the same sense may have different references in different situations.
4. In semantics, meaning of language is considered as the intrinsic and inherent relation to the physical world of experience.
5. The meaning of a sentence is the sum total of the meanings of all its components.

II Fill in the blanks in the following sentences.

1. Semantic can be defined as the study of _____.
2. _____ means what a linguistic form refers to in the real, physical world; it deals with the relationship between the linguistic element and the non-linguistic world of experience.

3. When two words are identical in sound, but different in spelling and meaning, they are called _____.

4. _____ are pairs of words that exhibit the reversal of a relationship between the two items.

5. _____ is based upon the belief that the meaning of a word can be divided into meaning components.

III Choose the best answer to each question.

1. The conceptualist theory is advanced by _____. ( )
   A. Ogden and Richards   B. Bloomfield
   C. Geoffrey Leech   D. Firth

2. The pair of words "give" and "take" are _____. ( )
   A. gradable opposites   B. relational opposites
   C. co-hyponyms   D. synonyms

3. A word with several meanings is called _____ word. ( )
   A. a polysemous   B. a synonymous
   C. an abnormal   D. a multiple

4. The word "sidewalk" and "pavement" are _____ synonyms. ( )
   A. near   B. dialectal
   C. collocationally-restricted D. stylistic

5. The words "literate" and "illiterate" are _____ opposites. ( )
   A. gradable   B. ungradable
   C. relational   D. complementary

6. The semantic components of the word "man" can be expressed as _____. ( )
   A. [+ANIMATE, +MALE, +HUMAN, –ADULT]
   B. [+ANIMATE, +MALE, +HUMAN, +ADULT]
   C. [+ANIMATE, –MALE, +HUMAN, –ADULT]
   D. [+ANIMATE, –MALE, +HUMAN, +ADULT]

7. The phenomenon that words having different meanings have the same form is called _____. ( )
   A. polysemy   B. hyponymy
   C. antonymy   D. homonymy

8. One way to analyze lexical meaning is _____. (   )
   A. predication analysis   B. stylistic analysis
   C. componential analysis   D. proposition analysis
9. Which of the following best describes the relation between "He is alone" and "He has no one to talk to"? (   )
   A. The former is synonymous with the latter.
   B. The former is inconsistent with the latter.
   C. The former entails the latter.
   D. The former presupposes the latter.
10. Synonyms are classified into several kinds. The kind to which "girl" and "lass" belong is called _____ synonyms. (   )
    A. stylistic   B. dialectal
    C. emotive   D. collocational
11. "Sweets" and "candy" are used respectively in Britain and America, but refer to the same thing. The words are _____ synonyms. (   )
    A. collocational   B. dialectal
    C. complete   D. stylistic
12. "Statesman" and "politician" are _____. (   )
    A. dialectal synonyms   B. collocational synonyms
    C. stylistic synonyms   D. synonyms that differ in affective meaning
13. "Eric's brother is in the U.K." _____ "Eric has a brother". (   )
    A. entails   B. contradicts
    C. presupposes   D. includes
14. The relation between "furniture" and "desk" is _____. (   )
    A. homophony   B. homography
    C. polysemy   D. hyponymy
15. The relationship between "John is married" and "John is a bachelor" is _____. (   )
    A. presupposition   B. inconsistency
    C. entailment   D. contradiction

IV Define the following terms.

1. semantics   2. sense   3. reference   4. synonymy
5. polysemy   6. homograph   7. perfect homonym   8. hyponymy
9. antonymy   10. componential analysis

V Answer the following questions.

1. What is componential analysis? Illustrate it with examples.
2. What distinction would you draw between sense and reference?
3. How do you distinguish between entailment and presupposition in terms of truth value?
4. How do you account for such sense relations between sentences as synonymous relation, inconsistent relation in terms of truth value?
5. According to the way synonyms differ, how many groups can you classify synonyms into? Illustrate them with examples.

Chapter 7

Pragmatics

The learning objectives of this chapter are:
1. to comprehend the relationship between pragmatics and semantics;
2. to master Speech Act Theory;
3. to familiarize students with the Cooperative Principle;
4. to understand the Politeness Principle.

语言学教程
A Coursebook for Linguistics

> **导言**
>
> 语用学是语言学的分支，它研究语言在具体语境中的意思。语言学家在不同层面上对意思进行研究，语义学研究的是词和句子本身所具有的意思，而语用学研究的则是在特定物理和社会环境中说话人所说话语的含义，以及听话人如何猜测说话人的含义。也就是说，如果句子中词语不改变，那么句子的语义意思就不会改变，但如果语境改变了，那么即使是同样的句子，也会有不同的语用意思。语用学中第一个重要理论是言语行为理论。这个理论是牛津哲学家奥斯汀提出的，他认为句子可以分成表述句和施动句，表述句只是陈述或描述事情，可真可假，而施动句是实施某种行为，没有真假。之后奥斯汀把一个言语行为分成三个层面：言内行为、言外之意和言外之果。言内行为是指说出一个有意义的句子，言外之意是指在说出句子时，人们实施的另一种行为、命令或请求等，言外之果是指句子最终实际产生的效果，可以是接受或者拒绝。语用学中第二个重要的理论是合作原则，由牛津另一位哲学家格莱斯提出。格莱斯注意到人们在日常会话中并不总是直接告诉对方，而是暗示。这另一层意思就是会话含意，由听话人根据格莱斯提出的合作原则推导出来。合作原则包括四条准则：质量准则、数量准则、关系准则、方式准则。人们在说话时总是有意无意地遵守合作原则，而刻意违背合作原则，实际是为了产生言外之意。和合作原则相关联的另一语用学理论是礼貌原则，由英国语言学家利奇提出。该原则阐述了礼貌对语言交际的重要作用。他把礼貌原则分为六大类：得体准则、慷慨准则、赞誉准则、谦逊准则、一致准则、同情准则。而人们在交际时刻意违背合作原则，有时是为了遵守礼貌原则。

Each utterance is a unique physical event created at a particular point in time for a particular communicative purpose.

—*J. S. Peccei*[1]

7.1 What Is Pragmatics?

The term "pragmatics" was coined in the 1930s by psychologist and philosopher Charles Morris. It was developed as a branch of linguistics in the 1970s. Generally speaking, pragmatics is a field of study to take care of the meaning of language in use.

---

[1] J. S. Peccei is a famous linguist with many published books, such as *Pragmatics* and *Child Language: A Resource Book for Students*. His masterpiece *Pragmatics* is commended for what it offers to all those wanting to gain insight into the use of language.

7.1.1 Pragmatics vs. Semantics

In the above definition, there is the word "meaning", which is closely associated with semantics. Consider this dialogue first.

A wife is washing her hands in the bathroom, while her husband is reading the newspaper in the hall. At this time, the telephone rings.

(1) Wife: Could you answer the phone?

　　Husband: I'm busy.

　　Wife: You're never free.

　　Husband: What do you mean?

In (1), the husband is reading the newspaper, so apparently, he is not illiterate, and for sure he can figure out the literal meaning of his wife's sentence "You're never free" from the perspective of seven meanings in semantics. However, he still raises the question "What do you mean?" So the meaning he wants is definitely not semantic. And this is the very reason that we should distinguish pragmatics from semantics.

Pragmatics and semantics are the two main areas of linguistics, which study the knowledge we use both to extract meaning when we hear or read, and to convey meaning when we speak or write. Within linguistics itself, the dividing line between these two disciplines is still under considerable debate.

Generally speaking, semantics concentrates on meaning that comes from purely linguistic knowledge, which can be words, sentences, etc. While pragmatics concentrates on those aspects of meaning that cannot be predicted by linguistic knowledge alone and takes into account our knowledge about the physical and social world, which is the key factor in understanding pragmatic meaning.

To sum up, semantics is the theoretical study with more attention to its superficial and abstract sentence meaning, while pragmatics is the applied study with more care about its speaker or utterance meaning in context. Pragmatics is the "meaning minus semantics", says Frank Brisard in his essay "Introduction: Meaning and Use in Grammar". He also notes that semantics refers to the literal meaning of a spoken utterance. Grammar involves the rules defining how the language is put together. Pragmatics takes context into account to complement the contributions that semantics and grammar make to meaning (2014: 5).

7.1.2 Definitions of Pragmatics

As a relatively new branch of linguistics, pragmatics has been defined in many ways. The diversity of definitions shows the different dimensions of language use and the different concerns of researchers. Generally, pragmatics is characterized by the consideration of the role both context and language speakers play in verbal communication. Consider the following two definitions of pragmatics.

a. Pragmatics is the study of contextual meaning in Yule's book *Pragmatics* (1996: 1) and it is also the meaning in context in Thomas's book *Meaning in Interaction: An introduction to Pragmatics* (1995: 1). There is the focal word "context" in both definitions.

Context refers to the background knowledge shared by the speaker and hearer, including general knowledge of the world, knowledge specific to the situation of communication, specific to the counterparts of communication, and the knowledge of the purpose of communication. Consider the following situation.

A little boy's mother asks him to wipe his feet before entering the house. Then the boy removes his muddy shoes and socks and wipes his feet on the doormat.

If you were the boy's parent, would you be mad at his reaction? Actually, the boy's knowledge of vocabulary and grammar does not appear to be the problem. When his mother asks him to wipe his feet, that is exactly what he does. So, the problem is that the boy appears to have understood what the words meant but not what his mother meant. As adults, we usually arrive at the speaker's meaning so effortlessly that we tend to be unaware of the context we use to accomplish this.

b. Pragmatics is the study of speaker meaning (Yule, 1996: 1). It is the study of how more gets communicated or interpreted than is said. That is, it deals with how listeners can make inferences about what is said in order to arrive at the interpretation of the speaker's intended meaning.

In modern linguistics, pragmatics has come to be applied to the study of language from the view of the users, especially the choices they make, the constraints they encounter in using language in social interaction, and the effects their use of language has on other participants in an act of communication (Crystal, 1985: 240). Take the following dialogue as an example.

(2) Teacher: Did you finish your reading list and research paper?
    Student: I finished my reading list.

Clearly, the student conveys the information that he or she has finished the reading list, but implicitly the student also delivers the message that he or she has not finished the research paper. Therefore, what the student communicates here is more than what he or she says.

7.2 Speech Act Theory

There are two proverbs that we are familiar with: "Actions speak louder than words" and "Easier said than done", which make a clear distinction between speaking and acting. However, contrary to popular belief, in Speech Act Theory (SAT for short), there is often no clear distinction between the two. That is to say, we are performing various kinds of acts when we are speaking.

Oxford philosopher John Langshaw Austin is one of the first modern scholars to recognize that words are in themselves actions and that these speech acts can and should be systematically studied. Austin began to give series of lectures on the theory in 1952. In 1955, he revised the notes and changed the title to "How to Do Things with Words", which was published posthumously in 1962.

7.2.1 Constatives vs. Performatives

Austin's first shot at SAT is the claim that there are two types of sentences: constatives and performatives. The constative sentence is used to describe or to state, and it can be true or false, while the performative sentence is used to perform an action, and it has no truth value. Compare the following two sentences:

(3) I'm a student.
(4) I declare the meeting open.

Clearly, (3) is a statement, which can be either true or false, so it's constative utterance. While (4) is a performative one, because at a meeting, as soon as the chairman says the sentence, the meeting has started.

Consider some other examples. In the case of a ship launching ceremony, after smashing the bottle against the stern, the mayor says (5) "I name this ship the Queen Elizabeth". At the meantime the ship gets its official name. And also in the court, the judge says to the defendant (6) "I sentence you to a maximum of five years in prison". Right after, the defendant gets the imprisonment sentence and is sent to jail. So we can see that the action is performed by the utterance.

7.2.2 Three Acts in Speech Act Theory

From all the examples above, we would agree that performative sentences can do things. But at the meanwhile, it is agreed that non-performative sentences can also do things. The sentence "It's cold" is a constative sentence to state, but on some occasions, in saying this sentence, someone may be performing the act of asking a favor to close the window.

In the latter part of the book *How to Do Things with Words*, Austin made a fresh start on what sense to say is to do something. In his opinion, there are three basic senses in which saying something may be understood as doing something. These are locutionary act, illocutionary act, and perlocutionary act, and the three kinds of acts are performed simultaneously.

The first sense is called locutionary act. Locutionary act means the basic literal meaning of the utterance which is conveyed by particular words and structures that the utterance contains. Or we can call it the act of saying something in the sense of "say". So the key point in locutionary act is the actual form of words used by the speaker and their semantic meaning.

The second sense is illocutionary act. It's the extra meaning of the utterance produced on the basis of its literal meaning, such as commanding, asking, offering, promising, threatening, thanking, etc. In other words, it's the act performed in saying something. Therefore, Speech Act Theory is most concerned with the illocutionary acts. When we speak, we not only produce some units of language with their certain meaning, but also make clear our purpose in producing them, and the way we intend them to be understood.

And the third sense is perlocutionary act. It's the effect of the utterance on the hearer, depending on specific circumstances. It may or may not be what the speaker wants to happen. We call it the act performed by or as a result of saying. By telling somebody something, the speaker may change the opinion of the hearer on something, or mislead him, or surprise him, or induce him to do something, etc. Whether or not these effects are intended by the speaker, they can be regarded as part of the act that the speaker has performed. Consider the following dialogue:

(7) Ann: It's cold here.

John: OK. I'll close the window.

In (7), the locutionary act is the saying of it with its literal meaning "The temperature is low in the room". The illocutionary act is Ann's request to close the window. The perlocutionary act is John's agreement to do so. In this way, actions are performed via utterances, which are common constative sentences.

Austin's proposal that speaking can be analyzed as action has made a major contribution to pragmatics. His basic analytic framework has stimulated an enormous amount of thinking and research about a previously neglected but very important area of interpersonal meaning.

7.2.3 Classification of Illocutionary Acts

Linguists generally have been most concerned with describing illocutionary acts, and John Searle, American philosophical linguist, has isolated five categories of such acts (1979).

Representatives or assertives are acts that represent a particular state of affairs, such as statements, descriptions, assertions, etc. Directives are acts that have the intent of getting the hearer to do something, such as orders, requests, instructions, etc. Commissives are acts that commit the speaker to some future actions, such as promises, threats, offers, etc. Expressives are acts that express an attitude of the speaker towards some state of affairs, such as thanks, apologies, welcomes, etc. Declaratives are acts that bring about some performance that corresponds to what is being said, such as declaring (a war), pronouncing (a couple husband and wife), firing (an employee), etc.

7.3 The Cooperative Principle

We know that quite often a speaker can mean a lot more than what is said. The problem is to explain how the speaker can manage to convey more than what is said and how the hearer can arrive at the speaker's meaning. Another Oxford philosopher Herbert Paul Grice believed that there must be some mechanisms governing the production and comprehension of these utterances. He began to give series of lectures on the theory in 1967. In 1975, he published part of the lectures under the title of "Logic and Conversation".

7.3.1 Four Maxims in the Cooperative Principle

Grice proposed that all speakers, regardless of their cultural background, adhere to a basic principle governing conversation, which he termed as the Cooperative Principle (CP for short). That is to say, the speakers will cooperate with each other when making their contributions in a conversation.

Then Grice summarized four basic maxims which go towards making a speaker's contribution to the conversation cooperative. And these four maxims are the maxim of quality, the maxim of quantity, the maxim of relation and the maxim of manner (1975).

1) The maxim of quality

    Try to make your contribution one that is true, i.e.:
    - Do not say what you believe to be false;
    - Do not say that for which you lack adequate evidence.

2) The maxim of quantity
    - Make your contribution as informative as is required (for the current purpose of the exchange);
    - Do not make your contribution more informative than is required.

3) The maxim of relation

    Be relevant.

4) The maxim of manner

    Be perspicuous.
    - Avoid obscurity;
    - Avoid ambiguity;
    - Be brief (avoid unnecessary prolixity);
    - Be orderly.

The key point in the maxim of quality is to say what is true. The key point in the maxim of quantity is to provide an appropriate amount of information. In the maxim of relation, we should say what is relevant to the conversation. And the key point in the maxim of manner is to say as clearly as we can.

We must make it clear that the CP is not to tell speakers how they ought to behave, while it is meant to describe what actually happens in conversation. That is, when we speak, we generally have something like the CP and its maxims in our mind to guide us, though subconsciously, or even unconsciously. We will try to say things which are true, relevant, as well as informative enough, and in a clear manner. Hearers will also try to interpret what is said to them in this way.

7.3.2 Flouting the Maxims

However, it does not mean that the CP and its maxims will be followed by everyone all the time. The second half of Grice's *Logic and Conversation* is devoted to the violations of the CP. That is, it is obvious to the hearer at the time of the utterance that the speaker has deliberately and quite openly failed to observe one or more maxims. And this triggers the conversational implicature. Consider this dialogue:

(8) Husband: Do you like my new hat, honey?

　　Wife: It's green.

According to the CP, the wife in (8) should answer the question directly with "yes" or "no". Instead, she replies with the color of the hat which is so apparent to both of them. So her answer is not that relevant to her husband's question and is not sufficiently informative. By deliberately violating the maxims of the CP, the wife implies that she doesn't like the new hat at all.

According to Grice, conversational implicature is something over the basic meaning of the words in conversations. It can arise from deliberately and openly flouting the maxims. And in the actual speech conversation, it is often the case that speakers cannot or do not observe the CP and its maxims.

In the maxim of quality, we should say what is true. But the sentence (9) "He is a tiger" is literally false, openly against the maxim of quality, for no human is a tiger. Therefore, the hearer needs to interpret it as a metaphor, meaning that the man has some characteristics of a tiger.

In the maxim of quantity, we need to say in an informative way. For example,

(10) Mark: Will George come to the party tonight?

　　Jane: If he comes, he comes.

(10) is a tautology, which means the use of different words to say the same thing twice in the same statement. This kind of sentence is uninformative by virtue of its semantic content. Hence, it violates the maxim of quantity, and on the level of what is implicated, it can mean that Jane doesn't care about whether George comes to the party or not.

In the maxim of relation, we should talk in a relevant way, otherwise, the conversation may not continue. But sometimes, in order to end the conversation in an implicit way, the speaker may violate this maxim. For instance, at a genteel tea party,

(11) Joshua: Mrs. Smith is a fat woman.

　　Alan: The weather has been quite delightful this summer, hasn't it?

In (11), Alan apparently refuses to make the answer relevant to Joshua's preceding remark. He thereby implies that Joshua's remark should not be discussed there.

In the maxim of manner, we need to say as clearly as we can. For example:

(12) Dad: Shall we get something for the girl?
Mom: OK, but I veto C-A-N-D-Y.

In (12), it's known to both dad and mom that she has no difficulty in pronouncing the word "candy". But the mother is still deliberately obscure, so that the girl cannot understand what her parents are talking about.

7.4 The Politeness Principle

From all the examples being mentioned in the CP, there arouses the question why people choose to imply rather than assert an idea. When the wife is asked whether she likes the hat or not, why doesn't she say "No, I don't" directly? And probably the answer lies in another theory in language use—the Politeness Principle (PP for short).

In most cases, the indirectness is motivated by considerations of politeness, which is usually regarded as a means or strategy used by a speaker to achieve various proposes, such as saving face, establishing and maintaining harmonious social relations in conversation. Following Grice's presentation of the CP, another British linguist Geoffrey Neil Leech put forward the PP in 1983 in his book *Principles of Pragmatics*.

Following the model of the CP, Leech (1983) put forward six maxims of the PP which run as follows: the maxim of tact, the maxim of generosity, the maxim of approbation, the maxim of modesty, the maxim of agreement, and the maxim of sympathy.

1) The maxim of tact
   - Minimize cost to other;
   - Maximize benefit to other.
2) The maxim of generosity
   - Minimize benefit to self;
   - Maximize cost to self.
3) The maxim of approbation
   - Minimize dispraise of other;
   - Maximize praise of other.

4) The maxim of modesty
   - Minimize praise of self;
   - Maximize dispraise of self.
5) The maxim of agreement
   - Minimize disagreement between self and other;
   - Maximize agreement between self and other.
6) The maxim of sympathy
   - Minimize antipathy between self and other;
   - Maximize sympathy between self and other.

It is argued that when the CP and the PP are in contradiction, it is generally the CP maxims that get sacrificed. For example, when Alfred and Carl are going to leave office in a company,

(13) Jack: We will all miss Alfred and Carl.

Rebecca: Yes. We will miss Carl.

In (13), Rebecca observes the maxim of agreement of the PP, but violates the first maxim of quantity of the CP at the same time. Thus, between the CP and the PP, there lies a relation of mutual challenge and concession when they are in conflict. Another interesting area of investigation is the study of different cultures and languages in relation to the social principles of conversation. For example, some cultures may place very high value on the maxim of agreement and speakers may show this by repeating every word the other speaker has just said, as if they agree totally, and then giving their own opinion. The British, for example, are supposedly well-known for the use of "Yes, but..." replies.

7.5 Summary

Pragmatics is the applied study with more care about its speaker or utterance meaning in context. The first theory is Speech Act Theory. Austin distinguished constatives from performatives, in which actions are performed by utterances. At the meanwhile, it is agreed that non-performative sentences can also do things. There are three basic senses in which saying something may be understood as doing something. The second theory is the Cooperative Principle. Grice proposed that all speakers adhere to a basic principle governing conversation which is classified into four maxims. When we speak, we generally have something like the CP and its maxims in our mind to guide us. But it is obvious to the hearer at the time of the utterance that the speaker has deliberately failed to observe one or more maxims. And in most cases, the indirectness is motivated by considerations of politeness. In the Politeness Principle, Leech put forward six maxims. And between the CP and the PP, there lies a relation of mutual challenge and concession when they are in conflict.

Exercises

I Define the following terms.

1. pragmatics
2. performative
3. locutionary act
4. illocutionary act
5. perlocutionary act
6. the Cooperative Principle
7. the Politeness Principle

II Answer the following questions.

1. What are the semantic and pragmatic meanings in the following sentence in the different contexts respectively?

   "Today is Sunday, John."

   Situation A: John gets up early during the workdays.

   Situation B: John never does housework in excuse of being busy at work.

   Situation C: John promised to go shopping with his wife on Sunday.

2. What are the locutionary act, illocutionary act and perlocutionary act in the following dialogue?

   A: It's such a fine day today.

   B: I have to handle the documents first.

3. Which maxim of the Cooperative Principle is flouted in the following dialogues and what are the conversational implicatures aroused?

   Dialogue one

   A: What do you think about John?

   B: He is a tiger.

   Dialogue two

   A: Will Smith come to the party tonight?

Chapter 7　Pragmatics

B: If he comes, he comes.

Dialogue three

A: Mrs. Smith is a fat woman.

B: The weather has been quite delightful this summer, hasn't it?

Dialogue four

A: Shall we get something for the kids?

B: Yes. But I veto I-C-E-C-R-E-A-M.

III Put the statement "You must cut the lawn" in a politer way.

IV Write a line of advertisement for each of the following sentences that slips in the claim via implicature.

1. ZONKO cures insomnia.
2. HAPPY HEAVEN INN has beautiful views.
3. KISSGOOD eliminates bad breath.
4. NO-ANT kills ants.
5. Dogs love YAPPY dog food.
6. Dentists use GRIN toothpaste.

Chapter 8

Discourse Analysis

The learning objectives of this chapter are:
1. to master the components of information structure and their realization;
2. to familiarize students with different language resources that achieve cohesion and coherence;
3. to identify the discourse markers and their functions;
4. to analyze the structure of daily conversations;
5. to analyze the structure of written texts.

语言学教程
A Coursebook for Linguistics

导言

语篇分析属于跨学科研究范畴，它不仅是语言学家研究的领域，也是其他人文学科和社会学科的研究路径之一。学者们从不同视角进行语篇分析，根据自身的研究焦点对语篇提出了不同的界定：有的关注语言本身，语篇被看作是大于句子的语言单位；有的关注语言的使用，将研究范围扩展到影响语篇生成和理解的众多因素，如社会语境和认知机制；有的认为语篇是一种社会实践，语篇分析成为揭示社会秩序和权利关系的重要途径。本章内容将关注语言本身的研究，所以我们使用狭义的语篇概念，将其视为句子之上的语言单位，语篇分析则研究口语和书面语中的句子如何形成更大的有意义的单位。语篇分析不仅有助于描述我们所使用语言的特征，还能够揭示语篇生产者在语境限定下如何组织语篇中的单词、短语和句子来实现特定的交际功能。语篇分析涵盖了许多研究领域。本章中，我们只关注以下五个领域：信息结构、衔接与连贯、话语标记语、会话分析和书面语篇结构。

A primarily linguistic approach to the analysis of discourse is to examine how humans use language to communicate and, in particular, how addressers construct linguistic message for addressees and how addressees work on linguistic messages in order to interpret them.

—Gillian Brown & George Yule[1]

8.1 What Is Discourse Analysis?

Discourse analysis concerns the language unit above sentence. It studies how discourse producers organize words, phrases and sentences to achieve specific communicative functions under context constraints. Discourse analysis covers many research areas. In this chapter, we only focus on the following five areas: information structure, cohesion and coherence, discourse markers, conversation analysis and textual patterns.

---

1 Gillian Brown is a British linguist and works in University of Edinburgh. She is known for her expertise on discourse analysis and sociology. Her representative works include *Listening to Spoken English*, *Questions of Intonation*, *Speakers, Listeners* and *Communication: Explorations in Discourse Analysis*. George Yule is a Scottish-American linguist and now works in University of Edinburgh. His areas of specialization are discourse analysis and pragmatics. His best-known works are *The Study of Language* and *Referential Communication Tasks*. They are the co-authors of *Discourse Analysis* and *Teaching the Spoken Language*.

Chapter 8 Discourse Analysis

8.2 Information Structure

Information structure is concerned about how information is distributed within discourse, and what resources are available to discourse producers for indicating the status of information which is introduced into discourse.

Information structure is composed of given information and new information. The former refers to the information that the producer believes is known to the recipients; the latter is the one the producer believes not known to the recipients. For example, in the following two-turn interaction, the noun phrase "Mary" in the answer is the message that Father wants to know; the word "door", in contrast, is the information shared by both participants. In other words, "Mary" is the new information to Father since it is just being introduced into the discourse, but "door" is given or old information to him because it is in his mind, who mentioned it in the previous turn.

(1) Father: Who left the door open?
    Son: Mary opened the door.

Sometimes, the given information need not be introduced into a discourse by a speaker when it has very close relation with the situation of an interaction. For instance, when you purchase a train ticket at the station, the "next train" in your question towards the clerk "When is the next train leaving?" is the given information, which is already in your mind and that of the clerk because of the shared setting of the communication. The new information is the departure time of the next train you want to know from the clerk. Similarly, "the door" in conversation (1) is given information to both participants if they are talking in the setting of the room.

Besides, given information has close association with something that has just been mentioned in the discourse. In the discourse (2), since "section" and "pie chart" form the part-whole relation, the referent of the subparts "each section" is regarded as given information.

(2) These pie charts show the world's production of renewable and non-renewable sources of energy. Each section represents a different source of energy.

Given information is commonly expressed in more attenuated ways—ways that are abbreviated or reduced, including pronouns and unstressed noun phrases. Sometimes, it is simply left out of a sentence together. For example, the answer in conversation (1) could be changed into the following form:

(3) Father: Who left the door open?

Son: Mary did.

The pro-verb "did" replaces the given information concerning the action of opening the door. There are more similar instances, such as the conversation (4):

(4) Jack: It's been a long time, Tom! Tell us—how is life in Kariba Town?
Toe: Pretty good, Jack.

In this conversation, the given information "life in Kariba Town" is omitted entirely from the answer. In contrast, new information is commonly expressed in a more elaborate fashion, with a full noun phrase instead of a pronoun, and sometimes with a relative clause or adjectival modifiers, just like "a tall man with an old-fashioned hat on, quite elegantly dressed" in the following discourse:

(5) When I entered the room, there was a tall man with an old-fashioned hat on, quite elegantly dressed.

8.3 Cohesion and Coherence

8.3.1 Cohesion

Cohesion is another important topic in discourse analysis. It refers to the grammatical and/or lexical relationships between the different elements of a discourse. This may be the relationship between different parts of a sentence. For example, there is a link between "a horse" and "him" in the sentence "You can lead a horse to water but you can't make him drink". Sometimes, the cohesive relationship is produced between different sentences. In the following text, the pronoun "it" at the beginning of the second sentence refers back to the nominal group "the kind of industrial revolution" in the first sentence.

(6) This is the kind of industrial revolution that needs to be repeated all across China. It will form the foundation of China's future economy.

In this way, "it" explicitly links the neighboring two sentences together in the discourse. There are many other cohesive devices like "it", which can be divided into grammatical and lexical categories. The former is composed of reference, substitution, ellipsis and conjunction; the latter is divided into reiteration and collocation.

Reference means the speech act of referring. Instead of being interpreted semantically in their own right, some linguistic elements, such as the word "it" at the initial position of the second sentence in the discourse (7) makes reference to something else for their interpretation—the word "monster" in the previous sentence. Here, "it" is the reference item and "monster" is the referent. One reference and one referent form a cohesive tie, giving rise to the nature of texture.

(7) I saw a monster. It is very large.

Reference can be personal reference, demonstrative reference and comparative reference. Personal references are realized by personal pronoun, possessive determiner and possessive pronoun. For example, all the three sentences a, b, c could form a cohesive discourse with sentence (8), since the personal pronoun "he" in a, the possessive determiner "his wife" in b and the possessive pronoun "his" in c refer back to the subject "John" in sentence (8).

(8) John has moved to a new house.
    a. He had it built last year.
    b. His wife must be delighted with it.
    c. I don't know it was his.

Reference could also be demonstrative, identifying the referent by locating it on a scale of proximity, realized by the demonstrative pronouns "this", "these", "that", "those" and demonstrative adverbs "here", "there", "now" and "then". There are some examples:

(9) Today mulberry tree plantations are being cleared. With the fruit now having been harvested, the leaves are to be used as animal feed. These trees play a role in improving the health of the Yangtze because their strong roots prevent soil runing off downhill.

(10) The success of this model along the Yangtze is catching on. And with support from authorities, local people here are now partners in reviving the river.

The pronoun "these" in (9) and the demonstrative adverb "here" in (10) are typical demonstrative references, indicating what trees and people are referred to in the discourse.

Sometimes reference is produced by expressing likeness or forming comparison between things. The former is realized by those expressions that show identity (same, equal, identical, identically), similarity (such, similar, so, similarly, likewise) and difference (other, different, else, differently, otherwise); the latter is realized by numeratives (more, fewer, less, further, additional, so, as) or epithets that highlight particular property (better...). The following discourses apply such comparative references to achieve cohesion between their different parts:

(11) "Ah, I can see you are a bookworm like myself. Now," he added, pointing to Mahony who was regarding us with open eyes, "he is different; he goes in for games." (*Dubliners*)

(12) Sure enough, there were two men just outside the stockade, one of them waving a white cloth; the other, no less a person than Silver himself, standing placidly by. (*Treasure Island*)

(13) "That's a fair young lady to be pitied by and wept for by! How does it feel? Is it worth being tried for one's life, to be the object of such sympathy and compassion, Mr. Darnay?" (*A Tale of Two Cities*)

(14) For a long time, though I certainly did my best to listen, I could hear nothing but a low gabbling; but at last, the voices began to grow higher, and I could pick up a word or two, mostly oaths, from the captain. (*Treasure Island*)

Apart from the categorization of references above according to the nature of referent, we can also divide them into different types based on the location of the referent concerned, as shown in Figure 8.1:

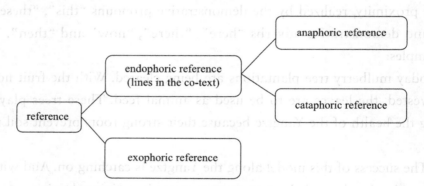

Figure 8.1 Categorization of reference

Sometimes, the addresser may refer to something in the situational context, and sometimes the addresser may refer to something that has already been introduced into the text. The former is exophora, and the latter is endophora, which is further divided into two subtypes: anaphoric reference where the referent lies in the prior text, and cataphoric reference where referent lies in the text to come. Here are some examples for each type of reference.

(15) Don't go; *the train*'s coming. (exophora)

(16) They broke a Chinese vase. *That* was valuable. (anaphora)

(17) I would never have believed *it*. They've accepted the whole scheme. (cataphora)

"The train" in (15) is an exophora, since it points to the approaching train in the situational context of the utterance. The initial reference "that" in sentence (16) belongs to anaphora by referring to the referent "a Chinese vase" in the previous sentence, while the pronoun "it" at the end of the first sentence in (17) is a typical cataphora, because we have to look forward to the next sentence in order to understand what it really means.

Another cohesive device is substitution. It is the process or result of replacing one word by another at a particular position in a structure. There are three types of substitution, that is, nominal, verbal and clausal substitutions. For instance, the substitute words "one" and "same" in (18) and (19) replace the noun phrases "axe" and "the roast duck" in nominal substitution; In (20), the substitute word "do" replaces the verb phrase "take that letter" in verbal substitution; the substitute word "so" in (21) replaces the clause "He is very clever" in clausal substitution.

(18) My axe is too blunt. I must get a sharper *one*.

(19) She chose the roast duck; I chose the *same*.

(20) Did Mary take that letter?

    She might have *done*.

(21) He is very clever. I don't think *so*.

The above pro-forms in different kinds of substitutions make these discourses more concise and highlight their central content. Different from reference, substitution is a kind of cohesive relation at the grammatical level rather than at the semantic level. The substitute item has the same structural function as that for which it substitutes.

Ellipsis is a special kind of substitution. We call it substitution by zero, in which a word or phrase of a sentence or a clause is omitted in a discourse. Similarly, there are three types of ellipsis, that is, nominal, verbal and clausal ellipses. The following discourses are typical examples of nominal, verbal and clausal ellipses respectively. All the omitted parts in them, such as "life", "watching" and "is he coming to the party" can be recovered from the previous discourses.

(22) The good life is one (life) inspired by love and guided by knowledge.

(23) A: Were you watching TV?

    B: No, I wasn't (watching).

(24) A: John's coming to the party.

    B: When? (= When is he coming to the party?)

Ellipsis can help us to avoid repetition in communication. For instance, in the discourse (25), the pro "ones" at the end of the first sentence replaces the nominal group "plant types", while "don't" in the next sentence avoid repeating the whole clause that modifies the word "leaves".

(25) The AI is capable of recognizing different plant types, so the drone can target the correct ones. And what's even more impressive, by using multi spectral imaging the drone can even identify which leaves on a plant need treatment, and which don't; which makes the whole technology environmentally friendly.

A fourth type of cohesive device is conjunction. It refers to an item or process whose primary function is to connect words or other constructions. The conjunction helps us to interpret the relation between different parts of a discourse, including additive, adversative, clausal and temporal relations, in which the latter part gives additional information to the preceding one or the information contrary to the expectation expressed by the preceding one or forms cause-effect relation and time sequence with the preceding one. For example, different conjunctive resources in a, b, in (26) can form different semantic relations with the same first sentence.

(26) For the whole day he climbed up the steep mountainside, almost without stopping.

    a. And in all this time he met no one. (additive)

    b. Yet he was hardly aware of being tired. (adversative)

    c. So by night time the valley was far below him. (causal)

    d. Then, as dusk fell, he sat down to rest. (temporal)

We can see the conjunction can be realized by conjunctives, such as "and" as well as "so" in a and c. It can also be realized by some conjunctive adverbs, including "yet" and "then" in b and d. Interestingly, one conjunctive could express different relations in different contexts, such as "and" in a–d in (27) can express different relations with the same preceding sentence.

(27) For the whole day he climbed up the steep mountainside, almost without stopping.

    a. And in all this time he met no one. (additive)

    b. And he was hardly aware of being tired. (adversative)

    c. And by night time the valley was far below him. (causal)

    d. And, as dusk fell, he sat down to rest. (temporal)

Apart from the grammatical cohesive devices above, cohesive relationship can also be realized by lexical cohesion, which is achieved by reiteration and collocation.

Chapter 8 Discourse Analysis

Reiteration means repeating the same word or the words with similar senses. So the sentences in the text can be connected with each other through recurrence of the same word, synonym, or near synonym, hyponym and superordinate, such as "cat", "gift" and "bird" in (28)–(30).

(28) There was a cat on the table. The cat was smiling.

(29) He got a lot of presents from his friends and family. All the gifts were wrapped in colored paper.

(30) Yesterday, a pigeon carried the first message from Pinhurst to Silbury. The bird covered the distance in three minutes.

Cohesion can also be achieved through the association of lexical items that regularly co-occur, such as "taxi" and "driver" in the following discourse, which often appear together in the human experience of taking a taxi.

(31) John went to school by taxi today. The driver was very rude.

We can come to the conclusion that sense relations between words contribute to the cohesion of discourse.

8.3.2 Coherence

Both grammatical and lexical relationships between the different elements of a discourse are crucial factors in our judgment on whether something is well organized or not. But they would not be sufficient to enable us to make sense of what we read or hear. For example, in the following discourse, there are a lot of connections in these neighboring sentences including "ford—the car", the repetition of "black", and "week". But it remains difficult to interpret. The whole discourse doesn't make any sense.

(32) I bought a ford. The car in which President Wilson rode down the Champs Elysees was black. Black English has been widely discussed. The discussions between the presidents ended last week. A week has seven days. Every day I feed my cat. Cats have four legs. The cat is on the mat. Mat has three letters.

This example reveals that there must be some other factor that leads us to distinguish connected discourses which make sense from those which do not. This factor is usually described as coherence. Coherence refers to the relationships which link the meanings of utterances in a discourse. It is not something which exists in the language, but something which exists in people. It is people who reach an interpretation which is in line with their experience of the way the world is. Let's consider the following conversation:

(33) A: Can you come to my birthday party on the weekend?
B: I will take an important exam on next Monday.

The two utterances seem to be entirely unconnected, but they constitute a very coherent conversation. The first speaker figures out that the second speaker can't go to the birthday party on the weekend, because the second speaker has to prepare for the exam and will have no time for the party. This process of interpretation is based on these two speakers' shared knowledge. As members of a discourse community and culture, we have built up expectations and background knowledge that can help us to understand the interlocutor even if he does not state everything explicitly.

8.4 Discourse Markers

Next, we will talk about a kind of connective element that figures prominently not only in pragmatics and discourse analysis but also in studies of language acquisition and in the research on sociolinguistic topics ranging from gender variation to code-switching. They are discourse markers, which are given a variety of labels by the scholars who carry out research from different perspectives: discourse particle, pragmatic particle, discourse connective, pragmatic expression, pragmatic marker and segmentation marker.

Discourse markers are realized by a rich group of lexico-grammatical forms, including such individual phonetic units as "uh", "oh" and "mm" and single words or lexical groups like "well", "anyway", "then", "now" and "as a result". They could be conjunctives, interjections, prepositions, adverbs and related phrases. Both definite and non-definite clauses can also be used as discourse markers in communication, such as "what's more", "I mean", "to begin with", "that is" and "you know."

Discourse markers are syntactically detachable from a sentence and do not affect the propositional content of the utterance in which they occur. Their positions in utterances are quite flexible. They are commonly used in the initial position of an utterance, like "however" in the following discourse.

(34) Archaeology can trace human history on earth back over two million years. However, the very evidence of any form of agriculture dates only 10,000 years.

They could appear in the middle position, such as "however" and "for example" in the next two discourses:

(35) For psychological studies, however, it is often necessary to study the whole animal and its relationship to the environment.

(36) We are inclined to forget, for example, that speech is an ingenious exploitation of a waste product—air charged with carbon dioxide as it is expelled from the lungs and that our organs of speech are able to produce purposeful noises only by interfering with this essential process.

Sometimes, a discourse marker is applied at the final position of an utterance, such as "you know" in (37).

(37) He is a good teacher. I've known him for three years, you know.

The main role of discourse markers is to guide speaker's interpretations of the discourses. In both written and oral discourses, discourse markers can frame the discourse, marking the boundary between different parts. Let's look at the following two examples:

(38) Teacher: So, we get energy from petrol and we get energy from food. Two kinds of energy. Now then, I want you to take your pen and rub it as hard as you can on something woolen.

(39) We do not yet have such a theory, and we may still be a long way from having one, but we do know many of the properties that it must have. Now, if you believe that the universe is not arbitrary, but is governed by definite laws, you ultimately have to combine the partial theories into a complete unified theory…

Example (38) is produced by a teacher in the middle of a lesson. The utterance of "now then" in combination with strong stress, high falling intonation and a following short pause frames the lesson, telling the students that they have finished one thing, and now they are going to start another thing in the next phase of the lesson.

Similar framing technique can also be found in the academic prose (39). Here, "now" is used as a device to shift the discussion into a new aspect of the topic. It does not signal a propositional relation between the two sentences but primarily indicates that there is a supplementary comment to be made by the author.

Discourse markers can also help the receivers to predict the content in the communication. For instance, (40) shows that the speaker wants to go together with the hearer, but he is too busy to do that. The discourse marker "however" shows the succeeding clause will counter the meaning produced by the previous one. Another example is the discourse marker "on the other hand" in (41). It lets the reader predict another aspect of the issue.

(40) I'd like to go with you; however, my hands are full.

(41) Goodhearted parents who aren't afraid to be firm when it is necessary can get good results with either moderate strictness or moderate permissiveness. On the other hand, a strictness that comes from harsh feelings or a permissiveness that is timid or vacillating can each lead to poor results.

Apart from framing and predicting functions, discourse markers can enable the speakers to continue their information transmission by indicating that their discourse is incomplete yet. They could use utterance incompletors, including such conjunctives and adverbs as "but", "and", "however" and hesitation fillers like "er", "well", "um", "you know" and "let me see". All these linguistic devices can show that the speakers have additional information to share with the hearers. For instance, the discourse marker in (42) indicates that the writer is more likely to offer further explanation next, while the series of hesitation fillers in (43) help the speaker to keep her floor in the communication.

(42) Typically, the programmer inserts an instruction that causes the computer to destroy an entire personnel data bank, for example, if the programmer's employment is terminated.

(43) Zelda: My older son was eh—was al—was twelve when she was born. And Samuel was s-seven. So that eh—y'd now it—it's different.

In conclusion, discourse markers play a significant role in constructing and interpreting discourses. Language users can make flexible choices according to their communicative purposes.

8.5 Conversation Analysis

This section will focus on conversation analysis, trying to discover what the linguistic characteristics of conversation are and how conversation is organized in ordinary life. It includes the study of how speakers decide when to speak during a conversation, how the utterances of two or more speakers are related, and the different functions that conversation is used for. We will deal with three main topics in the field, including adjacency pairs, the mechanism of the covert organization of conversation, preference structure and pre-sequences.

First, let's go to adjacency pairs. Conversations are not randomly produced, but follow certain rules that include both grammatical principles as well as cultural and social conventions. Speakers take turns in speaking in daily conversations. Certain turns have specific follow-up turns associated with them. For example, in conversation (44), A makes a complaint, and B replies with a denial. Here, the sequence of complaint–denial forms an adjacency pair.

(44) A: You left the light on.
   B: It wasn't me.

Adjacency pairs have the following properties: They consist of two utterances, a first part and a second part, which are spoken by different speakers. The form and content of the second part depend on the type of the first part. Adjacency pairs come in many types, such as question–answer, greeting–greeting, invitation–acceptance/non-acceptance, offer–acceptance/non-acceptance, complaint–apology/denial, and so on. However, not all first parts immediately receive their second parts. For instance, in conversation (45), a question–answer sequence is delayed while another question–answer sequence intervenes. The structure of the whole conversation takes the form Q1–Q2–A2–A1.

(45) Agent: Do you want the early flight?   (= Q1)
   Client: What time does it arrive?   (= Q2)
   Agent: Nine forty-five.   (= A2)
   Client: Yeah, that's great.   (= A1)

The middle pair is called an insertion sequence. There is a more complex instance of insertion sequence in (46). Three insertion sequences (Q2–A2, Q3–A3, Q4–A4) separate Q1 and A1.

(46) A: Are you coming to our party Tuesday evening?   (Q1)
   B: Can I bring a friend along?   (Q2)
   A: Male or female?   (Q3)
   B: What does that matter?   (Q4)
   A: Just a matter of balance.   (A4)
   B: Male.   (A3)
   A: OK.   (A2)
   B: I'll be there then.   (A1)

There is another problem with adjacency pairs. In conversation (47), there are many possible responses to the question "What does Joe do for a living?", including a question a, a partial answer b, a statement of ignorance c, a denial of the relevance of the question d, or a denial of its presupposition e.

(47) A: What does Joe do for a living?
      B: a. Do you need to know?
          b. Oh, this and that.
          c. I've no idea.
          d. What's that got to do with?
          e. He doesn't.

They are not expected answers but counted as second parts. It reveals there can be several second parts to one first part, but they are not of equal status. Preference structure divides them into preferred and dis-preferred ones. The preferred is the structurally expected next part and the dis-preferred is the structurally unexpected next part. The preferred second parts are more usual, more normal and less specific. For instance, agreement is a preferred second part to an assessment, while disagreement is a dis-preferred one. More examples can be seen in Table 8.1:

Table 8.1 The general patterns of preferred and dis-preferred structure

First part	Second part	
	Preferred	Dis-preferred
Assessment	Agreement	Disagreement
Invitation	Acceptance	Refusal
Offer	Acceptance	Declination
Proposal	Agreement	Disagreement
Request	Acceptance	Refusal
Criticism	Denial	Acceptance

It has been found that dis-preferred second parts contain more linguistic devices than preferred second parts. Take the invitation–non-acceptance conversation (48) for consideration. The dis-preferred second part has the elements of delay such as "Hehh", "well" and elements of appreciation ("thanks for the invitation"). It also provides an element of explanation ("You see I'm running an ad in the newspapers and I have to stay near the phone"). All these contribute to the politeness in the refusal of an invitation, which adheres to the social rules of human communication.

(48) A: Could you come to our party tonight?

B: Hehh, well, thanks for the invitation, but I'm afraid I can't make it this time. You see I'm running an ad in the newspapers and I have to stay near the phone.

Apart from adjacency pairs, conversations feature specific turns at the beginning. The opening sequences in a conversation usually set up some specific potential actions. They are called pre-sequences. For example, greetings are used to lead people into an oral interaction. There are many other types of pre-sequences, such as the pre-invitation in the following conversation, which helps the speaker to ensure the precondition for the forthcoming invitation:

(49) A: What are you doing this Sunday?

B: Nothing special. Why?

A: Why don't you come out with us then?

The pre-invitation is figured out by B who knows that something is forthcoming by asking "why".

8.6 Textual Patterns

Different textual patterns can be figured out according to various ways to combine the relations organizing (part of) a discourse. In the problem–solution pattern, the discourse consists of two parts: One part presents the problem, while the other part concerns the solution. The following newspaper article is an example in point. The dictions "violence", "concerns", "problems" and "solution" in the title and the first as well as the final paragraphs signal the problem–solution relationship between different parts of this article.

(50) TV Violence: No Simple Solution

There is no doubt that one of the major concerns of both viewers and broadcasters is the amount and nature of violence on our television screens.

...

The chief "lesson" of all our viewing, reading and discussion is that there is no simple solution to the problem of violence on television.

There are other typical textual patterns, including hypothetical–real or claim–reaction pattern, question–answer pattern, goal–achievement pattern and general–specific pattern. For example:

(51) People say Joe's stupid. But he's actually very clear. He's got a degree in psychology. (hypothetical–real pattern)

(52) London—too expensive? No surprise that London is the most expensive city to stay in, in Britain; we've all heard the horror stories. But just how expensive is it? According to international hotel consultants Horwath & Horwath's recent report, there are now five London hotels charging over £90 a night for a single room. (question–answer pattern)

(53) How to rub your stomach away? Here is a new method from China to flatten your stomach. There are two principal components to this exercise. The first part begins by…To order your copy of How TO RUB YOUR STOMACH AWAY, send your name, address and report title to Carnell plc. (goal–achievement pattern, general–specific pattern)

In some discourses, different textual patterns are mixed together, while in other discourses, the same textual pattern can be recycled. Let's take problem–solution pattern as an example. In the following discourse (example 54) about water supply in India, sentences ①–⑤ describe the problem. Then a solution is offered in sentence ⑥. However, the negative evaluation in ⑦ of the solution makes the problem unaltered. The problem remains until another different solution is presented in sentences ⑧–⑩ with the positive evaluation at the end of the discourse.

(54) ① The water supply in New Delhi doesn't look much better. ② Sometimes there's enough water for everyone, and sometimes there isn't. ③ Outside of New Delhi, getting water is even harder, where people have to walk for miles to get water from a well. ④ There is enough rain in the monsoon season, but they need water all year. ⑤ What can India do to solve its water problems? ⑥ Some in the government say the answer is to build more big dams. ⑦ However, many people disagree with that idea, pointing out that a large amount of money has been invested in water policy and big dams, but the dams have made the water problem worse by drying up rivers and wells and some villages still lack water. ⑧ Someone has a different idea to solve this problem. ⑨ He teaches villagers to collect stones and rocks to build small earthen dams and then make small holes near them and cover them with stones, earth and clay. ⑩ This stopped rainwater from running off and raised the level of the water under the ground. Because of such small dams, villagers can now produce food to raise their families.

8.7 Summary

So far, we have introduced only five topics in the discourse analysis due to the limitation of space. Information structure explores how discourse producers use language resources to distribute information within discourse to indicate their different status. Cohesion and coherence examine how different parts of discourse are connected and interpreted as a meaningful unit. Discourse markers, as a kind of connective element, help language users construct and interpret discourse. The structure of both oral and written forms of discourse is discussed through conversation analysis and typical textual patterns.

At the beginning of this chapter, we have mentioned that discourse analysis covers several different approaches. Nowadays, people study discourse in a broader view, considering social, cultural and cognitive factors that influence its production and understanding. Apart from language, other semiotic resources that can produce meanings are also considered in discourse analysis. In this way, new approaches of discourse analysis have emerged, such as critical discourse analysis and multimodal discourse analysis.

Exercises

I **Point out the new and given information in the following discourses.**

1. In the village of Chinchero, most people are farmers. But these days, they're also doing something new. They're entering the world of business. The new business begins with sheep.

2. Laura: What's assignment?
   Silvio: We have to give an oral summary of a movie or TV documentary. I watched a documentary about an archaeological site in Vietnam.
   Laura: That sounds interesting.

II **Pick out all the instances of discourse references in the following text.**

At one point the Brundtland report states that "The loss of plant and animal species can greatly limit the options of future generations; so sustainable development requires the conservation of plant and animal species". What, all of them? At what price?...At another point the Brundtland report says that economic growth and development obviously involve changes in the physical ecosystem. "Every ecosystem everywhere cannot be preserved intact." Well, that's a relief. But how can it be made consistent with the earlier objective? Does it mean that it is all right to deprive some people in some parts of the world of a piece of their ecosystem but not others? What justification is there for this discrimination?

III **Explain how the following discourses are organized.**

1. The engineers expected that the earthquake would have caused damage to their underground tunnel. It did; it was at least the magnitude of 6 on the Richter Scale.

2. Read the world's 100 Best Classics in less than 2 hours.
   Like most of us, you've always wanted to read the world's great classics of literature. But, because you have so much on, you just haven't been able to find the time. And right now, you cannot see when you will have the time. Now you can catch up on the world's greatest books in just 60 seconds per book, thanks to a new guide called "The 100 Best Classics at a Glance".

3. Horses are classified based on their height, which is measured in hands. Ponies are simply small horses or just under five feet. Draft horses are heavily built, can stand over 19 hands. Light horses such as racehorses fall in between.

Chapter 9

Sociolinguistics

The learning objectives of this chapter are:
1. to familiarize students with the correlation between language varieties and social variables;
2. to master the different kinds of language codes;
3. to analyze how the sets of language codes differ in language contact.

导言

社会语言学是语言学的重要研究领域之一。它的任务在于描述语言与社会的共变。语言与社会相互作用。一方面，语言在社会因素的影响下发生变异，产生变体，包括语言、标准语、方言（地区方言、社会方言、个体方言）、语域等。例如，社会阶层、种族、性别、年龄、受教育程度、职业等社会变量均会促成语言变异，衍生出稳定的或临时的语言变体，表现为语音、词汇、句子结构和语体等多方面的变异形式。语言变体是社会语言学重点研究的对象之一。另一方面，语言作为一种社会现象和社会行为也作用于社会现实。语言是信息的载体，交际的媒介，人类思维的方式，也是族群和国家的重要标志。社会发展和社会活动中的语言接触会导致语言变化，如洋泾浜语、克里奥尔语等，人们需要在双言、双语、多语等语言环境中进行语码选择和语码转换，以此维系社会运转，同时彰显个人和群体身份。语言接触也是社会语言学的重要研究部分。

In language there are only differences.

—*Ferdinand de Saussure*[1]

9.1 Introduction

Language provides a variety of ways of saying the same thing—greeting and addressing others, describing things, telling a story, paying compliments, etc. People vary the way of speech according to socio-cultural contexts. Therefore, language is not an autonomous system but a societal phenomenon.

Language also discloses aspects of our social identity through the way we talk. Our speech provides clues to others about who we are, where we come from, and perhaps what kind of social experiences we have had.

Sociolinguistics is the empirical study of how language is used in society, and an attempt to find correlations between social structure and linguistic structure and to observe any language changes that occur.

---

[1] Ferdinand de Saussure is a Swiss linguist, semiotician and philosopher. He is acknowledged as the founder of modern linguistics and semiology, and as having laid the groundwork for structuralism and post-structuralism.

9.2 Language Variety

A variety of language refers to a set of linguistic items with similar distribution (presumably, sounds, words, grammatical features, etc.) which can be uniquely associated with some external factors (presumably, a geographical area or a social group). A variety includes different accents, different linguistic styles, different dialects and even different languages which contrast with each other for social reasons. There are such varieties as standard English, Cockney, lower-class New York City speech, Oxford English, legalese, African American Vernacular English, slang, the language or languages used by a particular person, and so on. Each language exists in a number of varieties and is in one sense the sum of those varieties.

9.2.1 Standard Dialect/Variety

Language can be used to refer either to a single linguistic norm or to a group of related norms, and dialect refers to one of the norms.

In most of the cases, that a dialect becomes standard is an accident of history to meet the need that all people ruled by the government can understand and communicate by using the dialect. Historically, the standard variety of English is based on the dialect of English that developed after the Norman Conquest resulted in the permanent removal of the Court from Winchester to London.

A dialect is usually standardized by codification and elaboration, such as Caxton's establishment of printing in England, and Dr. Johnson's dictionary of English published in 1755. Codification is realized by the development of grammars and dictionaries. Elaboration is the use of the standard in literature, courts, education, administration and commerce.

Standard dialect/variety is usually based on the speech of the educated, used in print, in news broadcasts and other similar situations, and normally taught in schools and to non-native speakers learning the language. In China, the standard variety is standard Mandarin or Putonghua. It is estimated that up to 15% of British people regularly use standard British English. U.S. standard English is distinguishable from South African standard English and Australian standard English, for instance, and all three differ from the British standard dialect.

Standard dialect/variety not only reflects and symbolizes some kind of identity—regional, social, ethnic, or religious ones, but also unifies individuals and groups within a larger community. In essence, standard English is a typical social dialect.

9.2.2 Social Dialect

Dialects are linguistic varieties which are distinguishable by their vocabulary, grammar and pronunciation. Therefore, people in different social classes, ethnicities, genders and ages speak differently in these ways.

A New York City experiment on language and social stratification conducted by William Labov shows how the post-vocalic [r] varies in the three different department stores according to social stratification. The result demonstrates that pronouncing [r] is generally considered prestigious, and overall, the "posher" the department store is, the more people use post-vocalic [r].

The speech of blacks in the U.S.A. which is termed as African American Vernacular English (abbreviated as AAVE) has an interesting pattern in the verbal system, for example, the use of the zero copula. "He is nice" can be contracted to "He's nice" in standard English, and it can become "He nice" in AAVE.

In cross-gender conversation, women are inclined to be more collaborative and supportive, for example, to use more backchanneling signals (i.e., verbal and non-verbal feedback to show they are listening) to encourage others to continue speaking, and do not protest as much as men when they are interrupted. On the other hand, men interrupt more, challenge, dispute, and ignore more, try to control what topics are discussed, and are inclined to make categorical statements.

Young children in both Detroit and the Appalachian region of the U.S.A. use multiple negation more frequently than adolescents, and adolescents use it more frequently than adults. Children gradually acquire standard forms in the same way as they gradually acquire new vocabulary and control of grammatical constructions.

All varieties/dialects are inherently equal, although they are not socially equal. Some gain more respect, power and prestige in some situations than others do.

9.2.3 Regional Dialect

Varieties differing from each other based on geography are regional or geographical dialects. People are easily aware of pronunciation and vocabulary differences as well as grammatical differences. Speakers of Spanish can hear differences of pronunciation, vocabulary and grammar in the varieties of Spanish spoken in

Mexico, Spain, Argentina and Paraguay. South Africans use the term "robot" for British "traffic-light." Speakers of U.S. English tend to prefer "do you have", but in Britain the traditional British English adopts "have you got".

9.2.4 Idiolect

As every speech community has a dialect, every speaker has his own speech characteristics and linguistic behavior, including sounds, words, grammar and style. This language variety of individual users is called "idiolect". "Shakespeare's English" as a good example perfectly illustrates "The style is, to an extent, the man".

9.2.5 Register

A register refers to a language variety according to its context of use, in contrast with a dialect, a language variety, according to user. The same user may use different linguistic items to express more or less the same meaning on different occasions. One may write a letter to a business partner like "I am writing to inform you that…", but in another the same person may write to a friend like "I just wanted to let you know that…" One's dialect shows who (or what) he or she is, whereas the register shows what he or she is doing or how he or she is doing it.

M.A.K. Halliday analyzes register from three dimensions: field, tenor and mode. Field is about the purpose and subject-matter of the communication; mode refers to the means by which communication takes place—notably, by speech or writing; and tenor depends on the relations between participants. To put them simply, field refers to "why" and "about what" a communication takes place; mode is about "how"; and tenor is about "to whom". When any of the three features changes, there will be a different register. The two versions of the letter opening above differ in tenor, one being impersonal to keep formal relations and the other personal, but the field and mode are the same, i.e., the written letter.

Broadly, register is the combination of lexico-grammatical choices associated with particular groups of people or appropriate to the social setting and context, such as journalese, legalese, the language of auctioneers, race-callers and sports commentators, the language of airline pilots, criminals, financiers, politicians, baby-talk, disc jockeys, the language of courtroom and the language of classroom, etc.

A register helps one to construct an identity at a specific time or place. The developed lexical, syntactic and even phonological characteristics distinguish their communications from those of other groups. Eventually these specialized registers may be very difficult for outsiders to penetrate.

9.3 Languages in Contact

9.3.1 Diglossia

Diglossia denotes a situation where two varieties of a language exist side by side with clear functional separation throughout a speech community. One code is employed in one set of circumstances and the other in an entirely different set. Diglossia has three crucial features.

Firstly, two distinct varieties of the same language are used in the community, with one regarded as a high/H-variety and the other a low/L-variety.

In Arabic-speaking countries, Classical Arabic is H-variety and the various regional colloquial varieties are L-varieties. In Greece, Katharévousa is H-variety and Dhimotiki or Demotic is L-variety. In Haiti, the varieties are standard French (H-variety) and Haitian Creole (L-variety). In each case, the two varieties coexisted for a long period, sometimes, as Arabic and Greek, for many centuries.

L-variety is "learned" and H-variety is "taught". All children learn L-variety generally as the home language. H-variety is likely to be learned in some kind of formal settings, for example, in classrooms or as a part of religious or cultural indoctrination.

Secondly, each variety is used for quite distinct functions; H-varieties and L-varieties complement each other.

The H-varieties may be used for giving sermons and formal lectures, especially in a parliament or legislative body, for giving political speeches, for broadcasting the news on radio and television, and for writing poetry, fine literature, and editorials in newspapers. In contrast, the L-varieties may be used in conversation with familiars, in giving instructions to workers in low-prestige occupations or to household servants, in captions on political cartoons in newspapers, in soap operas and popular programs on the radio, and in folk literature. On occasion, a person may lecture in a H-variety but answer questions about its contents or explain parts of it in a L-variety so as to ensure understanding.

Thirdly, no one uses the H-variety in everyday conversation.

People seldom extend a H-variety into functions associated only with the L-variety, e.g., for addressing a servant; nor do they usually use a L-variety when a H-variety is called for, e.g., for writing a "serious" work of literature. The H-variety is the prestigious, powerful variety, which is more "beautiful" and "logical" than the L-variety. The L-variety lacks prestige and power although it is used far more frequently than the H-variety. In diglossia, the varieties do not overlap in their functions because of their status differences.

9.3.2 Pidgins

The particular combination of language and social contact gives rise to pidgins. Along the equatorial coastlines of the continents, two groups of people with no language in common usually find or improvise reduced language systems to communicate with each other in the long-standing contact, especially in trade, including trade in slaves. No group learns the native language of any other group because they lack mutual trust or close contact. Those simplified languages are pidgins which have no native speakers: It is no one's first language but is a contact language. In the 17–18th centuries, West African slaves in Caribbean slave plantations, who spoke different languages, communicated with each other and their bosses by developing a pidgin, a third language which was based on the native languages of the interlocutors. Many pidgins are mixed by the colonial languages, such as English, Portuguese, or Spanish and the local vernaculars, such as Indian African vernaculars.

The term "pidgin" is thought to come from the English word "business" as pronounced in the pidgin English which developed in China or perhaps from Hebrew "pidjom" meaning "trade or exchange".

To make them easier to learn and to use in contact situations such as trading, barter and administration, pidgins tend to have a simplified structure and a small vocabulary. Phonologically, Tok Pisin, one of the Pacific pidgin languages, has only five vowels, [a, e, i, o, u], which are fewer than those in English. There is no distinction between [ɪ] and [iː]. Speakers of Tok Pisin distinguish a ship from a sheep by calling the first a "sip" and the second a "sipsip". Morphologically, pidgins usually have a reduction of inflection in nouns, pronouns, verbs and adjectives. In Tok Pisin, pronouns are not distinguished for case, so there will be no "I–me" and "he–him" alternations, i.e., "me" is either "I" or "me". With more limited vocabulary, reduplicative pattern sometimes is adopted to express certain concepts, such as the pairs like "tok" (talk) and "toktok" (chatter), "look" (look) and "looklook" (stare), "cry" (cry) and "crycry" (cry continually). Consequently, pidgins tend to be full of structural irregularities.

A lingua franca refers to a language which is used habitually by people whose mother tongues are different in order to facilitate communication between them. Most pidgins are lingua francas, existing to meet temporary local needs. Pidgins often have a short life. If they develop for a restricted function, they disappear when the function disappears. In Vietnam, a pidgin English developed for use between the American troops and the Vietnamese, but it subsequently died out. A trading pidgin usually disappears when the trade between the groups dies out. Alternatively, if the trade grows, then more contact will generally lead to at least one side learning the other's language, so the need for the pidgin disappears. In some cases, however, pidgins go on to develop into fully-fledged languages or creoles.

9.3.3 Creoles

Once a pidgin is acquired as the first language of the next generation in a community, it gets nativized as a creole. Many pidgins have developed into creole languages.

Tok Pisin is a typical example of how a pidgin expands into a creole. Linguistically, pidgins become more elaborated and regularized grammatically during the process of creolisation. In 1960s, Tok Pisin was acquired as a first language by children and underwent a set of changes. A word-formation component has been developed; discursive devices are present; stylistic differentiation appears in verbs; grammatical categories such as time and number have become compulsory, for example, "bin" is used as a past time marker and "bai", from "baimbai" (by and by), as a future time marker.

Functionally, pidgins acquire more registers when they turn into creoles. Gradually, the expanded pidgins can be used in all social contexts, such as politics, education, administration, religion, agriculture, aviation, media, even original literature, and so on. Tok Pisin is frequently used as the language of debate in the Papua New Guinea Parliament, and it is used for the first three years of education in many schools. Creoles, like Tok Pisin, have become accepted standard and even national and official languages.

Thus, the role of first language acquisition is key to the development of creole languages from pidgin languages. The distinction of them lies in that pidgins are

Chapter 9　Sociolinguistics

non-native, simplified languages but creoles are native, fully elaborated languages. Creoles provide the laboratories of language change in progress and the study of pidgins and creoles clearly demonstrate the crucial role of social factors in language development.

9.3.4 Bilingualism and Multilingualism

Most nations have speakers of more than one language. In Canada, both French and English are official languages. In parts of Wales, both Welsh and English are spoken. This situation is bilingualism.

Israel has two official languages, Hebrew and Arabic. And Russian, Amharic, French and English are also widely spoken. Switzerland has four official languages: principally German, French, Italian and Romansh. In Belgium, people speak Flemish, French and German. India, Malaysia and Nigeria have the same complex stories. This situation is multilingualism. Take Singapore as an example. Singapore is effectively a multilingual nation. Although English is the first language of Singapore, there are also a multitude of other languages spoken in the country. As the year of 2008, there are more than 20 languages being spoken in Singapore. The Singapore government recognizes four official languages: English, Malay, Chinese (Mandarin), and Tamil. English is officially the only language of instruction in Singapore's educational system. The languages spoken in Singapore reflect its multiracial, multicultural and multilingual society.

Bilingualism—more generally, multilingualism—is a worldwide phenomenon. The world's estimated 5,000 languages are spoken in the world's 200 sovereign states, so that communication among the citizens of many of the world's countries clearly requires extensive bilingualism and multilingualism. More than half of Europeans are bilingual, while about 1/3 of the population in Great Britain, 1/3 in Canada, and 1/5 in the U.S.A. are bilingual. More than half of the world's population is bilingual or multilingual.

More frequently, multilinguals make language choice depending on a variety of social dimensions: location (city or country), social distance (stranger vs. friend), gender (male or female), relative status or role (doctor–patient), degrees of formality (formal wedding ceremony vs. lunchtime chat) and the function or goal of the interaction (getting a bargain vs. delivering a lecture). The choice of one code rather than the other is obviously related to the situation. Luxembourg is a trilingual country with three official languages: German, French and Luxembourgish. Each of them is used as the primary language in certain spheres. Luxembourgish is the language that Luxembourgers generally use to speak to each other, but it is not often written down. Most official (written) business is carried out in French. German is usually the first language taught in school and is the language of much of the media and of the church. Luxembourg's education system is trilingual: The first years of primary school are in Luxembourgish and then German, while in secondary school, the language of instruction changes to French. In addition to the three official languages, English is also taught in the compulsory schooling and much of the population of Luxembourg can speak English. Obviously, it is a daily pattern for multilinguals to make language choice. It is not only what you say that is important but which language you choose to say it in. They are bilinguals or multilinguals, who can use two or more languages effectively in their daily life and are able to switch from one to the other or others unconsciously when it is necessary.

Bilinguals/multilinguals have varying degrees of command of the different languages, which range from command of a few lexical items, formulaic expressions such as greetings, and basic conversational skills all the way, to excellent command of the grammar and vocabulary and specialized register and styles. Multilinguals develop competence in each of the codes to the extent that they need it and for the contexts in which each of the languages is used. Context determines language choice. In a society in which more than one language (or variety) is used one must find out who uses what, when, and for what purpose if one is to be socially competent.

In many parts of the world people speak a number of languages and individuals may not be aware of how many different languages they speak. They speak them because they need to do so in order to live their lives. Tukano, an Amazon tribe, gives us an interesting example of multilingualism. In the marriage tradition, the men must choose the women they marry from various neighboring tribes who speak other languages, that is, no man may have a wife who speaks his language, for that kind of marriage relationship would be viewed as a kind of incest. Consequently, children are born into this multilingual environment: The child's father speaks one language, the child's mother another, and other women with whom the child has daily contact perhaps still others. In such situations, language learning comes naturally and is quite unforced. They prize language learning, so most people can speak most of the languages. In fact, multilingualism is taken for granted, and moving from one language to another in the course of a single conversation is very common. Tukano are hardly conscious that they do speak different languages as they shift easily from one to another.

Bilingualism can be, and has been studied both as an individual and as a societal phenomenon. People tend to have a complex attitude towards people who speak a language different from theirs. Bilinguals/multilinguals may be admired and envied because they can speak different languages to fulfill more social functions. Nevertheless, bilinguals/multilinguals are usually regarded as "others" because they are likely to be immigrants, visitors, or children of "mixed" marriages, implying that they do not belong to the local cultures. Language choices forge one's social identity one claims for himself/herself and reflect one's loyalty to the culture or a nation.

In many multilingual societies, the languages enjoy different prestige. In certain Western societies, the languages that immigrants bring with them are downgraded because of the speakers' immigrant status. Multilinguals get little credit for speaking Swahili and, until recently at least, not much more for speaking Russian, Japanese, or Arabic. On the contrary, prestige is attached to only a certain few classical languages (e.g., Classical Greek and Latin) or modern languages of high culture (e.g., English, French, Italian and German).

There are three main reasons contributing to bilingualism/multilingualism. Firstly, when immigrants settle in a new community, they use their mother tongue over years along with the local language(s). The coexistence of the languages will result in bilingualism/multilingualism. Spanish in the U.S.A. is a good example of this. Secondly, cultural contact of the two or more societies over the years brings bilingualism/multilingualism. The use of Arabic and Western European languages, for example, English, French, Portuguese, Spanish, and Dutch in Asia, Africa, and Latin America bears testimony to this phenomenon. Thirdly, annexation, like colonialism, keeps the dominance of the colonial language over the vernaculars. Colonial languages such as Spanish, French, and especially English in many parts of Latin America, Asia, and Africa, become entrenched and continue to play crucial roles long after the cessation of colonial rule. Other reasons include the commercial, scientific and technological dependence of the speakers of certain languages on the speakers of other languages.

9.3.5 Code-Switching

It is inevitable for those bilinguals/multilinguals to switch from one code to another or to mix codes even within sometimes very short utterances, which is known as code-switching. Code includes languages, varieties and registers. Code-switching can occur in conversation between speakers' turns or within a single speaker's turn.

It is hard to account for the language choice, because the "right" choice is highly dependent on the social context and intent of the speaker, including solidarity, accommodation to listeners, choice of topic, and perceived social and cultural distance, etc.

Accordingly, there are two kinds of code-switching: situational and metaphorical code-switching. Situational code-switching occurs when the languages used change according to the situations in which the speakers find themselves: They speak one language in one situation and another in a different one. No topic change is involved. Typically, the four official languages of Singapore, which are English, the Mandarin variety of Chinese, Tamil, and Malay, are used in different sets. National policy promotes English as a trade language, Mandarin as the international Chinese language, Malay as the language of the region, and Tamil as the language of one of the important ethnic groups in the republic. What this means for a "typical" Chinese child growing up in Singapore is that he or she is likely to speak Hokkien with parents and informal Singapore English with siblings. Conversation with friends will be in Hokkien or informal Singapore English. The languages of education will be the formal varieties of Singapore English and Mandarin. Any religious practices will be conducted in the formal variety of Singapore English if the family is Christian, but in Hokkien if Buddhist or Taoist. The language of government employment will be formal Singapore English but some Mandarin will be used from time to time; however, shopping will be carried on in Hokkien, informal Singapore English, and the "bazaar" variety of Malay used throughout the region. The switches between languages always coincide with changes from one external situation to another. And each language has a social function which no other languages can fulfill.

When a change of topic requires a change in the language used, we have metaphorical code-switching. For example, in Shanghai, two negotiators in a business negotiation begin sorting out their business in Mandarin, but when they realize both of them come from Guangzhou and went to the same school, they switch to Cantonese to exchange stories about the school and their teachers. The topic "school" may be discussed in either code, but the choice of code adds a distinct flavor to what is said about the topic. The choice encodes certain social values. Changing the code is to redefine the situation—formal to informal, official to personal, serious to humorous, and politeness to solidarity.

Besides the context, motivation of the speaker is another important consideration in language choice. In Barcelona, all Catalans are bilingual. Catalans use Catalan only to each other; they use Castilian to non-Catalans and they will even switch to Castilian if they become aware that the other person is speaking Catalan with a Castilian accent. Catalan is only for Catalans. The case shows that one language expresses a we-type solidarity among participants, and is therefore deemed suitable for ingroup and informal activities, whereas the other language is they-oriented and is considered appropriate to outgroup and more formal relationships, particularly of an impersonal kind. It is the language that determines the situation.

It is worth mentioning that diglossia reinforces differences, whereas code-switching tends to reduce them. In diglossia, people are quite aware that they have switched from H-variety to L-variety or L-variety to H-variety. Code-switching, on the other hand, is often quite subconscious: People may not be aware that they have switched or which code they have used for a particular topic.

9.4 Summary

Language is closely intertwined with society. It is impossible to understand one without the knowledge of the other. Sociolinguistics studies language in relation to society by investigating how social variables contribute to language varieties and how language functions on society. A standard variety is usually chosen as the dominant prestigious variety to facilitate the speech community's internal mutual communication. The social dialects distinguish themselves on pronunciation, vocabulary, grammar and style, which are determined by social variables, like social class, ethnicity, gender and age. Dialects are varieties according to user whereas registers refer to varieties according to the context of use. Each variety works as H-variety or L-variety to serve different functions in social settings. Besides the inherent varieties, trading brings language contact and results in the simplified "mixed" language, pidgin. When a pidgin is acquired by the local children, it develops into a creole. Bilinguals/multilinguals may shift from one language to another/others in concord with the variation of situations or topics. To sum up, the primary sociolinguistic concern is the covariation between language use and social change.

Exercises

I Decide whether each of the following statements is true or false.

1. Social class affects the manner of how English is spoken and pronounced.
2. British standard English is the standard English of the world.
3. Regional dialect is inferior to standard dialect.
4. A register refers to a variety according to user.
5. Pidgins are, in essence, lingua francas.
6. If trade grows, pidgins go on to develop into fully-fledged languages or creoles.
7. No one uses the H-variety in everyday conversation.
8. Multilinguals make language choice mainly depending on situation.
9. Bilinguals/multilinguals have the same degrees of command of the different languages.
10. When a change of topic requires a change in the language used, we have a situational code-switching.

II Define the following terms.

1. lingua franca   2. language variety   3. idiolect
4. diglossia   5. code-switching

III Work out U.S. items vs. U.K. items in the following list. You should allow for the fact that some may use both.

1. When you go window-shopping, do you walk on the *pavement* or the *sidewalk*?
2. Do you put your shopping in the car's *trunk* or in the *boot*?
3. When the car's engine needs oil, do you open the *bonnet* or the *hood*?
4. Do you fill up the car with *gas* or with *petrol*?
5. How could he make warm water run from *tap* or *faucet*?
6. When the baby is wet, does it need a dry *diaper* or *nappy*?
7. Do you get to the top of the building in an *elevator* or a *lift*?
8. When the children are hungry, do you open a *can* or a *tin* of beans?
9. When you go on holiday, do you take *luggage* or *baggage*?
10. When you've made an error, do you remove it with an *eraser* or a *rubber*?

IV Read the following example of diglossia in Switzerland, and choose standard German (H-variety) and Swiss German (L-variety) to fill in the blanks indicating how H-variety and L-variety work in those situations.

In Eggenwil, a town in the Aargau canton of Switzerland, Silvia, a bank-teller, knows two very distinct varieties of German. One is the local Swiss German dialect (L-variety) of her canton which she uses in her everyday interactions. The other is standard German (H-variety) which she learned at school, and though she understands it very well indeed, she rarely uses it in speech. Newspapers are written in 1) _____, and when she occasionally goes to hear a lecture at the university it may be in 2) _____. The national TV news is broadcast in 3) _____, but weather broadcasts now use 4) _____. The sermons her mother listens to in church are generally in 5) _____, though more radical clerics use 6) _____. The novels Silvia reads also use 7) _____.

Chapter 10 Cognitive Linguistics

to language, which is rooted in the Aristotelian belief in classical definitions of categories, in objectivist realism (the existence of a mind-independent reality), and in the possibility of stating absolute truths. Cognitive linguistics holds that all individuals have an intentional relationship to the world and their access to the world or their consciousness is realized by their bodily experiences of that world. Secondly, cognitive linguistics is opposed to Saussurean and second-generation structuralist axioms, especially dichotomies such as langue vs. parole, synchrony vs. diachrony, syntax vs. semantics, lexis vs. grammar, etc. The claim of the arbitrariness of the linguistic sign is replaced by a search for motivation and iconic principles of linguistic organization. Thirdly, cognitive linguistics is opposed to generative linguistics, which sees language as an autonomous system, detached in principle from any other type of knowledge, especially encyclopedic knowledge. Cognitive linguistics, in contrast, holds that there is no clear-cut distinction between linguistic knowledge and encyclopedic knowledge.

Cognitive linguistics, as a new paradigm in linguistics, adopts a relatively new approach to the study of language and thought, which is based on the modern interdisciplinary framework of cognitive science. As it sees language as embedded in the overall cognitive capacities of mankind, there are some topics in which cognitive linguists are specially interested, including the natural language categorization, the functional principles of linguistic organization, the conceptual interface between syntax and semantics, the experiential and pragmatic background of language in use, the relationship between language and thought, etc.

In the following sections, some basic concepts and theories that are frequently used in cognitive linguistics will be introduced briefly.

10.2 Organizing Principles of Iconicity

Cognitive linguistics belongs to the functionalist tradition. Although Saussure saw linguistics as part of semiology or semiotics, he mainly emphasized one semiotic principle, symbolicity, as the organizing principle of linguistic structure. In a more balanced semiotic view of language, the two other semiotic principles (i.e., iconicity and indexicality), which are more perceptually and experientially based, are also shown to be important. The organizing principle of iconicity, which functions partly as one of the many direct manifestations of the interaction between perception and language, becomes visible in three sub-principles of linguistic organization. First, the principle of sequential order is that the order of the phenomena in our perceived or conceived world is reflected at all levels of linguistic structure. At discourse level, Caesar's wording "Veni, vidi, vici" reflects the temporal succession of these historical events. The same holds in advertising slogans such as "Eye it, try it, buy it". The second iconic principle of organization is the principle of proximity, or distance. What belongs together conceptually tends to stay together syntactically, and vice versa. The order in the adjective sequence "a large purple satin coverlet" reflects the primacy of material over color over size in the intrinsic nature of artifacts. The principle of quantity (more form = more meaning) is the third iconic principle of organization which is dictated by functional factors such as politeness, demands of informativity, rhetoric, etc. All these mean that extralinguistic factors and knowledge of them may have a direct bearing on linguistic structure.

10.3 Prototype Theory and Categorization

Categorization is the mental process of classification and its results are the categories or cognitive categories. The classical theory of categorization, i.e., the traditional view of categorization, can be characterized with the following points: (1) Categorization depends on a fixed set of conditions or features. (2) Each condition is absolutely necessary. (3) The conditions are binary (yes-or-no). (4) Categories have clear boundaries. (5) All members of a category are of equal status. According to this theory, everything either fulfills this set of conditions or it does not. If it does, it belongs to the category; otherwise, it does not. Therefore, categories have clear boundaries, and within their boundaries, all members have the same status of full members.

Indeed, in many cases, this classical theory does work in categorization. But sometimes it does not work, for in reality, categorization is far more complicated than what the classical theory of categorization assumes. Take the category "fruit" as an example. The classical theory of categorization assumes that all members of a category, e.g., fruit, share some essential feature(s), that all category members have equivalent status as members, and that category boundaries are clear-cut. Suppose that for the category "fruit", characteristics such as sweet, soft and having seeds are necessary and sufficient features. In this case, several types of fruit would remain outside the category: lemons (which are not sweet), avocados (which are not necessarily soft) and bananas (which have no visible seeds). Strawberries are more like rhubarb because both grow on the ground, not on bushes or trees. Are they fruits? Why is a strawberry a fruit, while rhubarb is not? All this fuzziness within or between categories points to a prototype view of categorization, which holds that categories do not reflect "objective" assemblies of features; rather, they are approximations consisting of clear, central or "prototypical" members such as apples, pears and oranges for fruit, and less central or even marginal members such as avocados, lemons and strawberries. Hence, members of a category do not have equivalent status, and category boundaries are not clear-cut (nuts grow on trees, but do not share any of the three basic features). Categories are to some extent also based on family resemblances, as Wittgenstein (1953/1968) showed for the German category "Spiele" (games). There is also psychological evidence for prototype effects in categorization. Statements about central members are processed far more quickly than statements about marginal members, and reasoning about any category is based on what is known about good examples of the category.

10.4 Polysemy and Radial Networks

In linguistic theorizing there is a huge cleft between monosemist and polysemist views of the lexicon. Generative linguists tend to subscribe to a monosemist view, according to which words have only one basic meaning and the different applications to various entities in the world are managed via an interface between language and thought. This may work nicely for words for artifactual entities, such as "university": A university can be categorized as a building, a place of learning, a period in a person's life, etc., but things are far more complicated in the case of the words for natural entities, such as "fruit". In its prototypical use, fruit 1 refers to "something such as an apple, banana, or strawberry that grows on a tree or other plants and tastes sweet" (*Longman Dictionary of Current English*). In this sense we can oppose fruit to vegetables, e.g., fresh fruit and vegetables. But in a technical sense, fruit 2 is "the part of a plant, bush, or tree that contains the seeds" (*Longman Dictionary of Current English*). In this sense, potatoes and all other root crops are fruits. Obviously, these two senses of one word are mutually exclusive. Fruit 2 is an instance of specialization, but the basic polysemy of lexical items does not end here. Each lexical item may undergo four different cognitive processes of meaning extension, i.e., generalization, specialization, metaphor and metonymy. Fruit 3 is an instance of generalization and means "all the natural things that the earth produces such as fruit, vegetables or minerals" (*Longman Dictionary of Current English*). Metaphorical extension applies to fruit 4 as in "the fruits of one's work", meaning "the good results from working very hard" (*Longman Dictionary of Current English*). The four senses of "fruit" are systematically related by the various cognitive processes discussed so far: Fruit 1 is the prototypical sense; fruit 2 is a more specific term, though only applicable to anything carrying or counting as seeds, hence also to grains, nuts, roots, tubes, etc.; fruit 3 is a more abstract generalization, including minerals; fruit 4 applies metaphorically to the abstract domain of the results of human endeavor. These four senses are clearly interrelated and can be represented in a radial network, in which the conceptual links between the senses of a term are revealed.

10.5 Metaphor and Metonymy

The human perceptual system is based on a number of pre-conceptual, most of all spatial, image schemas, which enable us to react to and manipulate the world. They include sensory-motor and visual schemas such as motion, containment, surface, contact, support, blockage, verticality, proximity-distance, etc. and, as the human mind and language develop, they serve as the basis for categorizing the physical world and, by a metaphoric leap, the abstract world as well.

Metaphor, for most of us, is regarded as a figure of speech in which one thing is compared to another by saying that one is the other, as in "My love is a red, red rose". Here, the word "rose" is used metaphorically to indicate the beauty, charm or passion of "my love". But in terms of cognition, metaphor is defined as understanding one conceptual domain in terms of another conceptual domain. Lakoff and Johnson (1980) claim that metaphors are not merely a matter of language, but just as much a matter of thought. The metaphorical mind seizes upon the world of spatial and concrete categories, and by means of metaphor, applies these concepts to less concrete, abstract entities such as emotion, time, event structure, causality, etc. For example, we tend to understand the emotion of anger in terms of the conceptual metaphor, HOT FLUID IN A CONTAINER, which may be expressed in various linguistic metaphors, e.g., "My blood was boiling"; "He was seething with anger"; "He blew his top". Time is experienced as A MOVING OBJECT (The years flew by.) or as A BOUNDED REGION FOR AN OBSERVER (We are coming up to Christmas.). The complex event structure metaphor consists of various subtypes such as states, changes, causes, actions, purposes, means, difficulties. All of these are conceptualized in spatial image schemas: STATES ARE LOCATIONS (be in doubt), CHANGE OF STATE IS MOTION, e.g., CHANGE OF LOCATION (get into trouble); ACTION IS SELF-PROPELLED MOTION; PURPOSES (OF ACTION) ARE DESTINATIONS; MEANS ARE PATHS (TO DESTINATIONS) and DIFFICULTIES ARE IMPEDIMENTS TO MOTION. Lakoff's claim is that such basic conceptual metaphors may well be universal, since human bodily experience is basically the same all over the world. This claim receives substantial support of Ning Yu (1998), who shows that the three domains of emotion, time and event structure are conceptualized both in English and Chinese by means of the same conceptual metaphors.

Metonymy is also a cognitive operation which is as fundamental as metaphor. The main claims made by cognitive linguists in the description of metaphor also apply to metonymy. Both metaphor and metonymy are conceptual in nature, which are major means of extending the resources of a language and can be explained as mapping processes. The main difference between them is that metaphor involves a mapping between two cognitive domains while metonymy is a mapping within one cognitive domain. The primary function of metaphor is to facilitate understanding, whereas that of metonymy is to enhance referential brevity. Thus, metonymy is defined as a cognitive process in which one conceptual entity provides mental access to another conceptual entity within the same domain. In other words, instead of mentioning an entity directly, we provide mental access to it through another entity. For example, we have several common conceptual metonymies such as (1) THE PRODUCER FOR THE PRODUCT (e.g., She likes to read Luxun. He loves Picasso.); (2) THE PLACE FOR THE EVENT (e.g., Diary-gate changed his life. America doesn't want another Pearl Harbor.); (3) THE PLACE FOR THE INSTITUTION (e.g., The White House refused to compromise. Wall Street is in a panic.); (4) PART FOR WHOLE (e.g., We need some new hands to participate in this project. Today we found some new faces in our classroom.); (5) WHOLE FOR PART (e.g., I heard the piano. England scored just before half time.); (6) CONTAINER FOR CONTENT (e.g., The kettle is boiling. Please drink a cup or two.); (7) INSTITUTION FOR PEOPLE RESPONSIBLE (e.g.,

You have to get permission from the university. The government's decision took effect.).

10.6 The Relation of Grammar to Cognition

Lakoff and Johnson mainly concentrate on abstract categorization and reasoning, and less on grammatical processes. As a highly abstract symbolic system, the grammar of a language is even more intimately linked with, and subject to, general cognitive processes than the lexical system. Talmy (1978, 1988a, 1988b) shows that the structure of grammar is related to principles of gestalt perception, one of which states that the perception of an overall shape comes about by dividing the perceptual field into a more prominent figure and a less salient ground, against which the figure moves, is moved or stands out otherwise. Talmy applies the perceptual principle of figure/ground alignment to complex sentences and shows that the main clause typically functions as figure and the subordinate clause as ground. Langacker (see 10.7 below) applies this principle to linguistic structuring at all levels. Probing into the relation of grammar to cognition, Talmy (1988b) treats the relations between lexicon, grammar and cognition in terms of a building metaphor. Whereas the lexicon can be compared to the single bricks of a building, the grammar is "the conceptual framework or, imagistically, a skeletal structure or scaffolding for the conceptual material that is lexically specified" (Talmy, 1988b: 165). The lexicon contains content words and reflects the tens of thousands of individual phenomena as single, conceptual categories, whereas the grammar develops more abstract, schematic categories. Thus, the schematic meaning of the plural morpheme—that is, a meaning applying to all possible contexts—is the notion of "multiplexity". This is found not only with count nouns (cups), but also with abstract nouns (fears, misgivings), uncountable nouns (ashes, waters) or event nouns (the silences between the two lovers). The concept "multiplex" is not limited to nouns and the plural morpheme, but can also be found with iterative verb forms, as in "He was hitting her". Thus, whereas the lexicon diversifies the conceptual world more and more, the grammar synthetizes under one common denominator quite different manifestations of "more than one", be it concrete entities, abstract entities, uncountable phenomena, or events. In this way grammatical "structuring is necessary for a disparate quantity of contentful material to be able to cohere in any sensible way and hence to be amenable to simultaneous cognizing as a Gestalt" (Talmy, 1988b: 196). Still, lexical and grammatical specifications are to be seen along a continuum ranging from content categories to schematic categories, which (like all categories) are by definition equal in nature.

10.7 Cognitive Grammar in Operation

According to Langacker (1995: 4), all linguistic meaning resides in conceptualization. All conceptual entities are either things like "book" or "linguistics", or relations like "about" or "know". They are joined to each other in relationships like "a book about linguistics" or "I know that book". A linguistic expression (be it word, phrase, sentence or text) always imposes a construal on somebody of conceptual content. When describing a conceived situation, a speaker must make choices as to the scope, i.e., which aspects of the situation are to be included, and as to the perspective adopted on the situation. Perspective involves three components.

First, it involves the choice of a vantage point, from which one looks at the situation.

Second, it involves the choice between an objective construal and a subjective construal. An objective construal is an explicit setting of the scene, e.g., the adverb "before now" defines the time reference point objectively as the speech act time (now). A subjective construal, in contrast, only implies a speaker-dependent reference point, as in the case of the past tense in "I saw him".

Third, perspective involves the choice of a direction of mental scanning, as in the opposition between "The roof slopes steeply upward" and "The roof slopes steeply downward". The cognizer/speaker selects things and relations in accordance with these cognitive processes, and assembles them into larger composite wholes such as relationships, clauses, sentences and texts. Not only clauses, but also things and relationships, are structured as gestalts, consisting of figure and ground. In the case of things, the figure/ground components are a profile and a conceptual base. Thus, for "strawberry", the ground or conceptual base is the domain of a "strawberry plant" with roots, leaves and fruit, and "strawberry" profiles the fruit. A relationship like "the strawberry on the plate" consists of the relation "on" and the two participants, "strawberry" and "plate". The relation "on" profiles contact or support with a surface in the domain of space. The figure/ground alignment holds between the first participant "strawberry" as a trajector—even though it does not move—and the second participant, "plate", as the landmark. Expressions that profile things are, prototypically, nouns, pronouns, determiners and higher-order expressions such as a full noun phrase; verbs typically profile temporal relations or processes, whereas prepositions, adjectives, and non-finite verbs profile atemporal relations.

These simple expressions can be assembled into complex expressions by grammatical patterns or constructions. A typical construction consists of two components that are integrated both semantically and phonologically. Such a composite structure, e.g., "the strawberry on my neighbor's plate", depends on correspondences between the subparts of the two components, i.e., "strawberry on X", and "my neighbor's plate". The corresponding entities "X" and "plate" are superimposed, i.e., their specifications are merged to form the composite structure. The figure/ground relation is also operative in the process of grounding the conceived situation in the speech event, comprising the speech act, its participants (speaker and hearer) and speech-act time. The speech event serves as the ground, and the linguistic expression communicated as the figure. The grounding of situations is achieved by means of the tense system for temporal relationships and by the determiner system for referential relations.

10.8 Construction Grammar

Langacker (1991: 8) characterizes the difference between his cognitive grammar and construction grammar as follows: Whereas cognitive grammar considers constructions to be reducible "to symbolic relationships", construction grammar assumes that "grammatical classes and other constructs are still thought of as a separate level of organization". Many other scholars have pointed to the existence of gestalt-like patterns or established configurations, which are both simpler to produce and also have meaning relations between the composing parts above their ad hoc composition. According to Goldberg (1995: 4), such patterns or constructions "carry meanings independently of the words in the sentence". A few instances of very frequently used constructions are the transitive construction, the intransitive construction, the passive construction, the ditransitive construction or double-object construction; less frequent, but still common, are the middle construction (This book sells well.), the incredulity response construction (What? Him write a novel?), the let-alone construction, etc. The middle construction is a special case of the intransitive construction, such as "The book fell down", which combines at least four semantic relations beyond the assembly of constituent parts. First, the verb is often a transitive verb (like "sell"), but used intransitively. Second, the subject "book" goes beyond the semantic value of a non-agentive intransitive in that it has some special properties that "enable" what is denoted by the predicate, "sell well". Third, unlike the intransitive construction, which may take all possible tenses, the middle construction prototypically occurs in the simple present, suggesting a kind of genericness. Fourth, the middle construction requires an adverbial or other modifier specifying the manner of what the predicate denotes. According to Taylor (1989: 21), constructions are thus schemas which have to be characterized by criteria such as the configuration of the parts, the contribution of the parts to the overall meaning of the construction, and the semantic, pragmatic and discourse value of the construction (the middle construction is especially favored in advertising). In a nutshell, the semantic relation of "property" does not come from the assembly of "book" with "sell", but originates from the gestalt of the construction as a whole. In other words, constructions are instantiated by linguistic expressions that "inherit" their (more) abstract relations from the higher sanctioning construction. Thus, the middle construction needs not only to use what would be a direct object in a transitive construction (sell a book), but it can, though marginally, also have a locative as in the following bookseller's exchange: "—Where shall we put the new travel book?", "—Well, the corner shop window sells very well." Obviously, we can observe prototypicality effects in this construction too, demonstrating that we witness the impact of the same very general cognitive principles at all levels of linguistic structure.

10.9 Mental Spaces

Cognitive linguistics is not only a lexico-grammatical theory of language; it also embraces the whole of language functions and structure, including pragmatic and discourse dimensions. In discourse, various knowledge frames, linguistic or non-linguistic, are invoked, which Fauconnier (1985/1994) called mental spaces.

Each utterance, even each content word, in discourse reflects and evokes a mental representation of some situations. For the encoding and interpretation of mental representations we draw not only on the linguistic expression, but also on the speech situation, and on encyclopedic knowledge, often called world knowledge. Each utterance is based in a mental space which is the speaker's perspective and possibly shared by other participants in the speech event. This is the base space (space 0). In base space we can open new spaces as illustrated in a much-discussed example "I dreamt I was Marilyn Monroe and kissed me". Here "I dreamt" is part of the base space, and the verb "dream" is a space-builder opening a new space (space 1), an imagined world, in which the second "I" (was Marilyn Monroe) is no longer identical with the first "I" (dreamt) in the base space, but is part of a new knowledge frame in which Marilyn Monroe is not kissing herself, but the speaker, i.e., the "I" in the base space. Mental space theory started out as a cognitive alternative to solve many of the referential problems left unsolved by logic-oriented trends in generative linguistics, but has, in the work of Fauconnier (1997) and Fauconnier and Sweetser (1996), developed into an encompassing cognitive theory of discourse and discourse management. In the development of the ongoing discourse, speaker(s) and hearer(s) have to keep track of all the mental spaces opened up and can at any time go back to any of them to elaborate them further.

10.10 Grammaticalization

For the understanding of grammaticalization, a distinction needs to be made between lexical items or content words, which carry specific lexical meaning, and grammatical items or function words, with little or no lexical meaning, which serve to express grammatical relationships between the different words in an utterance. Grammaticalization has been defined as the change whereby lexical items and constructions come in certain linguistic contexts to serve grammatical functions, and, once grammaticalized, continue to develop new grammatical functions. Simply said, grammaticalization is the process in which a lexical word or word cluster loses some or all of its lexical meaning and starts to fulfill a more grammatical function. Where grammaticalization takes place, nouns and verbs which carry certain lexical meaning develop over time into grammatical items such as auxiliaries, case markers, inflections, and sentence connectives. A well-known example of grammaticalization is that of the process in which the lexical cluster "let us", for example in "let us eat", is reduced to "let's" as in "let's you and me fight". Here, the phrase has lost its lexical meaning of "allow us" and has become an auxiliary introducing a suggestion, the pronoun "us" reduced to a suffix and then to an unanalyzed phoneme. It is the same case with the Chinese phrases such as "究竟" and "到底" in the sentence "你究竟/到底爱不爱我？". During the process of grammaticalization, such Chinese phrases as "究竟" and "到底" have lost their lexical meanings "追究原委" and "从一个地方到另一个地方为止" and become emphatic adverbials.

10.11 Summary

In a nutshell, cognitive linguistics involves the approach to language and language use that is based on human bodily experiences and the way that we conceptualize the world. The language we use to express the world is based on our cognitive conceptual structures and the worldly experience from which they come from. Cognitive linguistics provides many new perspectives for us to investigate language use and language itself. It seems that some unsolved problems in linguistic studies can be solved reasonably within cognitive linguistics.

Exercises

I Define the following terms.
1. cognitive linguistics
2. categorization
3. metaphor
4. metonymy
5. grammaticalization

II Answer the following questions.
1. What are the differences between classical theory of categorization and prototype theory of categorization?
2. What is construction grammar?

III **Comment on the following statement by George Lakoff.**

The metaphor is not in the words. The metaphor is not in the sentence. The metaphor is in the conceptual mapping on which the sentence is based.

Chapter 11

Psycholinguistics

The learning objectives of this chapter are:
1. to get to know the scope of psycholinguistics;
2. to comprehend the models in lexical access;
3. to get familiar with the models in sentence processing;
4. to master the models in discourse processing;
5. to understand the models in language production.

> **导言**
>
> 　　心理语言学是一门融合了语言学和心理学的交叉学科，主要关注言语交往中的编码和解码过程。也曾有学者使用语言心理学指代相关研究，目前较多采用心理语言学这一术语。由于研究对象的特点，它与诸多学科紧密相连，除心理学和语言学外，还有人类学、社会学等。脑科学技术和功能性磁共振成像技术的发展将心理语言学的研究带入了新高度。心理语言学的研究领域涵盖语言理解、语言产生、语言习得等，研究方法主要为实验法，研究目标是解释人类语言行为的内在心理机制。历经数十年发展，心理语言学已取得了丰硕成果。研究者针对语言理解、语言产生、语言习得等提出了诸多模型来解释语言使用者的认知加工过程。本章聚焦经典的心理语言学模型，主要涉及词汇通达、句子理解、语篇加工、语言产生过程等。

Language is the dress of thought.

—Dr. Samuel Johnson[1]

11.1 Overview of Psycholinguistics

　　Psycholinguistics is a hybrid term that involves the participation of psychology and linguistics. It is the scientific study of the psychological and neurobiological factors that enable humans to acquire, use, comprehend and produce language.

　　Traditionally, psycholinguistics addresses the questions related to language comprehension, language production and language acquisition. Language comprehension is about the process by which humans extract intended meanings from language. Psycholinguists are interested in exploring how humans comprehend the spoken or written language, ranging from a sound, a morpheme, a word, a sentence, to the whole discourse. Accordingly, models regarding the comprehension of the basic elements in linguistics have been proposed. Likewise, researchers may also explore the process by which humans produce spoken or written language, which is the major issue of language production. Both the study of language comprehension and language production can be done through psycholinguistic experiments. Language

---

[1] Dr. Samuel Johnson, usually known as Dr. Johnson, is an English author, poet, lexicographer, moralist and literary critic. He is regarded as one of the most prominent figures of the 18th century. One of Dr. Johnson's greatest contributions was his *Dictionary of the English Language*.

acquisition is also a hot topic in psycholinguistic research. It is meant to investigate the process by which humans acquire the capacity to perceive and comprehend language, as well as to produce and use words and sentences to communicate. How humans learn their mother tongue or a foreign language is the major concern of language acquisition research. Recently, the development of brain imaging methods and the event-related potential (ERP) technique has led to more precise measurements of brain activities and advanced the research of the link between the brain and language. These approaches to neurolinguistic exploration have enriched the discussion about language comprehension, production and acquisition. Neurolinguistics has become a promising branch of psycholinguistics.

Wilhelm Wundt, the father of experimental psychology, initiated the empirical research conducted on language after his founding of the first official research laboratory for psychological research at the University of Leipzig, Germany in 1879. Wundt also published a book entitled *Die Sprache*on (*Language*) which touched upon the topics such as child language acquisition, sign language, language perception and grammatical structure. These are still hot topics in today's psycholinguistic studies.

It is obvious that normal people like us can be recruited to participate in psycholinguistic experiments. Patients with language barriers also constitute a large proportion of participants for psycholinguistic studies. The relevant studies can be traced back to the ancient Greeks who noticed that brain damage could cause speech impairment (a condition known as aphasia). In 1861, French surgeon Paul Broca described a patient who could utter only one word "tan". Later, he found that there was severe damage to the left frontal lobes of the patient's brain, which has since been known as "Broca's area". Damage to this area can cause difficulty in speech production, yet with the ability to understand the language intact. In 1876, German psychiatrist Carl Wernicke found that patients with damage to the posterior part of the temporal lobe could lose the ability of language comprehension, but they could produce fluent and semantically incoherent speech. This area is known as "Wernicke's area". The foregoing brain-related studies promote the birth of psycholinguistics.

Under the auspices of the Social Science Research Council, U.S.A., a seminar that invited many of the most prominent psychologists and linguists was held at Cornell University in 1951. One result of this seminar was the monograph *Psycholinguistics: A Survey of Theory and Research Problems* (1954), which marked the emergence of psycholinguistics as an academic discipline.

11.2 Language Comprehension Models

Among the subfields of psycholinguistics, language comprehension is the most fruitful area, with many models related to lexical access, sentence processing and discourse comprehension proposed.

11.2.1 Lexical Access Models

Lexical access is the act to retrieve words in memory. Many prominent models concerning lexical access have been put forward in the development of psycholinguistics. For the sake of simplicity, we mainly introduce three of them, namely, the logogen model, the cohort model and the TRACE model.

1. The Logogen Model

In Morton's logogen model (1969), each word is represented by a logogen in memory, and it can be recognized when the activation levels of its corresponding logogen rise to or above the threshold level. The word "logogen" can be traced back to the Greek word "logos" which means "word" and "genus" which means "birth". Each logogen consists of several features about a word, like the phonological, orthographic, or semantic features, etc. The logogen model is applicable to the lexical access of both the auditory and the visual stimulus. The information flow of the logogen model is illustrated in Figure 11.1. For example, when the word "cat" is heard, the phonetic input enters the logogen system and fires the corresponding logogen stored in the brain. When the cat-related properties, such as the phonetic or semantic properties, reach or surpass the activation threshold, the word "cat" is recognized.

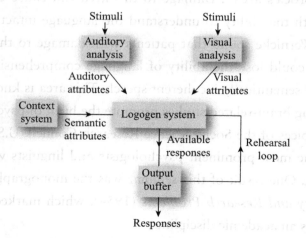

Figure 11.1 A schematic diagram of the logogen model (Traxler, 2012: 100)

Chapter 11 Psycholinguistics

The corresponding response is fed back into the logogen system via a rehearsal loop. Similarly, when a person views a picture of a cat, this visual input can activate the logogen threshold and the corresponding response is made available in the "output buffer" to produce either the spoken or the written form of "cat".

2. The Cohort Model

The cohort model was first proposed by William Marslen-Wilson around the 1980s. It was mainly developed to explain the lexical access of spoken words. A cohort means a whole group of matching candidate forms that are activated and become available or accessible at the initial stage of lexical access. The cohort model views that lexical access involves three stages: activation (or contact), selection and integration. During the initial activation or contact stage, the first one or two speech segments, or phonemes of the auditory inputs can activate every possible word which begins with the speech segment. As more speech segments unfold and enter the ear, the competitors no longer match the input, and the best matching candidate is selected. This is the selection stage. During the integration, features of the selected word, syntactic or semantic, are evaluated to see how well they fit with the prior discourse. Table 11.1 presents a schematic outline of the time-course for retrieving the word "candy" in light of the cohort model.

Table 11.1 Time-course of retrieving the auditory word "candy" in the cohort model

Time-course				
/k/	/kæ/	/kæn/	/kænd/	/'kændi/
cake	cattle	can	candle	candy
cool	can	candle	candy	
cattle	candle	candy		
can	candy			
candle				
candy				
etc.	etc.	etc.	etc.	

3. The TRACE Model

The TRACE model was proposed by McClelland and Elman in 1986. TRACE refers to the dynamic processing structure formed by the network of units, which serves as the perceptual processing mechanism. The TRACE model is also used to account for the comprehension of auditory inputs. In this model, there are three processing layers: feature, phoneme and word. Figure 11.2 shows a schematic diagram of the TRACE model for the lexical processing of the auditory stimulus "beaker". When people receive the auditory input, the corresponding phonetic features are activated, and accordingly, the phoneme-level processing units start to become active. An excited phoneme will excite the word unit to which it is connected. As the diagram shows, from input to features, features to phonemes, and phonemes to words, there are always excitatory connections. At the layers of features, phonemes, and words, there are also lateral inhibitory connections (within layers), that is, the activation of one unit (phoneme or word) inhibits the activation of other competing units (phonemes or words). The lateral inhibition turns "beetle" and "lamp" off and builds up "beaker". From words to phonemes, there are top-down feedback excitatory connections.

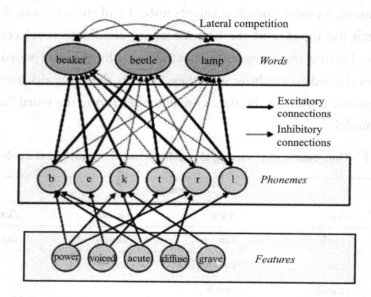

Figure 11.2 A schematic diagram for retrieving the auditory "beaker" in the TRACE model

11.2.2 Sentence Processing Models

1. Modular Model

Theorists who give priority to a quick representation of the syntactic or grammatical structure in sentence processing have constructed modular models. They believe that people can immediately build one or more representations of a sentence based on the range of grammatical information. According to Forster (1979), and Cairns and Kamerman (1980), the language processor is composed of separate subsystems in order to deal with different types of information. These subsystems are functionally modular because they only receive inputs from the subsystem inferior to them in the chain of processing, and their outputs are detached from the processing of other subsystems or by information from other cognitive domains. Modular theories hold that information processing follows a strict "bottom-up" manner, which does not allow "top-down" information flow. It means that a module's inputs can only be accessed and analyzed in its own databases and processes, and anything outside the module will not influence the processing in the domain. The information encapsulation and domain specificity enable the operation system to work automatically and quickly.

A typical modular account is the garden-path model proposed by Fraizer and Rayner (1982). The garden-path model claims that the syntactic processing follows the principles of minimal attachment and late closure. The principle of minimal attachment holds that the grammatical structure producing the fewest nodes is preferred. For instance, some previous studies have shown that when people read the sentence "The boy knew the answer was wrong", they tend to regard "the answer" as the direct object of the verb "knew", which is a mirror of the principle of minimal attachment. This in turn makes the sentence temporarily ambiguous. This type of sentence is metaphorically called a garden-path sentence because it seems that people are misled by different paths in a garden. A garden-path sentence can be defined as a temporarily ambiguous sentence that tricks the reader towards a seemingly familiar meaning in a processing failure and demands a recovery for its actual structure and meaning. The principle of late closure proposes that new words encountered in sentences are attached to the current phrase or clause if grammatically permissible. For example, according to late closure, when readers meet the sentence "The journalist interviewed the daughter of the colonel who was standing on the balcony", they tend to interpret the relative clause "who was standing on the balcony" as modifying "the colonel" rather than "the daughter".

2. Interactive Model

Contrary to modular modelists, interactive modelists hold that parsers are able to quickly draw on any useful information, whether it is syntactic, semantic, discourse, or even visual, to comprehend sentences, i.e., the contextual information of any kind can be employed to facilitate any stage of comprehension processing. They also claim that information can flow in an unrestricted way within the language system, and between the language system and other cognitive domains.

The most important interactive model is the constraint-based theory. The constraint-based theory assumes that language comprehension is an incremental one-stage process during which the processor can activate multiple sources of information in parallel. Parsers can immediately utilize all constraints (structural, discourse and lexical) available, both syntactic and non-syntactic, for sentence comprehension. The constraint-based theory predicts an eventually correct sentence interpretation. For example, some previous research using visual world paradigm has found that if the participants are given the visual context of two apples (one on a towel and the other on a napkin) and are asked to "put the apple on the towel in the box", they will not interpret the prepositional phrase "on the towel" as the place for the apple to be moved but as the modifier, and thus the visual context affects earlier than the syntactic structure in sentence processing, different from the prediction of the garden-path model.

3. The Good Enough Approach

Both modular and interactive models share a similar underlying assumption that eventually readers are able to work out a complete and accurate representation in sentence comprehension with the help of all relevant sources of information, getting rid of the initial misinterpretation. However, sentence reanalysis might not be an all-or-nothing process. For instance, previous studies have observed that after reading the sentence "While Anna dressed the baby played in the crib", people tend to give a high rate of erroneous answers "Yes" to such questions probing the initial, syntactically unlicensed interpretation as "Did Anna dress the baby?". This shows that sentence reanalysis might be a less detailed or complete representation, which is called a "good enough" instead of a thorough representation in language comprehension. According to the good enough hypothesis, readers process language based on two routes—semantic route and syntactic route. Monolingual research shows that it is the reconciliation between these two routes that gives rise to a merely good-enough instead of a totally faithful interpretation. A series of monolingual studies lend support to this good enough approach, such as the evidence found in garden-path sentence processing and passive sentence processing.

11.2.3 Discourse Comprehension Models

1. The Construction–Integration Model

The construction–integration model was proposed by Kintsch and his colleagues in the 1980s and has been modified ever since. This model assumes that two phases—

construction and integration of propositions—exist in discourse comprehension. A proposition can be understood as the semantic unit formed in readers' minds, which can be proved either true or false. At the phase of construction, readers construct the relevant preliminary propositions with the help of the words and sentences in the context. At the phase of integration, these propositions initially built by the readers will be incorporated with the prior context along with the background knowledge, and meanwhile, some irrelevant propositions formed in the construction phase are deactivated. In the process of construction and integration, three levels of mental representations can be created: the surface code, the text base, and the situation model. The surface code is a linguistic representation derived from the words and phrases in the text itself. With the help of surface code representation, the text base that includes macro and micro propositions can be established. Micro propositions are more related to local coherence, while macro propositions are more associated with global coherence. The situation model is the construction that integrates the text base and the relevant aspects of the comprehender's knowledge (Kintsch, 1998: 107). The surface code and the text base reflect the linguistic aspect in discourse processing. The propositions constructed therein will be cross-checked with the situation model which is stored in the long-term memory of the brain.

2. Structure Building Framework

The structure building framework was initiated by Gernsbacher in 1990. According to this framework, discourse comprehension is a process to build coherent mental representations by utilizing memory nodes. Memory nodes can be regarded as the building blocks of mental structures. The constructed building of discourse comprehension undergoes three stages. First, based on the early mentioned information, memory nodes are activated to lay a foundation for an intended mental representation. Second, by reactivating the same or related memory nodes, the incoming information is mapped onto this foundation. Third, when the new information is incongruent with the already built mental construct, new structures might be shifted or rebuilt. In Gernsbacher's opinion, if the subsequent information is not consistent with the prior discourse, additional memory nodes must be activated in order to create a foundation for a new mental substructure. The less coherent the incoming information is, the more processing efforts it takes and the longer processing time it costs.

11.3 Language Production Models

Compared with the well-documented models of language comprehension, the models put forward to account for language production are relatively few. The most cited ones have been proposed by Levelt and Dell.

11.3.1 Levelt's Speech Production Model

Levelt's model is the most influential among all the models of language production. It assumes that speech production begins in the conceptualizer (see Figure 11.3). It is in this domain that a message is generated. After the conceptualizer, the preverbal message arrives in the formulator. Three things happen to the message herein. Content words are selected from the lexicon, the message is given a surface form (grammatical encoding) and the message is phonologically encoded (phonological encoding). The lexicon contains lemmas, which are the abstract entities that represent words. They have access to the syntactic and semantic information of words and can be encoded into morphological and phonological forms. The output of the formulator is a phonetic plan. This plan is executed through the muscle movements of the articulator, which produces overt speech. In Levelt's speech production model, there is feedback so that while producing language, a speaker monitors both in the conceptualizer and through the speech-comprehension system whether the utterance makes sense. The audition system on the right hand of Figure 11.3 indicates that it can hear what the speaker has said.

11.3.2 Dell's Speech Production Model

In speech production, slips of the tongue, which refer to the unintended, nonhabitual deviations from a speech plan, are quite common. For example, "You have hissed all my mystery lectures" is a deviation from "You have missed all my history lectures". Dell's speech production model mainly copes with how speakers slip their tongues. It distinguishes three levels during speech production: semantic, lexical and phonological. Besides, speech production is a process of spreading activation (Dell & O'Seaghda, 1992), as shown in Figure 11.4. Dell's model allows information to flow in both a feedforward and a feedback direction. For example, in Figure 11.4, at the level of lexical nodes, when the word "dog" gains activation,

Chapter 11 Psycholinguistics

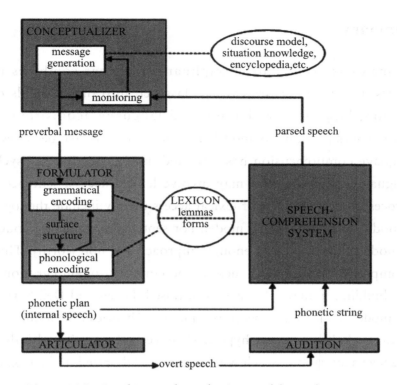

Figure 11.3 Levelt's speech production model (Levelt, 1989: 9)

it can feed back to the semantic level and reinforce the activation of the conceptual representation for "dog". The "dog" lemma also activates the corresponding phonological information. In turn, the appropriate pronunciation can feed back and reinforce the activation of the "dog" lemma.

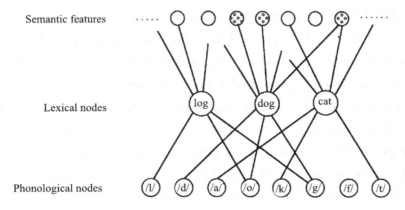

Figure 11. 4 A schematic diagram of Dell's speech production model (Knott et al., 1997: 1167)

11.4 Summary

Psycholinguistics is an interdisciplinary field that combines psychology and linguistics. Psycholinguistics can be classified into the subfields of language comprehension, language production and language acquisition. Ever since psycholinguistics was born, many models for each subfield have been developed. The issue of language comprehension has attracted much attention in psycholinguistic studies. Language comprehension may involve lexical access, sentence processing, discourse processing, etc. Models of lexical access mainly include the logogen model, the cohort model, and the TRACE model. For sentence processing, modular models, interactive models, and the good enough approach are noteworthy. The influential discourse comprehension models, such as the construction–integration model and the structure building framework, have been raised. Levelt and Dell have contributed much to the models concerning speech production. Theories like Skinner's behaviorist theory and Chomsky's innateness hypothesis have had a profound influence on the study of language acquisition, which will be further elaborated in the next chapter.

Exercises

I Answer the following questions.

1. Which field of psycholinguistics interests you most?
2. Can you talk about the main ideas of the lexical access models?
3. Which of the sentence processing models discussed in this chapter is more in line with the opinion presented in the following passage?

   In fact, this heuristic-based representation is not alone in language comprehension. It can be found extensively in cognitive psychology. For example, in the field of visual cognition, viewers do not build a veridical copy of the scene in their minds. Similarly, in the fields of judgment and decision-making, people make heuristic-based decisions in a reasonable time frame. Another famous heuristic or "good enough" processing example is the so-called "Moses Illusion". Suppose someone asks "How many animals of each sort did Moses put on the ark?", what will the answer be like? Most people tend to respond "Two" although the question should have "Noah" rather than "Moses" as the agent taking the animals onto the ark. Likewise, people always ignore the semantically anomalous sentences like "The authorities had to decide where to bury the survivors", although it should be "victims" rather than "survivors" to be buried.

4. What do you know about the speech production models proposed by Levelt and Dell?
5. Read the following excerpt from Kim and Pilcher's article "What Is Listening Comprehension and What Does It Take to Improve Listening Comprehension?" published in the *Journal of Experimental Child Psychology* (2016). How do the authors develop the construction–integration model for discourse comprehension? What can you learn from these research findings?

   We hypothesized that working memory, attention, vocabulary, and grammatical (or syntactic) knowledge are foundational language and cognitive skills needed for the surface representation, and that they provide input for establishing the text base representation. Furthermore, elementary and potentially inaccurate propositions in the text base representation have to be evaluated for accuracy and veracity, and inferences are needed to establish global coherence to ultimately establish the situation model (Kim, 2015, 2016). Therefore, comprehension monitoring would be involved to evaluate initial, local propositions, and inferencing and theory of mind would be involved to cross-check propositions and fill in missing information. Theory of mind, which is typically defined as the ability to infer others' mental states and predict behaviors, was hypothesized to capture inferences and reasoning about characters' intentions, thoughts, and emotions, which are critical aspects in comprehending texts.

   When we applied this model to data from Korean kindergartners and first graders, respectively, we found that the model fit the data very well and large amounts of total variance in listening comprehension, 74% and 85%, was explained (Kim, 2015, 2016). Working memory, vocabulary, and syntactic knowledge were all directly related to higher-order cognitive skills—comprehension monitoring and theory of mind, which, in turn, were directly related to listening comprehension. In addition, vocabulary and syntactic knowledge were directly related to listening comprehension after accounting for theory of mind and comprehension monitoring. In a follow-up study with children in Grade 1, we found that an inferencing skill (i.e., the ability to identify missing information in the text drawing on background knowledge) and theory of mind made independent contributions (Kim, 2016). A similar pattern was found for English-speaking children in Grade 2 as well.

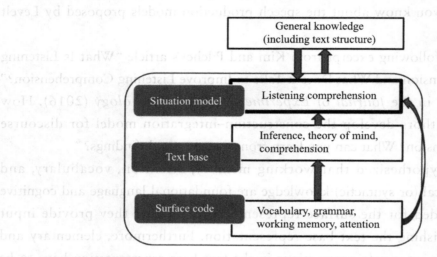

Figure 11.5　Direct and mediated relations model of listening comprehension (adapted from Kim, 2016)

Chapter 12

Language Acquisition

The learning objectives of this chapter are:
1. to master the basic concepts and theories of language acquisition;
2. to better understand first language acquisition;
3. to get some knowledge of what second language learners acquire and how;
4. to better understand instructions in second language learning.

语言学教程
A Coursebook for Linguistics

导言

语言习得是一个不断扩展又纷繁复杂的领域，本章呈现的是母语习得、二语习得和二语/外语教学中的基本概念、假设和理论。其中，母语习得主要涉及四个部分：行为主义语言习得观、先天论语言习得观、基于使用的语言习得观及语言习得发展阶段。行为主义语言习得观源自巴甫洛夫和斯金纳的基本概念，他们认为语言习得是通过刺激—反应—强化过程形成语言习惯。乔姆斯基的先天论语言习得观则认为，正常儿童均能够轻松掌握包含复杂语法规则的母语是由于人有先天的语言习得机制，生来就具有一种普遍语法知识。在接触现实语言素材的过程中，儿童认识到了母语的语言规则而获得语言能力，并进一步运用和创造语言。托巴塞罗等社会建构派主张从基于使用的视角理解和解释儿童语言习得。该习得观认为，语言知识源于语言使用体验，儿童在交际过程中能充分利用和加工输入频率特征，逐渐抽象出语言规则，儿童的语言随语言体验增加而发展。与先天论截然不同的是，基于使用的语言观认为人不存在先天的语言习得机制，语言是通过人类的一般认知能力习得的。语言习得发展阶段简要概述了儿童从咿呀学语到能说出句子的发展过程。二语习得包括三个部分：对学习者二语的描述、影响二语习得的外在因素以及二语学习者的个体差异。学习者二语描述部分简要介绍如何从对比分析、错误分析和中介语的视角理解学习者的语言变化。影响二语习得的外在因素部分阐释了输入假设、互动假设和输出假设在二语习得中的作用。二语学习者个体差异部分主要介绍了年龄、学习能力、认知风格、动机和学习策略等因素对二语学习影响的相关研究。二语/外语教学部分概述了认知派与社会派视角的二语教学理念。首先，针对教室环境的语言教学从认知和元认知两个方面展开讨论，认知教学目标分为以语言为中心的教学和以学习者为中心的教学；元认知教学目标则强调对学习者进行策略训练。其次，基于使用视角的教学强调语言学习是在互动体验中逐渐固化并达到形义映射的过程，具有系统性、概率性和动态性。

As a widespread, highly complex, uniquely human, cognitive process, language learning of all kinds merits careful study for what it can reveal about the nature of the human mind and intelligence.

—*Michael H. Long*[1]

---

1 Michael H. Long is a professor of SLA in the School of Languages, Literatures, and Cultures at the University of Maryland, U.S.A. He is an expert on SLA and his main research interests include epistemological issues and theory change in SLA, age differences, maturational constraints and sensitive periods, and SLA processes, e.g., stabilization/fossilization, interlanguage development, explicit and implicit learning, negative feedback, language aptitude, second language research methods, foreign language needs analysis, and task-based language teaching. He has been editors of various SLA research journals including *Studies in Second Language Acquisition, TESOL Quarterly, Language Teaching Research, Issues in Second Language Research*. He has published widely in the field of SLA and his publications mainly include: *The Handbook of Second Language Acquisition* (2003), *Second Language Needs Analysis* (2005), *Problems in Second Language Acquisition* (2007), *The Handbook of Language Teaching* (2009), *Sensitive Periods, Language Aptitude, and Ultimate L2 Attainment* (2013), and *Second Language Acquisition and Task-Based Language Teaching* (2014).

Chapter 12 Language Acquisition

12.1 First Language Acquisition

First language acquisition (FLA, L1 Language Acquisition) is the common term used to describe the process in which a child learns the primary language or the mother tongue. First language is also known as native language. By the time when children are three or four years old, they can use their first language to interact with others in many social settings. How and why does this happen? Theories of language acquisition are full of controversies. For decades there have been two representative views, that is, the behaviorist approach and the innateness approach. They account for children's remarkable linguistic accomplishments from different perspectives. In recent years, applications of a usage-based approach to language acquisition have become increasingly widespread. Researchers argue that usage-based approach may offer a more comprehensive understanding of the complex phenomenon of language learning.

12.1.1 Three Approaches

1. The Behaviorist Approach

Early research into language learning was heavily dependent on the dominant psychological paradigm—behaviorism. Within the behaviorist framework speaking consists of mimicking and habit-formation chiefly based on Pavlov's classical conditioning experiment and Skinner's operant conditioning experiment. Here we briefly present the two experiments.

I. P. Pavlov, a Russian physiologist, conducted the famous classical conditioning experiment. The dogs were first presented with meat powder (the unconditioned stimulus) and their unconditioned response was to salivate. The experimenter then rang a bell (the conditioned stimulus) before giving the dogs meat powder. Then the dogs began to salivate (the conditioned response) as soon as they heard the bell ringing. In this way, the dogs were "instructed" to respond to the bell as if it were the meat. Initially, the meat powder was the stimulus, and salivation was the response. But soon, the bell itself became the stimulus to evoke the salivation. According to this approach, it is believed that learning the meaning of a word follows a similar process. For instance, if each time an infant plays with a doll, her mother says "doll", the child will begin to associate the word "doll" with the object. Eventually, when someone says "doll", the child will respond to the word, uttering the sound "da". In this sense, she gradually learns the meaning of the word.

Operant conditioning (sometimes referred to as instrumental conditioning), carried out by the American psychologist B. F. Skinner, is a method of learning that occurs through rewards and punishments for behavior. In the experiment the rat was placed in a box and over the course of a few days, food was occasionally delivered through an automatic dispenser. Before long, the rat approached the food tray as soon as the sound of the dispenser was heard, clearly anticipating the arrival of more food. In the next step, researchers raised a small lever on the wall of the box and when the rat touched it, the food dispenser provided a snack. After the first self-induced meal, the rat repeatedly touched the lever in order to get more food. To the hungry rodent, the sound of the dispenser became a reinforcer when it was first associated with feedings and continued to be so until after a while, researchers stopped providing food when the lever was pressed. Soon after that, the rat stopped touching the lever. Through operant conditioning, an association is made between a behavior and a consequence for that behavior. Learner "operates" on the environment in order to get a reward. It follows that parents and other adults teach children language through operant conditioning by rewarding their attempts at early utterances.

2. The Innateness Approach

N. Chomsky, a famous American linguist, believes language is somewhat innate. According to him, children are born with what he calls a "Language Acquisition Device" (LAD), which is a unique kind of organ that fits them for language learning. Chomsky argues that on the basis of language input alone, children cannot attain the complexities of adult grammars. It is a child's biologically-equipped natural endowment that enables him or her to become a competent speaker. The Innatist Hypothesis is backed up by some observations (Chomsky, 1975): Children learn their native language very fast and with little effort, with very limited exposure to input they come to use and understand sentences that presumably never occur in their language learning environment, they learn the language independent of their family background, intelligence, motivation, emotional states and they receive no formal instruction, etc.

These are impossible without inborn linguistic knowledge. According to Chomsky, the principles that underlie all possible human languages are innate and constitute Universal Grammar (UG). The theory assumes that language consists of a set of abstract principles that characterize core grammar of natural languages. In addition to principles that are invariable in all languages, there are parameters that vary across languages. Here is an interesting analogy between driving a car and principles and parameters: Generally, there is a principle that drivers have to keep consistently to one side of the road, which is taken for granted by all drivers in all countries. The principle does not, however, say which side of the road people should drive on. A parameter of driving allows the side to be the left in England and Japan, and the right in the U.S.A. and France. So, a universal principle and a variable parameter together represent the essence of driving. The principle states the universal requirement on driving; the parameter specifies the variation between countries. As to language acquisition, what UG claims is that a child is born with universal language principles and thus has the potential to acquire all languages. Children are born into different speech communities and can pick up the language of the community they happen to be born into with equal competence. If a child of Chinese parents is born into America, he acquires English as his native language just as naturally as he would have picked up Chinese if he is brought into a Chinese-speaking community.

3. Usage-based Approach

Usage-based approach seeks to integrate the cognitive and social dimensions of human language in use. In the usage-based approach, the representation and processing of language is understood in terms of general psychological mechanisms such as categorization and entrenchment. Entrenchment refers to the strengthening of memory traces through repeated activation, so linguistic constructions that are used repeatedly and with high frequency will become highly entrenched. Categorization can be defined as a comparison between an established structural unit functioning as a standard and an initially novel target structure.

Usage-based theories propose that expressions in early child language are dominated by concrete expressions or item-based constructions limited to lexically specific patterns (e.g., Cut _____, Give me _____). These item-based constructions are gradually organized into lexical group constructions and finally move into more abstract representations through schematization and analogical processes (MacWhinney, 2008; Tomasello, 2003). According to the usage-based approach, language learning is initially exemplar-based. As the child/learner is exposed to an increasing number of exemplars in the course of learning, repeated encounters with known exemplars gradually change the learner's mental representations, allowing for abstractions over instances to be derived. These abstractions are referred to as schemas, with schema formation defined as "the emergence of a structure through reinforcement of the commonality inherent in multiple experiences" (Langacker,

2000: 4). To put it differently, a schema emphasizes the commonalities of a number of exemplars while at the same time leaving aside specific exemplars of words describing actions or events producing observable change such as "Laura passed her the book", "Harry sends his mother a birthday card", "You can fax me the document", and so on will eventually enable the child/language user to abstract away from the specific differences between these constructions and focus on their commonality: the constructional schema of the ditransitive "X causes Y to receive Z" (Goldberg, 1995). To sum up, language learning is a bottom-up process during which the child/learner moves from exemplar-based formulas or chunks, that is, entirely specific linguistic constructions (e.g., Laura passed her the book.) via item-based schemas (e.g., pass-NP-the book) toward partially or wholly abstract schemas, that is, more abstract linguistic constructions (e.g., pass-NP-NP, or the wholly abstract V-NP-NP). This developmental trajectory, which describes an essentially implicit process, has been posited for both L1 and L2 learning. Nevertheless, due to L1 transfer and other factors, L2 learning is different from L1 acquisition.

12.1.2 Language Development

Learning first language is an amazing task for a child. Anyone who has a baby is aware of the various means that he or she uses to express his or her needs. There are roughly four stages of language development: cooing and babbling, one-word stage or holophrastic stage, two-word stage and telegraphic utterances (Gass & Selinker, 2008).

1. Cooing and Babbling

The earliest means are crying, smiling and cooing, etc. For example, from approximately 4 to 7 months, infants utter these cooing sounds to play with such language-related phenomena as loudness and pitch.

When infants reach approximately 6 months of age, they turn to more language-like sounds in what is called babbling. Babbling commonly consists of consonant and vowel sequences, e.g., bababa, dadada. It is often the case that some of these early babbling sounds are taken to be words by adults. For example, "bababa" is interpreted as referring to the child's father and "mamama" to his or her mother.

Children commonly use sounds to express meaning at about age 1. According to the data from Vihman (1996, cited in Foster-Cohen, 1999), during the five-month period three children are found to decrease in babbling and increase in words although the increase and decrease are not always stable. They relate the concept of words to something when two of them are 14 months and one 15 months.

2. One-word or Holophrastic Stage

When children begin to produce words at about 12 to 18 months, there is hardly any grammar at all since only single words are involved. However, by using intonation and gestures, these words function as if they were sentences. For example, a child can use the word "dada" at least in two ways: When he or she says "dada" with the stress on the second syllable with his or her arms outstretched, one can imagine that the child intends to give a command like "Pick me up, daddy!"; When the child hears a door opening and says "dada" with rising intonation, this might be a question such as "Is that daddy?" So, these two utterances function as the "command" and "question".

Another point is that words in an adult's language do not always correspond to those in a child's language. One word for children might reflect more than one word in the adult language. For example, "allgone" is one word for a child even though it comprises two words in the adult language.

There are other aspects of child and adult words that do not totally correspond. Children often overextend the meanings of words they know. For example, a child probably uses "bear" to refer to a stuffed toy lion and a picture of a pig. In addition to overextension, children sometimes underuse or underextend words. For example, a child may use the word "tree" to refer to a tree with green leaves while he or she does not associate the word "tree" with a leafless tree.

3. Two-word Stage

Usually around the age of 1 and 2 years old, children start to combine words. What is typical of this stage is that the words that are used are content words (e.g., nouns and verbs) instead of function words (e.g., articles, prepositions, etc.). They might say something like "Mommy cry" or "no bed".

4. Telegraphic Utterances

Between 2 and 3 years old, the two-word utterances soon become telegraphic. The utterances are much like the ones commonly used when sending a telegram, that is, only the bare minimum is used so as not to have to "pay" for any more than is necessary. For example, "Aaron go home", "Seth play toy", "Ethan no go". Later, there are some stages that are found in further syntactic development. By the age of 5, the child becomes a competent speaker.

12.2 Second Language Acquisition

How do we distinguish language acquisition and language learning? Do they refer to the same thing? Krashen (1982) assumed that second language learners have two independent means of developing knowledge of a second language: acquisition and learning. Language acquisition is a subconscious process and acquirers use the language for communication, while language learning refers to conscious knowledge of a second language and learners are aware of the rules, know and talk about them. Because of the difficulty in differentiating the two terms in reality, many second language acquisition researchers use them interchangeably.

Second language acquisition (SLA) refers to the process of learning another language after the native language has been acquired. Sometimes the term refers to the learning of a third or fourth language. Comparatively, foreign language learning is differentiated from second language acquisition in that the former refers to the learning of a nonnative language in the environment of one's native language. This is most commonly done within the context of the classroom. In this part we will cover three aspects: the description of learner language, external factors affecting second language acquisition and individual differences in second language acquisition.

12.2.1 Description of Learner Language

In order to understand what second language learners acquire, SLA researchers describe how learner language changes over time and try to explain why learners learn a second language the way they do. Initially the main approach is studying learners' errors, seeking to predict errors by identifying the differences between learners' L1 and the target language. Later, Error Analysis involves a comparison of learners' idiosyncratic utterances with a reconstruction of those utterances in the target language. However, they were superseded by Interlanguage Theory which proposes that learners construct and draw upon a series of interlanguages or mental grammars in producing and comprehending L2.

1. Contrastive Analysis

Researchers from the 1940s to the 1960s conducted Contrastive Analysis, systematically comparing the first language and the target language. The assumptions are as follows (Lado, 1957: 59):

- Language learning is a matter of habit formation.
- L2 learning is a matter of changing the habits of L1 into the habits of L2.
- Errors are a consequence of interference from the learners' L1 habits.
- Interference occurs when L1 and L2 differ.

According to Contrastive Analysis Hypothesis, identifying these linguistic differences between L1 and L2 can help predict learner errors, but it is not often the case. For instance, the placement of object pronouns in English and French differs: Whereas English speakers say "I like them", French speakers say "Je les aime" (I them like). Contrastive Analysis would predict that object pronoun placement would be difficult for both English learners of French and French learners of English. This is not the case, however; whereas English learners of French do have problems with this construction and produce errors such as "*J'aime les" in initial stages, French learners of English do not produce errors of the type "*I them like", as would be predicted by Contrastive Analysis.

The assumptions of Contrastive Analysis that all errors would be caused by interference from the first language were shown to be unfounded, as many studies showed that many errors could not be traced to the first language.

2. Error Analysis

What is Error Analysis? As the name suggests, it is a type of linguistic analysis that focuses on the errors learners make. Unlike Contrastive Analysis, the comparison made is between the errors a learner makes in producing the target language and target language form itself. A shift in interests began to emerge during the 1950s and 1960s. Researchers began to make the systematic investigation of second language learners' errors. Corder (1967) was the first to focus attention on the importance of studying learners' errors. Errors, in Corder's view, are not just to be seen as something to be removed, but rather can be important in themselves.

Error Analysis provides a broader range of possible explanation than Contrastive Analysis for researchers/teachers to use to account for errors, as the latter only attributed errors to the native language. In comparison, there are two main error types within an error analysis framework: interlingual and intralingual. Interlingual errors are those which can be attributed to the native language, i.e., they involve cross-linguistic comparisons. For example, the sentence "*We just enjoyed to move and to play" made by French learners of English is probably due to the fact that in French verb complements are in the infinitival form and there is no "-ing" equivalent in French. Intralingual errors are those that are due to the language being learned, independent of the native language. For example, regularization leads to the error in the sentence "*He comed yesterday" made by learners of English.

3. Interlanguage

In second language acquisition, as researchers try to understand learner errors, interest in the overall character of the second language system was also growing. The term "interlanguage" was coined by Selinker (1972) to refer to the language produced by learners. It relies on two fundamental notions: (1) The language produced by the learner is a system in its own right, obeying its own rules; (2) It is a dynamic system, evolving over time.

Interlanguage studies proceed one step beyond Error Analysis, by focusing on the learner system as a whole, rather than just on its non-target-like features.

12.2.2 External Factors Affecting Second Language Acquisition

The second issue focuses on the role of environmental language in promoting second language learning, in the form of second language input received by the language learner, second language output produced by the learner and second language interaction between the learner and some other conversational partners. There are three hypotheses: Input Hypothesis advanced by Stephen Krashen, Interaction Hypothesis by Michael Long and Output Hypothesis by Merrill Swain.

1. Input Hypothesis

According to Input Hypothesis, humans acquire language in only one way—by understanding messages, or by receiving "comprehensible input". We move from i (i.e., our current level), to $i + 1$ (i.e., the next level along the natural order), by understanding input containing $i + 1$ (Krashen, 1985: 2). In other words, input can facilitate learning only when it is comprehensible. Krashen used the formula $i + 1$ to propose the idea. In the formula, i stands for the present proficiency level of the learner, and $i + 1$ refers to input slightly above the present level.

2. Interaction Hypothesis

According to Interaction Hypothesis, language acquisition requires or greatly benefits from interaction, especially negotiation of meaning (Long, 1985). Long (1985: 378) argues that interaction can lead to acquisition in the following way:

Step 1: (a) Linguistic/conversational adjustments promote (b) comprehension of input.

Step 2: (b) Comprehensible input promotes (c) acquisition.

Step 3: Deduce that (a) linguistic/conversational adjustments promote (c) acquisition.

Long stresses the importance of the interactional modifications that occur in negotiating meaning when a communication problem arises. Linguistic adjustment means that the interlocutor uses simpler syntax and vocabulary, etc. Conversational adjustment refers to repetition, confirmation checks, comprehension checks, clarification requests, etc. to achieve mutual understanding and keep a conversation going between two speakers. For instance, NS–NNS interaction and teacher talk seem to be rich in comprehension checks like "You understand?", "OK?" and requests for clarification "Sorry?", "Huh?", "I beg your pardon".

3. Output Hypothesis

Comprehensible Output Hypothesis is based on Swain's investigation of immersion programs in Canada (1985). Output, or the act of producing language (speaking or writing), under certain circumstances, facilitates second language learning. Opportunities to produce the target language are highly important for L2 acquisition. Swain argues that when learners experience communicative failure, they are pushed into making their output more precise, coherent and appropriate. The role of the output in SLA is independent of that of the comprehensible input. Thus, to be successful, both comprehensible input and comprehensible output are needed.

12.2.3 Individual Differences in Second Language Acquisition

Our understanding of SLA will not be complete if we don't take the learners into consideration. We have to ask ourselves: How different are we? What are the ways in which learners can differ from each other? Individual differences in learners determine whether and how each learner engages in learning. Here we just briefly introduce five of them.

1. Age

People generally believe that children do better than adults in language learning. Such a belief is supported by the Critical Period Hypothesis which basically states that individuals exceeding a certain age are less capable of learning a language than younger individuals.

In an early study, Penfield and Roberts (1959) suggested that the optimum age for acquiring another language is in the first ten years because it is during this time that the brain retains its maximum plasticity or flexibility. At around puberty, the brain loses this flexibility and it becomes difficult to learn another language. Long (1990) presented evidence to show that the acquisition of a native-like accent is not possible for children who start learning a second language after the age of 6. He also pointed out that it is difficult for teenage beginners of a second language to acquire a native-like grammatical competence. Scovel (1988), based on different evidence, argued that the critical period for acquiring a native-like pronunciation is before 12 years of age. Yet in contrast with Long (1990), Scovel (1988) questioned the possibility of a critical period for grammatical development. Is there a critical period for acquiring a second language? The following are what the researchers generally accept (Ellis, 1994: 491–492):

(a) Adult learners have an initial advantage where rate of learning is concerned, particularly in grammar. They will eventually be overtaken by child learners who receive enough exposure to the L2. This is less likely to happen in instructional than in naturalistic settings because the critical amount of exposure is usually not available in the former.

(b) Only child learners are capable of acquiring a native accent in informal contexts provided they receive massive exposure to the L2. Adult learners may be able to acquire a native accent with the assistance of instruction, but further research is needed to substantiate this claim.

(c) Children may be more likely to acquire a native grammatical competence. The critical period for grammar may be later than for pronunciation (around 15 years). Some adult learners, however, may succeed in acquiring native levels of grammatical accuracy in speech and writing and even full "linguistic competence".

(d) Irrespective of whether native-speaker proficiency is achieved, children are more likely to reach higher levels of attainment in both pronunciation and grammar than adults.

(e) The process of acquiring an L2 grammar is not substantially affected by age, but that of acquiring pronunciation may be.

2. Language Aptitude

Some people seem to be better language learners than others. The capability to learn a second language is referred to as language aptitude. To be specific, language aptitude is thought to be a combination of various abilities, such as the ability to identify sound patterns in a new language, the ability to recognize the different grammatical functions of words in sentences, and the ability to infer language rules, and so on. There are two language aptitude tests which are well-known in SLA. One is Carroll's Modern Language Aptitude Test (MLAT) and the other is Pimsleur's Language Aptitude Battery (PLAB).

Four components of language aptitude have been identified (Ellis, 1994: 495–496):

(a) Phonemic coding ability which helps the learner to identify foreign sounds and to form associations of these sounds with the symbols that represent them so that they can be remembered and retrieved later.

(b) Grammatical sensitivity which helps the learner to recognize the grammatical functions of words in sentences.

(c) Inductive language learning ability which helps the learner to identify patterns and relationships between form and meaning.

(d) Rote learning ability which helps the learner to learn the associations of sounds and meanings and to retain them.

To sum up, language aptitude involves both an underlying language learning capacity and a capacity to handle decontextualized language. Language aptitude has been consistently found to be among the best predictors of success in L2 learning.

3. Cognitive Style

Cognitive style refers to the way an individual processes information or approaches a task. Several cognitive styles have been identified in the psychological literature and investigated to see if they have any effect on L2 acquisition. The distinction between field dependence and field independence is probably the most often studied dichotomy in cognitive style.

The instruments measuring cognitive style include Group Embedded Figures Test (GEFT) (Witkin et al., 1971), the Cognitive Style Analysis (Riding & Cheema, 1991), and the Learning Style Questionnaire (Ehrman & Leaver, 2003). Originally, learners were asked to look at complex patterns and identify a number of simple geometric figures that were hidden within them. The purpose is to see whether they are able to separate the parts from the whole. Then the learners were asked to identify the words, phrases and sentences and understand how the parts form the whole text. Field independent students are usually good at summarizing the main ideas of a lecture even though the lecturer may not have presented in a very well-structured way. Field dependent students will be lost completely if a lecture is not well-organized.

Some approaches involve a more complex view of cognitive style. For example,

(a) the wholist-analytic learning dimension, which distinguishes individuals in terms of whether they preferred to organize information as an integrated whole or as a set of parts making up the whole; (b) the verbal-imagery dimension, which distinguishes individuals in terms of whether they are outward going and represent information verbally or are more inward looking and think visually or spatially; (c) the reflective-impulsive dimension, which distinguishes individuals in terms of whether they tend to think deeply about things before making any decisions or act on their intuitions.

It is commonly accepted that the cognitive style of an individual is along a continuum between the poles. Research to date has not found a convincing link between certain cognitive styles and success in L2 acquisition, but it is interesting to discuss them and to consider what cognitive styles each of us may have. We can then look for learning methods that suit us best.

4. Motivation

Motivation has been explored by many researchers in second language acquisition. All of them agree that learners learn more efficiently if they are motivated to learn. Motivation refers to directed effort individual learners make to learn the language. Gardner and Lambert (1959) suggested that motivation could fall into two types: integrative motivation and instrumental motivation.

A learner is said to be integratively motivated when he or she likes the culture of the target language and wants to identify with the people from the target language culture. A learner is said to be instrumentally motivated if he or she learns an L2 for utilitarian purposes such as passing an important exam, finding a good job, or improving social status.

To sum up, motivation serves as a powerful predictor of L2 achievement, but may itself be the result of previous learning experiences. Integrative motivation has been shown to be strongly related to L2 achievement. It combines with instrumental motivation to serve as a powerful predictor of success in formal contexts. Learners with integrative motivation are more active in class. Actually, learners with an instrumental reason for learning an L2 can also be successful. Learners with either integrative motivation or instrumental motivation, or a mixture of both, will manifest greater effort and perseverance in learning.

5. Learning Strategy

"Strategy" is defined by Collins COBUILD as "general plan or a set of plans intended to achieve something, especially over a long period". The term "learning strategies" has kept this meaning of planning but also added techniques and devices used to learn an L2. In O'Malley and Chamot's framework, three major types of strategy are distinguished.

Metacognitive strategies help learners plan and manage their study of the L2; cognitive strategies are the ones used by learners to deal with various specific problems in L2 learning, and social mediation helps learners to learn in groups. As Table 12.1 indicates, metacognitive strategies include advance organizers, directed attention, selective attention, etc. Cognitive strategies include repetition, resourcing, directed physical response, translation, grouping, note-taking, deduction, etc. Social mediation has two strategies: cooperation and question for clarification. Please refer to the detailed descriptions of different strategies.

Table 12.1 Typology of learning strategies (O'Malley & Chamot, 1990: 119–120)

Learning strategies	Descriptions
Metacognitive	
Advance organizer	Making a general but comprehensive preview of the concept or principle in an anticipated learning activity.
Directed attention	Deciding in advance to attend in general to a learning task and to ignore irrelevant distracters.
Selective attention	Deciding in advance to attend to specific aspects of language input or situational details that will cue the retention of language input.
Self-management	Understanding the conditions that help one learn and arranging for the presence of those conditions.
Advance preparation	Planning for and rehearsing linguistic components necessary to carry out an upcoming language task.
Self-monitoring	Correcting one's speech for accuracy in pronunciation, grammar, vocabulary, or for appropriateness related to the setting or to the people who are present.
Delayed production	Consciously deciding to postpone speaking to learn initially through listening comprehension.
Self-evaluation	Checking the outcomes of one's own language learning against an internal measure of completeness and accuracy.
Cognitive	
Repetition	Imitating a language model, including overt practice and silent rehearsal.
Resourcing	Defining or expanding a definition of a word or concept through use of target language reference materials.

(Continued)

Learning strategies	Descriptions
Directed physical response	Relating new information to physical actions, as with directives.
Translation	Using the first language as a base for understanding and/or producing the second language.
Grouping	Reordering or reclassifying and perhaps labeling the material to be learned based on common attributes.
Note-taking	Writing down the main idea, important points, outline, or summary of information presented orally or in writing.
Deduction	Consciously applying rules to produce or understand the second language.
Recombination	Constructing a meaningful sentence or larger language sequence by combining known elements in a new way.
Imagery	Relating new information to visual concepts in memory via familiar easily retrievable visualizations, phrases, or locations.
Auditory representation	Retention of the sound or similar sound for a word, phrase, or longer language sequence.
Key word	Remembering a new word in the second language by (1) identifying a familiar word in the first language that sounds like or otherwise resembles the new word, and (2) generating easily recalled images of some relationships with the new word.
Contextualization	Placing a word or phrase in a meaningful language sequence.
Elaboration	Relating new information to other concepts in memory.
Transfer	Using previously acquired linguistic and/or conceptual knowledge to facilitate a new language learning task.
Inferencing	Using available information to guess meanings of new items, predict outcomes, or fill in missing information.
Social/affective	
Cooperation	Working with one or more peers to obtain feedback, pool information, or model a language activity.
Question for clarification	Asking a teacher or other native speakers for repetition, paraphrasing, explanation and/or examples.

Generally, successful learners appear to use learning strategies more frequently and in qualitatively different ways than learners who are less successful. For example, successful adult beginners seem more adept at the use of memory strategies.

Metacognitive strategies involving goal identification, planning, monitoring, and evaluation assume considerable importance at least for adults. The learning strategies used by children and adults may differ; social and interactional strategies may be more important for younger learners.

12.3 Instruction and Second Language Learning

Instruction and second language learning includes two orientations: cognitive and social, which will be briefly reviewed in the following two parts.

12.3.1 Two Types of Formal Instruction

There are two second language learning settings: naturalistic SLA and classroom SLA. A major goal for SLA research is to inform L2 instruction in the classroom. This is especially true in the Chinese EFL context.

The following figure displays two types of formal instruction.

Figure 12.1 distinguishes between formal instruction directed at cognitive goals and metacognitive goals. The former focuses on developing linguistic or communicative competence; the latter focuses on the use of effective learning strategies. Cognitive goals can be divided into two types, depending on whether the instruction is language-centered or learner-centered. In language-centered instruction, the goal is pronunciation, lexis, grammar, or discourse. In learner-centered instruction, the instruction is still directed at some aspect of language, but an attempt is made to match the type of instruction to the learner, so that different learners are taught in

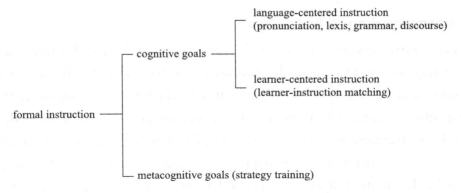

Figure 12.1 Types of formal instruction (Ellis, 1994: 612)

different ways. Formal instruction directed at metacognitive goals is concerned with attempts to train learners to use effective learning strategies.

Researchers try various ways to draw learners' attention to the forms and structures of the language within the context of communicative interaction. For example, form-focused instruction that encourages learners to pay attention to the formal properties of language in the context of trying to communicate may facilitate acquisition. However, the results of the studies are so far inconclusive. It is probably premature to reach any conclusions regarding what type of formal instruction works best. There is a need for much more research.

As to learner-centered instruction, it is possible that the optimal type of instruction will be one that matches the individual learner's preferred approach to learning. Learner-instruction matching involves an attempt to ensure that the teaching style is suited to the learner. It is based on the assumption that learners have different learning styles, language aptitudes, and so on. Different learners may be able to achieve success if the instruction enables them to maximize their strengths. Therefore, there is a need for research to examine how the instructions affect different kinds of learners.

The study of learning strategy has been motivated by the desire to identify how to assist learners to become more effective. It is for this reason that a number of researchers have attempted to design learner training programs. Some studies investigated the effects of vocabulary strategy training. Others explored the effects of cognitive strategy like imagery or grouping, and metacognitive strategy like self-evaluation on language learning. The research findings are not generally convincing in demonstrating the effectiveness of strategy training. Nevertheless, this has not prevented a number of researchers proposing strategy instruction schemes.

12.3.2 Usage-inspired L2 Instruction

Many discoveries have occurred in cognitive science, psycholinguistics, first language acquisition, and linguistic theories which have changed the way we think about human cognition and how this relates to the nature of language, language learning and language teaching. From the perspective of social school, usage-inspired L2 instruction rests on the following five tenets (Tyler & Ortega, 2018). A first usage-based tenet is that language and language learning are meaning-based. Contrary to the traditional axiom that the linguistic sign is arbitrary, in usage-based approach, language from lexis to syntax to discourse is gradually built up from smaller chunks to fully formed entrenched schemas or constructions, that is, form–meaning mappings. The language a learner constructs is intimately based on the language to which the learner is exposed; this is driven by the processing of meaning. A second usage-based tenet posits that meaning is grounded in the physical world and is embodied. Therefore, language and language learning are based on groundedness and embodiment too. The oft-cited illustration is that humans' physical experience of upright stance and gravity shapes metaphors pervasive in everyday language involving the two orientations "up" and "down" as positive and negative respectively, e.g., "Keep up the good work!" "I feel down." A third usage-based tenet is that language and language learning are critically situated in contextualized social interaction. Actual language use is culturally, socially and contextually embedded, because all usage events are tied to particular speech communities. A fourth tenet is that language and language learning emerge from the same general cognitive mechanisms involved in all aspects of learning, driven by various aspects of input, particularly frequency. Frequency-driven learning crucially involves implicit learning processes of category formation constructed by the learner bottom-up on the basis of contextualized, iterative language use. However, there is room for explicit instruction concerning L2 learning. The fifth usage-based tenet is that language and language learning are open to variability and change all throughout the life span. No linguistic unit is ever produced exactly the same in exactly the same context; the input itself is constantly variable. Thus, language learning is ever open to change and variation. Though usage-inspired L2 instruction displays powerful insights into language and language learning, SLA researchers and L2 teachers need more empirical evidence to provide benefits from the five tenets beyond their familiar teaching approaches.

12.4 Summary

This chapter began by defining the term "first language acquisition" and accounting for its relevant theories, that is, the behaviorist approach, the innateness approach and the usage-based approach. The language features at four stages of L1 development are also discussed. Second language acquisition research is reviewed from three interrelated aspects: description of learner language, external factors affecting second language acquisition, and individual differences in second language acquisition.

Instruction and second language learning concentrates on instructions involving cognitive goals and metacognitive goals in second language acquisition and usage-inspired instruction emphasizing social interaction and meaning construction. FLA and SLA research is characterized by data, opinions, facts, explanations and perspectives that exist in a state of complementarity and opposition. Based on the previous studies, progress has been made in broadening the scope of FLA and SLA, in understanding essential issues in need of investigation, in developing methods for studying them and in the ways of giving effective language learning instructions. No doubt, over time, the pictures about learner language, language learners and factors affecting learners and learning will become clearer.

Exercises

I Define the following terms.

1. first language acquisition
2. behaviorist approach
3. innateness approach
4. babbling
5. telegraphic utterance
6. second language acquisition
7. Contrastive Analysis
8. Error Analysis
9. interlanguage
10. Input Hypothesis
11. Interaction Hypothesis
12. Output Hypothesis
13. language aptitude
14. cognitive strategy

II Answer the following questions.

1. What are the stages of child first language acquisition? Give some examples of each stage.
2. Consider age as a factor in language learning and age may make a significant difference in language learning. What is your view about it?
3. Describe possible reasons for the following misuse. Had the lesson been a waste of time? How might you go about finding answers to these questions?
   A teacher has drilled students in the structure known as indirect questions:
   Do you know where my pen is?
   Do you know where he is?

Chapter 12　Language Acquisition

Did he tell you what time it is?

As a direct result of the drills, all students in the class were able to produce the structure correctly in class. After class, a student came up to the teacher and asked, "Do you know where is Ms. Lin?" Only minutes after the class, in spontaneous speech, the student used the structure practiced in class incorrectly.

◀ References

Anderson, S. 1992. *A-Morphous Morphology*. Cambridge: Cambridge University Press.

Aronoff, M. 1994. *Morphology by Itself*. Cambridge: The MIT Press.

Aronoff, M. & Rees-Miller, J. 2001. *The Handbook of Linguistics*. Beijing: Foreign Language Teaching and Research Press.

Ashby, M. 2015. *Introducing Phonetic Science*. Cambridge: Cambridge University Press.

Austin, J. 1962. *How to Do Things with Words*. Oxford: Oxford University Press.

Badecker, W. & Caramazza, A. 1998. A lexical distinction between inflection and derivation. *Linguistic Inquiry*, 20: 108–116.

Baker, M. C. 2001. *The Atoms of Language: The Mind's Hidden Rules of Grammar*. New York: Basic Books.

Bauer, L. 1983. *English Word Formation*. Cambridge: Cambridge University Press.

Bauer, L. 2008a. Exocentric compounds. *Morphology*, 18: 51–74.

Bauer, L. 2008b. Les composes exocentrique de l'anglais. In D. Amiot (Ed.), *La Composition Dans Une Perspective Typologique*. Arras: Artois Presse Universite, 35–47.

Baugh, A. C. & Cable, T. 2012. *A History of the English Language*. London & New York: Routledge.

Beard, R. 1995. *Lexeme Morpheme Base Morphology: A General Theory of Inflection and Word Formation*. Albany: State University of New York.

Bloomfield, L. 1933. *Language*. London: George Allen & Unwin Limited.

Booij, G. 2010. *Construction Morphology*. Oxford: Oxford University Press.

Brisard, F. 2014. Introduction: Meaning and use in grammar. In F. Brisard et al. (Eds.), *Grammar, Meaning and Pragmatics*. Shanghai: Shanghai Foreign Language Education Press, 1–12.

Brown, G. & Yule, G. 2000. *Discourse Analysis*. Beijing: Foreign Language Teaching and Research Press.

Cairns, H. S. & Kamerman, J. 1980. Lexical information processing during sentence comprehension. *Journal of Verbal Learning & Verbal Behavior*, 14: 170–179.

Carney, A. 2007. *Syntax: A Generative Introduction*. Cambridge: Blackwell Publishing.

Catford, J. C. 2002. *A Practical Introduction to Phonetics*. Cambridge: Cambridge University Press.

Chalak, A. & Asfahani, N. 2012. The effects of text-structure awareness on reading comprehension of Iranian EFL learners. *Journal of Language, Culture, and Translation*, 1: 35–48.

Chamot, A. 1987. The learning strategies of ESL students. In A. Wenden & J. Rubin (Eds.), *Learner Strategies for Second Language Acquisition*. Englewood Cliffs: Prentice Hall, 71–83.

Chomsky, N. 1965. *Aspects of the Theory of Syntax*. Cambridge: The MIT Press.

Chomsky, N. 1972. *Language and Mind*. New York: Harcourt Brace Jovanovich.

Chomsky, N. 1975. *Reflections on Language*. Glasgow: Pantheon Books.

Chomsky, N. 1986. *Knowledge of Language: Its Nature, Origin, and Use*. New York: Praeger.

Chomsky, N. 1995. *The Minimalist Program*. Cambridge: The MIT Press.

Chomsky, N. 2002. *Syntactic Structures*. Berlin & New York: Mounton de Gruyter.

Chomsky, N. & Halle, M. 1998. *Sound Pattern of English*. Indianapolis: Addison Wesley Educational Publishers.

Clark, J. et al. 2007. *An Introduction to Phonetics and Phonology*. Oxford: Blackwell Publishing.

Corder, S. P. 1967. The significance of learners' errors. *International Review of Applied Linguistics*, 5: 161–170.

Crystal, D. 1985. *A Dictionary of Linguistics and Phonetics*. Oxford: Blackwell Publishing.

De Saussure, F. 2001. *Course in General Linguistics*. Beijing: Foreign Language Teaching and Research Press.

Dell, G. S. & O'Seaghda, P. G. 1992. Stages of lexical access in language production. *Cognition*, 42: 287–314.

Dooley, R. A., & Levinsohn, S. H. 2008. *Analyzing Discourse: A Manual of Basic Concept*. Beijing: Foreign Language Teaching and Research Press.

Ehrman, M. & Leaver, B. L. 2003. Cognitive styles in the service of language learning. *System*, 31, 393–415.

Ellis, R. 1994. *The Study of Second Language Acquisition*. Oxford: Oxford University Press.

Fant, G. 1960. *Acoustic Theory of Speech Production*. The Hague: Mouton de Gruyter.

Fauconnier, G. 1985/1994. *Mental Spaces: Aspects of Meaning Construction in Natural Language*. Cambridge: Cambridge University Press.

Fauconnier, G. 1997. *Mappings in Thought and Language*. New York: Cambridge University Press.

Fauconnier, G. & Sweetser, E. (Eds.). 1996. *Spaces, Worlds and Grammars*. Chicago: University of Chicago Press.

Fill, A. F. & Penz, H. 2018. *The Routledge Handbook of Ecolinguistics*. New York & London: Routledge.

Firth, J. R. 1957. *Papers in Linguistics*. London: Oxford University Press.

References

Forster, K. I. 1979. Levels of processing and the structure of the language processor. In W. E. Cooper & E. C. T. Walker (Eds.), *Sentence Processing: Psycholinguistic Studies Presented to Merrill Garrett*. Hillsadale: Erlbaum, 27–85.

Foster-Cohen, S. 1999. *An Introduction to Child Language Development*. London: Longman.

Frazier, L. & Rayner, K. 1982. Making and correcting errors during sentence comprehension: Eye movements in the analysis of structurally ambiguous sentences. *Cognitive Psychology, 14*: 178–210.

Gardner, R. & Lambert, W. 1959. Motivational variables in second language acquisition. *Canadian Journal of Psychology, 13*: 266–272.

Gass, S. M. & Selinker, L. 2008. *Second Language Acquisition—An Introductory Course*. New York: Routledge.

Goldberg, A. E. 1995. *Constructions: A Construction Grammar Approach to Argument Structure*. Chicago: University of Chicago Press.

Grice, H. 1975. Logic and conversation. In P. Cole (Ed.), *Syntax and Semantics: Speech Acts*. New York: Academic Press, 41–58.

Gussenhoven, C. & Jacobs, H. 2017. *Understanding Phonology*. London & New York: Routledge.

Halliday, M. A. K. 1978. *Language as a Social Semiotic*. London: Edward Arnold.

Halliday, M. A. K. & Hasan, R. 2001. *Cohesion in English*. Beijing: Foreign Language Teaching and Research Press.

Halliday, M. A. K., McIntosh, A. & Strevens, P. 1964. *Linguistic Science and Language Teaching*. London: Longman.

Hatch, E. & Brown, C. 2001. *Vocabulary, Semantics and Language Education*. Beijing: Foreign Language Teaching and Research Press.

Hewlett, B. & Beck, J. 2006. *An Introduction to the Science of Phonetics*. Mahwah: Lawrence Erlbaum Associates.

Hockett, C. F. 1958. *A Course in Modern Linguistics*. Hampshire: Macmillan.

Hoey, M. 1983. *On the Surface of Discourse*. London & Worcester: Billing and Sons.

Holmes, J. 2013. *An Introduction to Sociolinguistics*. London & New York: Routledge.

Hudson, R. A. 2000. *Sociolinguistics*. Beijing: Foreign Language Teaching and Research Press.

Jackendoff, R. S. 1994. *Patterns in the Mind: Language and Human Nature*. New York: Basic Books.

Jones, D. 1976. *An Outline of English Phonetics*. Cambridge: Cambridge University Press.

Kenstowicz, M. & Kisseberth, C. 2014. *Generative Phonology: Description and Theory*. Waltham: Academic Press.

Kim, Y.-S. G. 2015. Language and cognitive predictors of text comprehension: Evidence from multivariate analysis. *Child Development*, 86: 128–144.

Kim, Y.-S. G. 2016. Direct and mediated effects of language and cognitive skills on comprehension or oral narrative texts (listening comprehension) for children. *Journal of Experimental Child Psychology*, 141: 101–120.

Kim, Y.-S. G. & Pilcher, H. 2016. What is listening comprehension and what does it take to improve listening comprehension? In R. Schiff & M. Joshi (Eds.), *Handbook of Interventions in Learning Disabilities*. New York: Springer, 159–174.

Kintsch, W. 1998. *Comprehension: A Paradigm for Cognition*. Cambridge: Cambridge University Press.

Knott, R. et al. 1997. Lexical and semantic binding effects in short-term memory: evidence from semantic dementia. *Cognitive Neuropsychology*, 8: 1165–1216.

Krashen, S. 1982. *Principles and Practice in Second Language Acquisition*. Oxford: Pergamon.

Krashen, S. 1985. *The Input Hypothesis: Issues and Implications*. London: Longman.

Ladefoged, P. 2006. *A Course in Phonetics*. Stanford: Cengage Learning.

Ladefoged, P. & Johnson, K. 2014. *A Course in Phonetics*. Boston: Cengage Learning.

Lado, R. 1957. *Linguistics Across Cultures*. Ann Arbor: University of Michigan Press.

Lakoff, G. & Johnson, M. 1980. *Metaphors We Live By*. Chicago & London: University of Chicago Press.

Langacker, R. W. 1987. *Foundations of Cognitive Grammar: Theoretical Prerequisites*. Stanford: Stanford University Press.

Langacker, R. W. 1991. *Foundations of Cognitive Grammar: Descriptive Application*. Stanford: Stanford University Press.

Langacker, R. W. 1995. Cognitive grammar. In J. Verschueren, J.-O. Östman & J. Blommaert (Eds.), *Handbook of Pragmatics Manual*. Amsterdam & Philadelphia: John Benjamins, 105–111.

Langacker, R. W. 2000. A dynamic usage-based model. In M. Barlow & S. Kemmer (Eds.), *Usage-based Models of Language*. Stanford: CSLI, 1–64.

Leech, G. 1981. *Semantics*. London: Penguin Books.

Leech, G. 1983. *Principles of Pragmatics*. London: Longman.

Levelt, W. J. M. 1989. *Speaking: From Intention to Articulation*. Cambridge: The MIT Press.

Levelt, W. J. M. 1993. Lexical selection, or how to bridge the major rift in language processing. In F. Beckmann & G. Heyer (Eds.), *Theorie und Praxis des Lexikons*. Berlin: Mounton de Gruyter, 164–173.

Levinson, S. C. 2001. *Pragmatics*. Beijing: Foreign Language Teaching and Research Press.

References

Liamas, C., Mullany, L. & Stockwell, P. 2007. *The Routledge Companion to Sociolinguistics*. Oxford: Routledge.

Long, M. 1985. Input and second language acquisition theory. In S. Gass & C. Madden (Eds.), *Input in Second Language Acquisition*. Rowley: Newbury House, 368–378.

Long, M. 1990. Maturational constraints on language development. *Studies in Second Language Acquisition, 12*: 251–286.

Lyons, J. 1981. *Language and Linguistics*. Cambridge: Cambridge University Press.

MacWhinney, B. 2008. A unified model. In P. Robinson & N. C. Ellis (Eds.), *Handbook of Cognitive Linguistics and Second Language Acquisition*. New York: Routledge, 341–371.

McCarthy, C. A. 1992. *Current Morphology*. London: Routledge.

McCarthy, J. J. 2008a. *Doing Optimality Theory: Applying Theory to Data*. Oxford: Wiley-Blackwell.

McCarthy, J. J. 2008b. *Optimality Theory in Phonology: A Reader*. Oxford: Wiley-Blackwell.

McClelland, J. L. & Elman, J. L. 1986. The TRACE model of speech perception. *Cognitive Psychology, 18*: 81–86.

Miller, G. 1991. *The Science of Words*. New York: Scientific American Library.

Morton, J. 1969. Interaction of information in word recognition. *Psychological Review, 76*: 165–178.

Mugglestone, L. 2006. *The Oxford History of English*. Oxford: Oxford University Press.

Napoli, D. J. 1996. *Linguistics*. Oxford: Oxford University Press.

Narayanan, S., Alwan, A. & Haker, K. 1995. An articulatory study of fricative consonants Using MRI. *JASA, 98*: 1325–1364.

Ning, Y. 1998. *The Contemporary Theory of Metaphor: A Perspective from Chinese*. Amsterdam & Philadelphia: John Benjamins.

Ogden, C. K. & Richards, I. A.1923. *The Meaning of Meaning*. London & New York: Harcourt Brace Jovanovich.

O'Malley, J. M. & Chamot, A. U. 1990. *Learning Strategies in Second Language Acquisition*. Cambridge: Cambridge University Press.

Peccei, J. 1999. *Pragmatics*. London: Routledge.

Penfield, W. & Roberts, L. 1959. *Speech and Brain Mechanisms*. New York: Atheneum Press.

Peter, B., Denes, P. B. & Pinson, E.N. 1993. *The Speech Chain: The Physics and Biology of Spoken Language* (2nd ed.). Oxford: Freeman and Company.

Pinker, S. 1999. *Words and Rules: The Ingredients of Language*. New York: Harper Collins.

Poole, S. C. 2000. *An Introduction to Linguistics*. Beijing: Foreign Language Teaching and Research Press.

Prince, A. & Smolensky, P. 1993/2004. *Optimality Theory: Constraint Interaction in Generative Grammar*. Malden: Blackwell Publishing.

Quirk, R., Greenbaum, S., Leech, G. & Svartvik, J. 1989. *A Comprehensive Grammar of the English Language*. Beijing: World Publishing Corporation.

Radford, A. 2004. *English Syntax: An Introduction*. Cambridge: Cambridge University Press.

Radford, A. 2009. *Analysing English Sentences: A Minimalist Approach*. Cambridge: Cambridge University Press.

Raymond, K., Patterson, K. & Hodges, J. R. 1997. Lexical and semantic binding effects in short-term memory: Evidence from semantic dementia. *Cognitive Neuropsychology, 14*: 1165–1216.

Rekema, J. 2009. *Introduction to Discourse Studies*. Shanghai: Shanghai Foreign Language Education Press.

Riding, R. & Cheema, I. 1991. Cognitive styles—An overview and integration. *Educational Psychology: An International Journal of Experimental Educational Psychology, 11*(3–4): 193–214.

Riemer, N. 2010. *Introducing Semantics*. Cambridge: Cambridge University Press.

Robins, R. H. 2000. *General Linguistics*. Beijing: Foreign Language Teaching and Research Press.

Saeed, J. I. 2000. *Semantics*. Beijing: Foreign Language Teaching and Research Press.

Salmi-Tolonen, T. 2013. Legal linguistics as a line of study and an academic discipline. In C. Williams & G. Tessuto (Eds.), *Language in the Negotiation of Justice. Contexts, Issues and Applications*. Farnham: Ashgate, 259–278.

Sapir, E. 1921. *Language*. New York: Harcourt Brace.

Scovel, T. 1988. *A Time to Speak: A Psycholinguistic Enquiry into the Critical Period for Human Speech*. Rowley: Newbury House.

Searle, J. 1979. *Expression and Meaning: Studies in the Theory of Speech Acts*. Cambridge: Cambridge University Press.

Selinker, L. 1972. Interlanguage. *International Review of Applied Linguistics, 10*: 209–231.

Small, L. 2019. *Fundamentals of Phonetics: A Practical Guide for Students*. London: Pearson.

Stubbs, M. 2002. *Words and Phrases-corpus Studies of Lexical Semantics*. Oxford & Malden: Blackwell Publishing.

Swain, M. 1985. Communicative competence: Some roles of comprehensible input and comprehensible output in its development. In S. Gass & C. Madden (Eds.), *Input in Second Language Acquisition*. Rowley: Newbury House, 235–253.

Sweet, H. 1891. *A New English Grammar: Logical and Historical*. Oxford: Clarendon.

Talmy, L. 1978. Figure and Ground in Complex Sentences. In J. H. Greenberg (Ed.), *Universals of Human Language: Syntax* (Vol. 3). Stanford: Stanford University Press, 627–649.

References

Talmy, L. 1988a. Force dynamics in language and cognition. *Cognitive Science*, 12: 49–100.

Talmy, L. 1988b. The relation of grammar to cognition. In B. Rudzka-Ostyn (Ed.), *Topics in Cognitive Linguistics*. Amsterdam: John Benjamins, 14–24.

Taylor, J. R. 1989. *Linguistic Categorization: Prototypes in Linguistic Theory* (2nd ed.). Oxford: Oxford University Press.

Thomas, J. 1995. *Meaning in Interaction: An Introduction to Pragmatics*. London: Longman.

Tomasello, M. 2003. *Constructing a Language*. Cambridge & London: Harvard University Press.

Traxler, M. J. 2012. *Introduction to Psycholinguistics: Understanding Language Science*. Oxford: Wiley-Blackwell.

Tyler, A. E. & Ortega, L. 2018. Usage-inspired L2 instruction: An emergent, researched pedagogy. In A. E. Tyler, L. Ortega, M. Uno, & H. Park (Eds.), *Usage-inspired L2 Instruction: Researched Pedagogy*. Amsterdam & Philadelphia: John Benjamins, 3–26.

Verschueren, J. 1999. *Understanding Pragmatics*. London: Edward Arnold.

Vihman, M. 1996. *Phonological Development: The Origins of Language in the Child*. Oxford: Basil Blackwell.

Wardhaugh, R. 2006. *An Introduction to Sociolinguistics*. Oxford: Blackwell Publishing.

Wardhaugh, R. & Fuller, J. M. 2015. *An Introduction to Sociolinguistics*. Oxford: Wiley-Blackwell.

Widdowson, H. G. 1996. *Linguistics*. Oxford: Oxford University Press.

Witkin, H., Oltman, O., Raskin, E. & Karp, S. 1971. *A Manual for the Embedded Figures Test*. Palo Alto: Consulting Psychology Press.

Wittgenstein, L. 1953/1968. *Philosophical Investigations*. Oxford: Basil Blackwell.

Yule, G. 1996. *Pragmatics*. Oxford: Oxford University Press.

陈建平. 2017. 语言与社会. 北京: 高等教育出版社.

陈新仁. 2007. 英语语言学实用教程. 苏州：苏州大学出版社.

戴炜栋，何兆熊. 2010. 简明英语语言学教程. 上海：上海外语教育出版社.

胡壮麟. 2001. 语言学教程. 北京：北京大学出版社.

胡壮麟，李战子. 2014. 语言学简明教程. 北京：北京大学出版社.

胡壮麟，刘润清，李延福. 1996. 语言学教程. 北京：北京大学出版社.

刘润清，文旭. 2006. 新编语言学教程. 北京：外语教学与研究出版社.

沈阳，贺阳. 2015. 语言学概论. 北京：外语教学与研究出版社.

汪榕培，卢晓娟. 2004. 英语词汇学教程. 上海：上海外语教育出版社.

吴宗济，林茂灿. 1989. 实验语音学概要. 北京：高等教育出版社.

张韵斐. 2006. 现代英语词汇学概论. 北京：北京师范大学出版社.

语言学术语表

A

abstraction	抽象化
acoustic phonetics	声学语音学
acronym	首字母拼音词
acronymy	首字母缩略法
activation	激活
active articulator	主动调音器官
adjacency pair	毗邻对
affective meaning	情感意义
affective strategy	情感策略
affixation	词缀法
affricate	破擦音/塞擦音
African American Vernacular English (AAVE)	美国黑人英语
air stream mechanism	气流机制
allomorph	词素变体
allophone	音位变体
alveolar	齿龈音
ambiguity	歧义
antonymy	反义（关系）
aphasia	失语症
apocope	词尾省略
applied linguistics	应用语言学
approximant	通音/近音
arbitrariness	任意性
artifactual entity	人造实体
articulation	调音
articulator	调音器官/调音器
aspiration	送气
assimilation	同化

audition 听觉

B

back-formation 逆生法
base 基体
behaviorist approach 行为主义观
bilabial 双唇音
bilingualism 双语现象
blending 拼缀法
bottom-up 自下而上的
bound morpheme 粘着词素
Bow-Wow Theory 拟声说
breathy voice 喘气音
Broca's area 布罗卡区

C

cataphora 后指
categorization 范畴化
click 喷音
clipping 截短法
coda 音节尾音
code-switching 语码转换
cognitive grammar 认知语法
cognitive linguistics 认知语言学
cognitive strategy 认知策略
cognitive style 认知风格
cognizer 认知体
coherence 连贯
cohesion 衔接
cohort 词汇群集
cohort model 词汇群集模型
coinage 创造新词
collocative meaning 搭配意义
commissive 承诺类
competence 语言能力
complementary antonymy 互补反义关系
complementary distribution 互补分布
componential analysis 成分分析法
compounding (composition) 复合法

conceptual metaphor	概念隐喻
conceptualization	概念化
conceptualizer	概念形成器
configuration	配置
conjunction	连接；连词
consonant	辅音
constative sentence	表述句
constituent	成分
constraint	制约条件
construal	识解
construction	建构，构式
construction grammar	构式语法
construction-integration model	建构整合模型
context	语境
contrastive analysis	对比分析
conversational implicature	会话含意
converse antonymy	相反反义关系
conversion	转类法
Cooperative Principle	合作原则
creaky voice	嘎裂音
Creole	克里奥尔语
Critical Period Hypothesis	关键期假设
cultural transmission	文化传递性

D

declarative	宣告类
degree of stricture	摩擦程度
Dell's speech production model	戴尔的言语产生模型
dental	齿音
derivation	派生法
derivational affix	派生词缀
descriptive	描述性的
design feature	设计特征
diachronic	历时的
dialect	方言
dichotomy	二分法
diglossia	双言制，双重语体
diphthong	双元音

directive	指令类
discourse analysis	语篇分析
discourse marker	话语标记语
displacement	移位性
dominance	支配
duality	二重性

E

egressive glotallic air stream	外向声门气流
ejective	喷音
Electropalatography (EPG)	电子颚位
elision	删音
ellipsis	省略
encapsulation	封装
encode	编码
entailment	蕴涵
epenthesis	增音
error analysis	错误分析
esophagus	食管
event-related potential (ERP)	事件相关电位
exophora	外指
expressive	表达类

F

family resemblance	家族相似性
feedback	反馈
feedforward	前馈
field	语场
field dependence	场依存
field independence	场独立
figure/ground alignment	焦点/背景对齐
first language acquisition	第一语言习得，母语习得
flap	闪音
formant	共振峰
form-focused instruction	形式聚焦教学
formulator	构成器
free morpheme	自由词素
fricative	擦音
frontal lobe	额叶

functionalist	功能派；功能主义者
fundamental frequency (F0)	基频
fuzziness	模糊性

G

gap	闭塞空白段
garden-path model	花园路径模型
garden-path sentence	花园路径句
generative linguistics	生成语言学
genericness	种属性
geographical/regional dialect	地域方言
Gestalt Perception	格式塔感知
glottal	声门音
glottal stop	声门塞音
glottis	声门
gradable antonymy	等级反义关系
grammaticalization	语法化
Great Vowel Shift	元音大迁移
grounding	背景化

H

hard palate	硬腭
hierarchical ordering of constituents	成分的阶层结构
high variety/H-variety	高变体
historical sound change	历史音变
homograph	同形异义词
homography	同形异义
homonym	同音异义词
homonymy	同音异义
hyponymy	下义关系

I

iconicity	像似性
idiolect	个人方言
illocutionary act	言外之意
image schema	意象图式
implicature	含意
implosive	内爆音
indexicality	指示性
individual difference	个体差异

inflectional affix	屈折词缀
information structure	信息结构
informative function	信息功能
ingressive glottalic air stream	内向声门气流
ingressive velaric air stream	内向软腭气流
inhibit	抑制
initialism	首字母缩略词
innateness approach	先天观
Input Hypothesis	输入假设
instrumental motivation	工具型动机
integrative motivation	融入型动机
Interaction Hypothesis	互动假设
interactive model	交互作用模型
interchangeability	互换性
interface	界面
interlanguage	中介语；过渡语
International Phonetic Alphabet (IPA)	国际音标表
interrogative function	疑问功能
intonation	语调

L

labiodental	唇齿音
language aptitude	语言能力，语言学能
language barrier	语言障碍
language comprehension	语言理解
language perception	语言感知
language production	语言产生
language variety	语言变体
langue	语言
larynx	喉
lateral	边音
lateral approximant	边近音
learning strategy	学习策略
lemma	词目
lexical access	词汇通达
lexical tone	词汇声调
lexicon	词汇
linear ordering of constituents	成分的线性结构

lingua franca	通用语
linguistics	语言学
logogen	词汇发生器
logogen model	词汇发生器模型
long-term memory	长期记忆
low variety/L-variety	低变体

M

macrolinguistics	宏观语言学
macro proposition	宏观命题
magnetic resonance imaging (MRI)	磁共振成像
manner of articulation	调音方式
maxim of agreement	赞同准则
maxim of approbation	赞扬准则
maxim of generosity	慷慨准则
maxim of manner	方式准则
maxim of modesty	谦逊准则
maxim of quality	质量准则
maxim of quantity	数量准则
maxim of relation	关系准则
maxim of sympathy	同情准则
maxim of tact	得体准则
meaning extension	意义引申
measurement	测量
mental representation	心理表征
mental scanning	心理扫描
mental space	心理空间
mental space theory	心理空间理论
meronymy	整体部分关系
metacognitive strategy	元认知策略
metalingual function	元语言功能
metaphor	隐喻
metaphorical code-switching	喻意型语码转换
metaphorical extension	隐喻引申
metonymy	转喻
microlinguistics	微观语言学
micro proposition	微观命题
minimal pair	最小对立对

mode	语式
modular model	模块化模型
monitor	监控
monophthong	单元音
monosemist view	单义观
morpheme	词素
morphology	形态学
multilingualism	多语现象

N

nasal	鼻音
nasal cavity	鼻腔
nasalization	鼻化
neurolinguistics	神经语言学
neutralization	中和
node	节点
nucleus	音节核

O

objectivist realism	客观现实主义
onomatopoeia	拟声法
onset	音节首音
Optimality Theory	优选论
oral	口腔音
oral cavity	口腔
organ of speech	发音器官
orthographic	正字法的
output buffer	输出缓冲区
Output Hypothesis	输出假设

P

palatal	硬腭音
palatography	颚位
paradigmatic relation	纵聚合关系
parole	言语
parser	解析器
participant	参与者
passive articulator	被动调音器官
performance	言语行为
performative sentence	施动句

perlocutionary act	言外之果
perspective	视角
pharynx	咽
phatic function	寒暄功能
phonation	声带发声
phoneme	音位
phonetics	语音学
phonological process	音系过程
phonological rule	音系规则
phonology	音系学
phonotactics	语音配列
pidgin	皮钦语/洋泾浜语
place of articulation	调音部位
plosive	塞音/爆破音
Politeness Principle	礼貌原则
polysemy	多义关系
Pooh-Pooh Theory	感叹说
postalveolar	齿龈后音
pragmatics	语用学
pre-conceptual	前概念的
preference structure	首选结构
presequence	前序列
prescriptive	规定性的
presupposition	预设
principle of late closure	迟关闭原则
principle of minimal attachment	最小附加原则
processor	处理器
productivity	多产性
profile	侧显
proposition	命题
prototype theory	原型理论
proximity	相邻性
psycholinguistics	心理语言学

R

radial network	辐射网络
reference	指称
referent	指称对象

reflected meaning	反射意义
regional/geographical dialect	地域方言
register	语域
rehearsal loop	复述回路
representation	表征
representative	阐述类
response	反应
retrieve	提取
retroflex	卷舌音
romanization	拉丁化

S

scope	辖域
second language acquisition	第二语言习得
semantics	语义学
semiology/semiotics	符号学
sense	意义
sentence stress	句重音
sign language	手语
situational code-switching	情景型语码转换
situation model	情景模型
slip of the tongue	口误
social dialect	社会方言
social meaning	社会意义
social strategy	社交/情感策略
sociolinguistics	社会语言学
soft palate	软腭
space-builder	空间建构语
spectrogram	频谱图
speech act theory	言语行为理论
speech chain	言语链
speech event	言语事件
speech segment	言语语段
spike	冲直条
standard dialect	标准语
stimulus	刺激
stop	塞音，爆破音
strategy training	策略训练

stress	重音
structuralist	结构派；结构主义者
structure building framework	结构构建框架
stylistics	文体学
subglottal vocal tract	声门下声道
substitution	替代
supraglottal vocal tract	声门上声道
suprasegmental feature	超音段特征
surface code	表层代码
syllabicity	音节化
syllable	音节
symbolicity	象征性
synchronic	共时的
synonymy	同义（关系）
syntagmatic relation	横组合关系
syntax	句法学

T

tap	拍音
temporal lobe	颞叶
tenor	语旨
text base	文本基础
textual pattern	语篇模式
thematic meaning	主位意义
time-course	时间进程
tone	声调
tone sandhi	变调
tongue back	舌背
tongue blade	舌叶
tongue dorsum	舌面
tongue root	舌根
tongue tip	舌尖
top-down	自上而下的
trace model	轨迹模型
trachea	气管
trajector	射体
tree diagram	树型图
trill	颤音

triphthong	三合元音

U

unaspirated	不送气的
usage-based approach	基于使用观
usage-inspired L2 instruction	使用驱动二语教学
utterance	语句
uvular	小舌音

V

velar	软腭音
velarization	软腭化
velum	软腭
visual world paradigm	视觉情境范式
vocal fold	声带
vocal tract	声道
Voice Onset Time (VOT)	浊音起始时间
voiced sound	浊音
voiceless sound	清音
vowel	元音
vowel backness/fronting	元音前/后度
vowel height	元音高度
vowel length	元音长度
vowel roundedness	元音圆唇度

W

waveform	波形图
Wernicke's area	韦尔尼克区
whispery voice	耳语音
word stress	词重音

X

X-ray photography and cinematography	X光照相和录像

Y

Yo-He-Ho Theory	劳动喊声说